Religion and Secularities

Religion and Secularities

Reconfiguring Islam in Contemporary India

Edited by

Sudha Sitharaman
Anindita Chakrabarti

Orient BlackSwan

RELIGION AND SECULARITIES: RECONFIGURING ISLAM IN CONTEMPORARY INDIA

ORIENT BLACKSWAN PRIVATE LIMITED

Registered Office
3-6-752 Himayatnagar, Hyderabad 500 029 (Telangana), India
e-mail: centraloffice@orientblackswan.com

Other Offices
Bengaluru, Bhopal, Chennai, Guwahati,
Hyderabad, Jaipur, Kolkata, Lucknow, Mumbai,
New Delhi, Noida, Patna, Visakhapatnam

First published by Orient Blackswan Private Limited 2020

ISBN 978-93-90122-00-4

Typeset in
Adobe Jenson Pro 11/13 by
Shine Graphics, Delhi 110 094

032402

Printed in India at
Glorious Printers, Delhi

Published by
Orient Blackswan Private Limited
3-6-752 Himayatnagar, Hyderabad 500 029, Telangana, India
e-mail: info@orientblackswan.com

Contents

Abbreviations

AIML	All-India Muslim League
AWPS	All-women police station
CPI(M)	Communist Party of India (Marxist)
CrPC	Criminal procedure code
INC	Indian National Congress
IUML	Indian Union Muslim League
KNM	Kerala Naduvathul Mujahideen
LDF	Left Democratic Front
NDF	National Development Front
NGO	Non-governmental organisation
NNPC	Neighbourhood Network in Palliative Care
MLA	Member of legislative assembly
PIL	Public interest litigation
SIO	Students Islamic Organisation
SIMI	Students Islamic Movement of India
SSF	Sunni Student Federation
SYM	Solidarity Youth Movement
UCC	Uniform civil code
UDF	United Democratic Front
VHP	Vishwa Hindu Parishad
WHO	World Health Organisation

Glossary

aanchalik	pertaining to a particular region
adab	etiquette
adhatyatmaka	devotional
adil	justice
akhlaq	morality
akhrat	afterlife
alim	an expert in Islamic law and theology
amal	good practice
amalukal	rites and rituals
amir	president
anal haqq	I am the truth
anandravan	nephew
anustanikata	ritualism
aravana payasam	the *prasadam* at the Sabarimala temple
archaka	priest
ashurkhana	place of mourning for Shia Muslims
avakasham	right
awqaf	plural of waqf
azan maghrib	call for compulsory prayer just after sunset
bahs karna	argue
batil	false or unacceptable
bhadralok	'gentlefolk'; as a social category, it emerged in colonial Bengal, comprising the landed elite mainly from the upper-caste Bengali Hindu community
bhoomi	earth
bida	an innovation regarded as un-Islamic
biradari	caste group; among Muslims, members who follow a particular occupation
chador	tomb-cloth sheet

Chandanakkudom	a form of *urs*; a ritual in which sandalwood paste is made and Quran suras are recited on that, and they are taken to the concerned shrines
chattram	feeding house that provides free food to travellers; also known as *musafirkhana*
chillah	a place of 40-days' retreat, involving religious seclusion and meditation
dar-al-ifta	an institution of Islamic legal jurisprudence where fatwa-seekers approach a *qazi/mufti* for queries in their religious and ethical matters; also functions as a space for dispute resolutions in matters related to the sharia
dar-ul-qaza	sharia *adalat*; religious forum for adjudication of personal disputes
dargah	a shrine or tomb built over the grave of a revered religious figure, often that of a Sufi saint
dawa	invitation to the path of Allah
desham	country
devasthana	temple
dharmakartha	a person entrusted with the custody and worship of the idol
dharmam	duty
dharna	protest
dikr	a ritual of remembrance of God
din	belief/religion
dua	collective prayer
faisla	a judicial decision
fariq	party to the lawsuit
farista	angel
farz	duty
faskh	divorce invoked by a qazi where the husband's consent is not required
fatwa	religious verdict
fiqh	the four schools of Islamic jurisprudence

fitina	distress
gaddi	office of a pir
gaddinashin	a tradition popular in Sufi shrines where after the death of the Sufi pir, the senior-most disciple becomes the spiritual head of the shrine
ghar-makan	shelter
haj	pilgrimage to Mecca
halal	prescribed food for Muslims
haqq	obligation; right
haram	proscribed activities for Muslims
hukmat-e-ilahi	rule of God
hukum	divine rule
ibada	worship
iblis	devil
iddat	the obligatory waiting period that a wife has to observe following her divorce
idgah	occasional place of worship
iftar	the evening meal that breaks the daily fast during Ramzan
ijtihad	to carry out independent interpretation in Islamic discourses
ikhlaq	conduct
ilhad	heresy
imam	leader of the prayer
imamate	leadership
iman	faith
isale swahab	transferring of rewards to the dead and reciting the Quran for the dead
isnad	holy transmit
istislah	seeking public good
jalsa	sermon
jamaat	local council
jatra	a traditional theatrical performance
juma	Friday

kaftan	shroud
karar	deed or consensus that is arrived at between contesting parties
karnavar	the senior-most male member in a matrilineal *tharavad*
karnoti	the eldest female member in the tharavad
khalifa	representative of Allah
khamoshi	silence
khan-pan	food
khanqah	hospice
kharcha	finances
khilafat	divine deputy
khuda ka khidmat	religious service
khula	a mode of divorce in which a wife appeals her husband for marriage dissolution
kirtan	devotional songs
lakkhibar	day of Goddess Lakkhi (Lakshmi in Hindi)
lok adalat	informal judicial unit within the family/civil court that pronounces the verdict in cases that have already been settled out of court through compromise
mahila mandal	women's committee organised by the women from a neighbourhood/locality
mahila thana	all-women police station
mahr	an entitlement that is accrued to a woman on her marriage; dower
mannu	soil
maslak	the schools of jurisprudence
matha	Hindu monastic establishment
mathasamoohikatha	religious sociality
mathetharatvam	the Malayalam equivalent of secularism
mazar	tomb
minhaj	clear way/method
miskeen	destitute
mohalla	neighbourhood

moulid	celebrating the Prophet's birthday
muamalat	social dealings
mufti	an Islamic scholar who responds to those seeking solutions to ethical dilemmas by issuing fatwas
mujawar	person who performs rituals in the dargah
mutavalli	manager, trustee or governor for the waqf
nafaka	the maintenance due to a divorced woman from her husband during the period of *iddat*
namaz	compulsory prayer
nanma	virtues
Nercha	anniversaries of saints
nikah	marriage
niyom	practices and rituals informed by scriptures
niyyat	intention
olima	objects like a stone or a tree can be venerated as a pir by Muslims
panipoda	sacred water
paraloka	otherworldly
parampara	local traditions
paristhiti	environment/nature
paura dharmam	citizens' responsibility
peetha	rostrum or seat
pir	Sufi master who is responsible for guiding disciples by following a specified path or *tariqa*
prakriti	nature
prasadam	transvalued religious offering by Hindu worshippers
putravakasam	property/estate acquired by members of a *tavazhi* by way of gifts from their fathers
qabar	grave
qabarstan	the common burial ground of Muslims
qanuni adalat	civil court
qasm	oath-taking

qazi	the one who adjudicates and arbitrates
qiyas	principle of analogy used in interpreting Islamic law
qutba	public sermon
rabbul-alameen	nurturer/lord of the worlds
rahmat	mercy
rakat	ritual cycle just after the second *sujud*
rathib	a ceremonial practice conducted in the name of a saint
ray	judgement
sadaqa	voluntary giving of alms
sadar	national headquarters of a legal school
sahaba	companions of the Prophet
sahih	correct
sajda	prostration
sajjadah nashin	custodian of the dargah
salafiya	movements urging Muslims to return to the religion's origins and the practices of the first generations of Muslims
salat	prayer
salisi	arbitration
samaravum sevanavum	struggle and service
samjhauta	agreement
sammelanam	conference
sanatana moolyaghal	eternal universal values
saum	fasting during the month of Ramzan
seva ashram	council organised by local committees as an endeavour towards social service
shahada	testifying to one's faith
sharia	Islamic law
shebait	manager
shirk	attributing divine qualities to any worldly being or objects
silsila	Sufi order
sinni	a sweet made of wheat-flour and sugar

sramadanam	an individual/collective act of helping others without expecting any monetary returns and for fulfilling social and/or divine commitment
stanam	position
strisothu	a custom of settling property on females and their female descendants; also known as *henummula*
sujud	prostration
Sunnah	the normative example of the Prophet
tafsir	exegetical reinterpretation of the Quran
taghoot	to cross the limits, to overstep boundaries or to rebel
tahqiq talav	investigation
tahqiqat	investigation
tajdid	renewal of faith
takhia	the residence of fakirs and saints
talaqnama	divorce agreement in written form
taqlid	adherents to the tradition
tavazhis	branches
tawheed	indivisible oneness of Allah
taziya	a miniature mausoleum signifying the tomb of Ali, the grandson of Prophet Muhammad, and his sons—Hasan and Husayn
telpoda	sacred oil
tharavad	group of individuals who claim descent in the female line from a common female ancestress
ulema	Sunni Islamic scholars
ummah	Islamic community
urs	annual festivals at Sufi shrines to commemorate the death anniversaries of saints
vajah	grounds
vakala	plural of *vakil*
vakil	advocate; person representing a case before the qazi on behalf of the litigant
virasat	inheritance
vishvasi	true believer

waaz	long speech at mosques
waqar	reverential behaviour
waqf	an endowment made by a Muslim to a religious, educational or charitable cause
waqif	an individual creating a waqf
wasiyatnama	will
zakat	giving alms; derived from the word *zaka,* which means 'to purify'
zakat-ul-fitr	a charity given to the poor at the end of the fasting in the month of Ramzan
zaum	fasting during Ramzan
zubani maslah	enquiry

Acknowledgements

The book is based on a seminar held at the Department of Humanities and Social Sciences, IIT Kanpur, in October 2014. As the essays in the volume reflect, at this seminar, a small group of researchers working on sociology of religion came together to discuss the field's theoretical as well as methodological concerns. J. P. S. Uberoi in his opening talk 'Why Study Religion?' dwelled on the theme of the seminar as he drew on his fieldwork in Afghanistan. Unfortunately, soon after the seminar, he had to slow down due to a stroke and could not complete the paper that he intended to contribute. We thank all the participants of the seminar who contributed to an engaging debate. The essays in the volume have been a truly collective and collaborative effort in exploring the many lives of Islam as they negotiate reform, revival, personal law and everyday piety within the constitutional framework of a postcolonial nation state.

Patricia Uberoi has constantly encouraged us and reminded us of the paucity of research on sociology of Islam in the Indian context. The financial support for the seminar came from the Department of Humanities and Social Sciences, IIT Kanpur. Surajit Sinha, who was the head of the department at that time, deserves special mention for his support and for handling all the administrative nitty-gritties with much care. We thank the anonymous referee for the comments and suggestions. Special thanks are in order to the editorial team at Orient BlackSwan for their interest in publishing the manuscript and also for their patience.

We would also like to thank Hashim, Saravanaraja and Suchandra for their help in the final stage of the book. Part of the writing was done during a sabbatical that Anindita spent at the HCAS 'Multiple Secularities: Beyond the West, Beyond Modernities' programme at Leipzig University in the summer of 2017. She is thankful to the colleagues at the Multiple Secularities project for their engagement with this research.

Sorted out as 'false consciousness' and antithetical to anything that is progressive, religion has remained grossly marginal to academic curiosity and attention in the Indian universities, especially so in the departments of sociology. Professor J. P. S. Uberoi has inspired generations of (unsuspecting) students to conduct ethnographic research on religion at a time when no one knew that religion would make such a comeback.

This book is dedicated to him for the sabotage.

Sudha Sitharaman
Bangalore
Anindita Chakrabarti
Kanpur

Introduction: Anthropology of Islam in Contemporary India

A Conceptual Overview

Sudha Sitharaman and **Anindita Chakrabarti**

The academic debates and discussions around Muslim communities and Islam in contemporary times traverse a minefield of issues, and it has become increasingly difficult to write on this topic without engaging with the current polemics that surround us. It is a truism that religion's reversal of fortune and its militant mixture with politics has been a ubiquitous feature of our times. Since the events of 9/11, any discussion on religion, particularly Islam, must countenance the polemics that have followed the events of the past decades—the rise of political Islam, the war on terror and the rise of religious politics globally. The most obvious target of these strident calls is Islam, particularly those practices and discourses within Islam that are suspected of fostering fundamentalism and militancy. And even when there is no direct violence, Islam appears as the bearer of a frightening tradition that insists upon mixing politics with religion. Moreover, practices such as veiling and the issue of

Muslim personal law, especially triple talaq and polygamy, have also contributed to the construction of stereotypes that render Islam as an anachronistic anathema in the modern world. As Mamdani (2002) has pointed out, since 9/11 there has been much 'culture talk' about Muslims and their politics. Such essentialist characterisations of Islam are sometimes carried out sympathetically and at other times with hostile intent. While academic discourse and media alike have produced reified views of Islam and Muslims, such views have also emerged from within Islam itself, via Muslim subjects' interpretations and representations of their own religion as unitary, timeless and unchanging (Launay 1992; Parkin 2000).

This volume brings together a collection of essays focusing on the theme of reconfiguration of Islam in the world's largest democracy, India, where Islam has a long history and Muslims are categorised as a minority community. The thread that connects these essays is the critique they pose not only to the theories of secularisation and modernisation, but also to the analytical dualism that has permeated the study of religion in the Indian context. We begin with some of the theoretical antecedents of understanding of Islam by locating the series of binaries that have been dominant in the study of Islam in India. A rigid concept of 'Islamisation'—which, in turn, is based on the dualism of centre and periphery, text and context, or reform and syncretism—has guided much of the research on Islam in India. These well-accepted binaries, we argue, have led to more theoretical opacity than clarity. The essays in this volume go beyond the comfort zone of these accepted dualisms as they investigate the relation between religion, civil society and the state in contemporary India.

The ethnographic sites documented in this volume show how articulations of religiosity and reshaping of the practices of Islam/religion invite us to rethink the modalities through which both religion and the state negotiate the normative imperative of secularity. The essays explore the relationship between the state, civil society institutions and religious actors, animated by diverse social groups and their religious praxis in varying contexts. Based on ethnographic work conducted in different regions—West Bengal, Uttar Pradesh, Karnataka and Kerala—they address diverse issues of religious piety such as community activism and civic participation; disputes and debates around visitation and commemoration of historic religious sites and saints; changing contours of matrilineal practices of a Muslim community in Malabar; and how Muslim women negotiate personal/Islamic law in a legally plural context. In sum, the book focuses on the impossibility of understanding contemporary Islam outside the logic of modern, secular, liberal governance—a standpoint that takes the secularism debate forward and explores the modern state's sovereign power to reorganise substantive features of religious life and the intractable tensions of secular rule that involves determining where to draw the line between religion and politics. Yet, in many ways, it is precisely this instability and the need for boundary-drawing decisions that constitute and reconstitute secular power.

What also connects the essays in the volume as they explore these negotiations is their methodological commitment to ethnography while paying attention to historical details. The Introduction is divided into four sections that look into the substantive theoretical debates in four key areas in the anthropology of Islam. We begin by revisting the debates on 'Indian Islam' to situate some of the issues in sociology of Islam in the Indian context, and then move on to critically engage with the trope of syncretism that has shaped much of the academic writings on Islam in the subcontinent. The discussions in this section help us unpack some of the intricacies of the concept of secularism/secularity. The essays in the volume, in one way or another, engage with the boundaries between religion and the non-religious, offering insights into what could be described as an ethnography of the secular in contemporary India. How the interactions between different religious groups and drawing of boundaries between religion and the secular take the form of debates and contestations in the public sphere is discussed in the section on the Islamic public sphere. The contributions of the individual essays to these theoretical debates are outlined in these four sections.

Debating 'Indian Islam'

A fact that is known to sociologists and anthropologists of Islam in India but not necessarily to others is the paucity of ethnographic work on Islam in India.[1] Historians and political scientists dominate the scholarly work that exists on Islam in the subcontinent.

Anthropologists, on the other hand, have focused on the questions of kinship, family and caste within Muslim communities. Emphasising this diversity, they have addressed the question: What have been the ways of explaining the existing diversity among the Muslims? What is the uniqueness of Indian Islam? Imtiaz Ahmad (1973, 1976, 1981) in his edited volumes has explored the diversity as well as local features of 'Indian Islam' that range from 'caste-like social stratification' to 'saint worship'. Ahmad (1981: 15) writes, 'indigenous tradition encouraged Islam in India to accept and retain the local tradition, but adapt them to its own requirements and needs by putting Islamic content into them'. Emphasising the local facets in the practice of Islam, Ahmad and his colleagues describe Islam as an 'indigenised' category, which has much to do with the local cultural practices rather than Islamic textual traditions.

The publication of Ahmad's work led to an important debate in the journal *Contributions to Indian Sociology*. Robinson (1983) offered a critique of the syncretism thesis, alluding to the disciplinary boundaries between sociologists and Islamists. While Ahmad harps on the difference between Islamic law and Muslim practice and on the ability of the sociologists to decipher the latter, Robinson criticises him of behaviourism on the one hand, and Indianism on the other. Moreover, he argues that the commitment of Ahmad and his associates to a notion of 'Indian Islam' has prevented them from looking at these issues from a comparative perspective (ibid.: 189–90). Though the observation regarding comparative sociology is important, Robinson's own analysis remains curiously predetermined as he articulates how the 'Islamic' finally triumphs over the diversity, be it within Islam or the culture within which it has to accommodate itself. In this analysis, Islamisation remains a minimally contested and unilinear process.

Das (1984: 293–94) criticises Robinson for upholding the view of Islam as a 'single unified tradition' and the knowledge of this tradition leading to the straight path of Islamisation. Though on opposite sides of the spectrum, Das detects a deeper similarity between Ahmad's notion of syncretism and Robinson's thesis of Islamisation, as they both believe that normative or orthodox Islam constitutes a single pattern of perfection, which contains an unchanging essence. Yet, the quranic science of *tafsir* that involves exegetical reinterpretation of the Quran acknowledges a plurality of meaning. Whereas both Ahmad and Robinson equate orthodoxy with the practices of the elite, Das urges us to think in terms of what she calls a 'folk theology' for studying the phenomenon of Islam in its interpretative multitude, beyond the binary of elite versus folk (ibid.: 297–98).[2]

In a similar vein, Minault (1984) also questions Robinson's march of Islamisation thesis. Minault points out that Islamisation does not do away with local practices but generates divisions within Muslim society, a condition that Robinson glosses over and therefore fails to anticipate its full implication. Moreover, citing Mines' (1975) work, Minault points out how the same people move between the two worlds of Islamic and customary practices. Most importantly, she draws attention to the doctrinal difference and antagonism between groups like the Deobandis and Barelwis who work for greater Islamisation. She argues that the issue of divisiveness is something that the proponents of Islamisation and reassertion have not adequately addressed (Minault 1984: 303–04).[3] The argument, as we can see, has revolved around the corrosion of syncretic traditions as a natural corollary to the process of Islamisation. Reform movements, such as the Tablighi Jamaat, have often been portrayed within this framework (for details, see Chakrabarti 2018).

Mines' (1975) work has drawn attention to the societal dynamism involved in the making of Islamic reform movements among Muslim ethnic groups in the northern cities of Tamil Nadu. Through an ethnography of 'Islamic revival', he shows how Tamil Muslims adapt to participate in the emerging new urban space and thereby situates the processes of Islamisation in the specificities of class and locality.[4] However, the questions posed by Mines—the interaction between religious movement, caste and politics on the one hand, and internal dynamism of Islamic revival in urban space on the other—were rarely addressed in the later decades. The scholarly endeavour remained predictably preoccupied with discussions on the impact of Islamic reform upon the syncretic society/culture.

Without initiating a theoretical discussion on the topic, much of the anthropological work on syncretism investigated practices associated with rites of passage, customs and beliefs, and accounted them as 'survivals' or as 'accretions' from Hindu customs. Rituals especially were described as 'syncretic', thus indicating a certain identity and continuity in the social practices of Muslims and Hindus. The concept of syncretism, by and large, simply flagged the interaction between Hinduism and Islam, and it was made operational with no clear theoretical understanding of the religious pluralism and diversity that exist as a fact of social life in India. It displayed two recurring themes: first, the relationship between 'purist' and 'syncretic' religious behaviour within Muslim communities; and second, the relationship of Muslim believers to the wider non-Islamic society. Yet, the meaning of the terms 'purist' and 'syncretic', and whether they were useful categories to apply to the historical study of Muslim communities in India, were not interrogated. Syncretism came to be a 'gatekeeping concept' to discuss Indian Islam, largely at the expense of other ways of approaching this area of sociological inquiry. In the next section, we will outline the contours of the syncretism debate in the Indian context.

Limits to Syncretism

'Syncretism' is a term most often used to describe religious communities that have assimilated rituals or concepts from other religious communities.[5] The most important representation of Hindu–Muslim syncretism in India is always the dargah[6] and/or Sufi saint veneration. Muslims and non-Muslims frequent dargahs and Muslim shrines in India (as elsewhere), praying for the saint's intercession by participating in the rituals. The meeting of 'Hindu' and 'Islamic' features in the dargah has often been understood as a 'mixture' of religions—'fusion', 'amalgam', a 'patchwork model' or a form of religious 'synthesis', and sometimes even as 'confluence' or 'convergence'. Arguments concerning 'Hindu–Muslim syncretism' flow from two distinct registers, that of religious fundamentalism and of liberal secularism. A review of scholarship reveals that the word 'syncretism' is used variedly: bringing together *people* of different religions, a *place* where various religious traditions of the subcontinent converge, sharing of a *metaphoric world*, mutual adaptation of *religious vocabulary* and *ritual*. Much of the discussion on shrines and saint veneration begins with a liberal secular understanding that 'syncretism' is, by definition, progressive and liberating. The scholars advocating this position believe in the unchanging essence of religion and religious identities, and have treated this inter-religious convergence as a powerful resource to combat communalism and other forms of sectarian strife. The secular engagement with the romance of syncretism, as a solution to sectarianism, nationalism, ethnocentrism and religious intolerance, evokes a euphoric intellectual nostalgia. What makes for secularist (liberal) reading is that the recent rise of fundamentalism in India has obliterated the deep-rooted syncretism in Indian culture, and therefore there is an urgent need for its recovery. However, the term is Janus-faced, carrying a negative charge for those concerned with analysing or maintaining putatively 'pure' or 'authentic' rituals and a positive one for those who criticise concepts such as cultural purity or authenticity, or favour the idea of 'multiculturalism' (Stewart and Shaw 1994). Accordingly, syncretism is also understood as a 'lax' and 'spurious' form of religion, a corrupt and 'Hinduised form of Islam', an institutional form of Sufism, the worship of local saints and graves, etc.

The response of the Muslims to revive/reform differs from the secular response; they base their arguments on an understanding that any religion that is conceived in terms of pure essence will, if mixed with another religion, yield 'debased', 'diluted' or 'distorted' offspring, which may be termed the revivalist/reformist position, often dubbed conservative. The practice of worshipping saints at their tombs and praying for their intercession has remained an issue for a number of theological debates among Muslims for centuries (see, for instance, Osella 2015). A long-standing argument against the worship of saints is that the imputation of divine powers to the saint and his tomb goes against the fundamental concept of *tawheed,* which considers worship of anything other than Allah as amounting to *shirk* and a *bida,* an innovation contrary to Sunnah, the normative example of the Prophet. The fundamental issue here is whether 'mediation' of the saints amount to shirk.[7] However, the Sufi orders maintain that since all prayer is directed to Allah, the saint is merely a messenger, and the practice is therefore not un-Islamic. It has been reiterated by many ulema (Sunni Islamic scholars) as well. In fact, the Barelwi movement,[8] a movement of ulema, developed to defend the practices at saint shrines and the belief in intercession. Anthropologists, however, often privilege dargah practices like the *urs* (shrine festivals) and saint veneration against the reformists who deplore tombs, saints, shrine festivals, intercessionary prayers, *dikr* (remembrance chants), *moulid* (celebrating the Prophet's birthday) and so on.[9]

The ambiguous nature of syncretism increases with the growth of polarisation between communities captured by the term 'communalism' in Indian academic as well as popular discourses. In this context, Bayly (1989: 463) has noted a 'paradox' in which 'there has been a growing tendency for groups and corporations to confront each other with growing hostility' while at the same time 'links of syncretic religious practices or overlapping religious beliefs have persisted or even been reinvented'. This phenomenon is paradoxical only if syncretism is presumed to require amity between the groups so linked. It is precisely this assumption that seems to underlie the view that syncretism indicates tolerance. However, this assumption has been questioned. Peter van der Veer (1994: 200–01), for example, has suggested that '"syncretism" in India ... is a trope in the discourse of "multiculturalism"' and that scholarly discussion of 'syncretic' phenomena such as Hindu worship of Sufi saints usually omits consideration of conflict or of the processes of expansion and contraction of religious communities. The key here is in the reference to processes. What is seen as a *condition* of synthesis may be better viewed as a *temporal manifestation* of relations between social groups, which continue to differentiate themselves from each other. The first view, that syncretism represents tolerance, presumes stasis, while the second brings time into the analysis. Of course, from the standpoint of secular politics, this static view of relations between groups is preferred, since secularism presumes that competition between religiously defined groups is an impermissible basis for politics, electoral as well. However, insofar as a politics is based on stasis, it cannot match changes in society.

Moving beyond syncretism and away from the dargah, there are studies describing community identities and Hindu–Muslim interactions, critical of syncretism (for instance, Assayag 2004a, 2004b; Eaton 1978; Gottschalk 2001; Mayaram 1997a, 1997b).

The scholarship here demonstrates how syncretism presupposes two or more self-contained and static essences, of the Hindu and the Muslim, categories that remain internally singular and absolutely exclusive, so that their resemblance to each other is rarely in evidence. In this scholarship, religious traditions blend automatically, keeping questions of power away. Against this position, for instance, Stewart and Shaw (1994), explore a range of ways in which people promote or resist syncretism. They understand syncretism and anti-syncretism as continually created and recreated in conditions of contestation and struggle. This raises the question of whether syncretism refers to an operation or a result, a process or a structure. Fazalbhoy (1997) rightly points out that syncretism was not a concept that was of general sociological interest and application. It appeared much more in the discussions on Islam in India, perhaps also of other minority religions (for instance, Sikhism was often referred to as 'syncretic'), but it seemed as if the problematic was the impact of Hinduism on Islam, that is the majority culture on the minority culture, and not vice versa. In fact, in the sociological discussions of religious syncretism, there is hardly any study which looks at the impact of Islam on Hinduism or considers the question of syncretism from the point of view of Hinduism. It appears that the problem of syncretism is a problem of the minority religions.

Aditya Kapoor, in Chapter 1, addresses the issue: How do Muslims negotiate their 'Muslim' identity as they draw on what they think to be a right balance between customary obligations, religious duties and traditions of the Prophet? Based on fieldwork in a Muslim community in West Bengal, he demonstrates how Muslims in their everyday lives negotiate their identity of 'being a Muslim' and other identities like that of 'being a Bengali'. They do not see their religious identity in tension with their other identities, but rather the play of multiple identities in everyday life is strategic and situational. A religious tradition acquires new forms, functions, meanings and modes of expression that require legitimisation and confirmation of new identities. When and why a particular religious custom is deemed syncretic and therefore is to be replaced by something authentic and true would reveal the work of socio-cultural contexts (Stewart and Shaw 1994). The question then is, does syncretism truly offer inclusive possibilities for a merging of religious difference, or is it a code word for the incorporation and assimilation of 'minority' cultures into the culture of the dominant group? Sufi shrines should be syncretic, more cultural, since Hinduism is assumed to be universal already. Is syncretism compatible with dogmas of 'Truth' or is it closer to a form of cultural relativism that in fact *dilutes* truth (Viswanathan 1998)? Most importantly, is syncretism possible as a subjectively experienced idea or is it only the stance of the outside observer, the social scientist, the privilege of the dominant or majority group making incorporative gestures in the name of a harmonious integration of all faiths? The question then is, what makes something syncretic? Does it also involve inquiring into the discursive and historical conditions that gave rise to this concept? Scholars have often asked the question of the 'when' and 'how' of 'syncretism' without answering the 'what': What is 'syncretism'? This is not simply a definitional question but one which delineates our object of study—Islam (Sitharaman 2013). An important issue is to see how Islam itself is constituted as an object of inquiry. These questions are posed in the spirit of negotiating the difficult and often perilous terrain between syncretism and separatism as vastly different cultural solutions to problems of religious difference.

The respective analytical frameworks developed in debating syncretism foreground issues that are central to questions of the secular and secularism. What kind of religion is acceptable in a secular age? The notion of 'the secular' employed in speaking of syncretism does not stand in opposition to 'the religious'. As part of rethinking the possibilities of modern secularism, it would seem worthwhile to ask how it might be possible to draw resources from 'religious' traditions that have been excluded by the various modes of secularism. The claim that religious movements may well have a legitimate place in modern politics if they agree to confine themselves to rational debate and persuasion and not resort to intolerant practices that circumscribe secular rights shows only a plea for a particular kind of religion. The debate on syncretism brings to light a process in which a certain kind of religion is determined to be compatible with liberal, democratic modernity, while others are not. An answer to these questions could be very useful for getting a better grasp of the secular.

Secular, Secularism and Secularity[10]

For more than two decades now, theorists of modernity have grappled with the resurgence of religion and the contemporary salience of politico-religious movements, along with their cognate processes, secularisation and modernisation, across the world (see, for instance, Asad 2003; Casanova 1994; Taylor 2007). One response was to turn the secularisation thesis into a normative rather than a sociological claim: secularisation had to happen if modernity was to be achieved; if some countries were not becoming secular, it was because they were insufficiently modern or because their modernising project had gone astray (Chatterjee 2006: 58). The exposition of the fallacies of linear, deterministic narratives of secularisation theory, ineluctably anchored in the separation of state and church and the private–public divide, foreground the dynamic nature of the public-ness of religious imagery and values that universalise not only European experiences of the Western development path, but also the transferability of the concepts in studying colonial and postcolonial societies. It is worth remembering that the current wave of theorising secularism was initially situated within a postcolonial context, both geographically and theoretically. And therefore, a spate of studies began to interrogate the monolithic understanding of secularism, and the variation of forms that this separation of state/politics and religion may take, thus, providing a picture of secularism that better fitted the actual practices of modern secular states (see, for example, Asad 2003, 2006b; Bilgrami 2006; Connolly 1999; Sullivan 2005). The strategy employed to dislodge a Eurocentric way of being secular was to espouse multiple secularities.

As opposed to the concept of secularism, an ideological–philosophical project, and secularisation that signifies both the process of differentiation, including diminishing mutual influences between religion and other social domains, as well as the decline in religious participation and belief, Wohlrab-Sahr and Burchardt (2012: 876) have initiated a discussion on secularity in terms of the *cultural meanings* underlying the differentiation between religious and non-religious spheres. In contrast to the political ideologies of separation, the concept of multiple secularity detects a variety of combinations of religion, national politics and the claims of religious groups and secular agents carried into the public sphere. They frame the concept not around the question of whether secularism/secularity are culturally inauthentic and a Western import, but in terms of how the boundaries between religion and the secular spheres are negotiated, challenged and redrawn in secular democracies.

As a number of scholars have shown, the categories of secular and the religious are not opposites of each other, but are closely intertwined in paradigmatic ways in modern nation states (see, for example, Agrama 2012; Asad 2003; Baubérot 2000; Connolly 1999; Keane 2007; Taylor 2007). The emergence of the modern category of the secular (in contrast with the pre-modern Latin term *saeculum*) is constitutively related to the rise of the modern concept of religion wherein it is impossible to track the history of one without simultaneously tracking the history of the other (Mahmood 2008: 462). Religion thus needs to be unpacked just as much as secularism as a concept.[11] Apart from the fact that 'religion' and 'secular' interpenetrate, it is modern law that is crucially involved in defining and defending the distinctness of social spaces, especially the legitimate space for religion. Thus, endorsing Asad (2006a: 209), what is of interest to us is the point that, '(L)aw finds itself continually having to redefine the space that religion may properly occupy because the reproduction of secular life ceaselessly disturbs the clarity of its boundaries'. In India, with its widely divergent religious traditions, both religious beliefs and practices, historically, have taken the form of politically negotiated religious settlements and varying religion–state arrangements. These movements also constitute the necessary tensions from which the modern nation state derives its own identity, as that of the supreme legislator and arbitrator (Viswanathan 1998: 16; see also Chakrabarti 2016; Sitharaman 2010).

An irreducible pluralism of beliefs, values and commitments, and the myriad ways in which state and religion are juxtaposed and the secularities that this bequeaths, requires 'some kind of neutrality, or "principled distance"' towards 'religious and nonreligious beliefs' which may offer us a foothold to deepen our understanding of secularism of what is been termed as 'the democratic state's response to diversity' (Taylor 2011: 310). Incidentally, these questions can be seen to be either bearing upon or issuing forth from the essays in this volume as well. Three essays in this volume look at some of these negotiations and challenges of secularism through a consideration of state law, politics and religion in colonial as well as contemporary times. In accordance with the current surge of theorising about secularism, both geographically and theoretically, for all the authors, law is a modality of secular power through which the state extends its reach into religious and social life, constantly blurring the line between religion and politics, and fostering religious–political conflict rather than mediating it.

Aleena Sebastian, in Chapter 2, looks at the interface between religion and law, and how secularity takes shape at the 'local' and how the matrilineal *tharavad* of the Mappila Muslims of Kerala came to be refashioned along new forms of familial relations in colonial and postcolonial Malabar through legal reform of Mappila custom and usage. The study foregrounds the 'courtroom' as a site where the court of law engages with the socio-cultural pluralities in Malabar. Through a close reading of court cases and legislative interventions in colonial and postcolonial Malabar, the author initiates a context-specific historical analysis of the contestations and negotiations between the state, religion, customary practices and legal pluralities. The essay also illustrates how the legal reforms were informed by Islamic reformist interventions in colonial Malabar and the changing power relations in tharavad, as well as the socio-economic aspirations of the Mappila Muslims.

Sudha Sitharaman, in Chapter 3, explores how the secular principles of religious freedom and the state's claim to religious neutrality, embedded in liberal democracies, are shot through with tensions, generating their own peculiar set of problems as they routinely intervene through a variety of injunctions to regulate the domain of religion as to how it should be practised in public life. Through the case study of a shrine in Bababudhan hills in Chickmagalur, south India, a common place of worship for two religious communities, where a dispute has now ensued, the essay attempts to illustrate the indeterminacies that exist in establishing legal categories—'Hindu', 'Muslim' and/or 'syncretic'—and demonstrates how the attempt at securing a religious framework by the state's sovereign authority denies traditions of their vitality. By focusing on the legal shapings of religion, the essay illustrates the distortions that occur in and through the process of translating social realities into legal categories and of how law produces normative conceptions of religion. The essay emphasises that secularism involves less a separation of religion and politics; rather religion is made an object of the state's regulatory capacity to intervene, thereby fashioning religious life and sensibility to fit the presuppositions and ongoing requirements of liberal governance. It further suggests that, perhaps, it would be more useful to rethink secularism as a constant interrogation, modelling and refashioning of religious subjectivities and practices wherein secularism's constitutive indeterminacies, integral to its workings, consolidate and extend the state's sovereign power of decision over social life. This rethinking of secularism would thereby give rise to a modular conception of religion and a concomitant religious subject compatible with rationality and liberal political rule.

Suchandra Ghosh and Anindita Chakrabarti, in Chapter 6, bring an ethnographic account to the question of Muslim personal law in India. By exploring the patterns and the processes of dispute resolution in marriage, divorce and inheritance among the Muslim litigants at a *dar-ul-qaza* (also known as sharia *adalat*) in a large Muslim locality in Kanpur (Uttar Pradesh), the authors draw our attention to the negotiations between what is considered to be 'Islamic rights and duties' and their religio-legal praxis. While family and marriage relations are embedded in a network of religiously sanctioned rights and duties, such obligations are subject to constant negotiation and interpretation. The legal–plural landscape offers avenues for Muslim women to exercise their agency in resolving a range of disputes covered under personal law. The ethnography depicts a complex terrain of inter-legality where both the religious and secular judicial authorities function in collocation. This process of institutionalised inter-legality once again shows how the concept of secularity functions not by circumscribing the role of religion in the public domain but by first creating a domain of religious personal 'law' and then by governing it. In the next section, we will foreground some of the debates on the Islamic public sphere as we discuss two essays in the volume that directly contribute to this debate.

The Islamic Public Sphere

The dominance of the privatisation thesis of religion was challenged by the pioneering work of José Casanova in his book *Public Religions in the Modern World* (1994). Casonava coined the term 'public religion' and argued that instead of an increasing privatisation, religion would assume a public role in many modern societies and it was actually 'deprivatisation' of religion that was on the cards (ibid.: 41).[12] Ever since the publication of his seminal work in 1994, Casanova has made several changes and critical revisions to his approach, and he only saw functional differentiation as an inevitable requirement for secularisation. However, the assumption of functional differentiation from the religious sphere, constituting the 'core of the theory' of secularisation, suffered criticism, as in the historical process of secularisation, the religious and the secular are inextricably bound together and mutually condition each other. In Asad's (2003: 182) view, when religion becomes an integral part of modern politics, it is not indifferent to debates about how the economy should be run, which scientific projects should be funded or what the broader aims of a national education system should be. The stress here is not merely that religion and the secular inter-penetrate but that (a) both are historically constituted; (b) this happens through accidental processes bringing together a variety of concepts, practices and sensibilities; and (c) in a modern society, the law is crucially involved in defining and defending the distinctiveness of social spaces, especially the legitimate space for religion. Asad (2003: 207–10) criticises Casanova for drawing an analytical distinction between those kinds of public religion that are compatible with modern differentiated structures, liberal democratic norms and individual liberties, and those that are not.

How has the concept of public religion unfolded in the anthropological literature on contemporary Islam? A close reading of the scholarly works in the field suggests that they begin by contesting the idea of the public sphere as the central locus in which to determine the nature of Muslim life. There have been many compelling new theories on the emergence of an 'Islamic public sphere' associated with new kinds of politico-religious movements. Spearheaded by scholars such as Salvatore (2007), Salvatore and Le Vine (2005), Eickelman and Anderson (2003), and Göle and Amman (2006), these theories have sought to simultaneously rethink the characteristics of the public sphere and to broaden our understanding of who participates in it and how, entering the conversation following the recalibration of Jürgen Habermas's concept by his critics and interlocutors.[13]

Contemporary Muslim socio-religious movements attempt to reformulate and implement the discourses on the idea of 'common good', which aspires to legitimise specific forms of political community, based on distinctive methods of public reasoning. Salvatore and Le Vine (2005) explain this in one of their edited volumes, giving as a key example the plethora of literature published on Islamic public spheres in the first decade of this century. In seeking to expand the definition of the public sphere, they state that sharia notions such as *istislah* (which they define as seeking public good) are at the heart of Muslim understanding of the public sphere (ibid.: 5). The new imaginaries of the Islamic public sphere are often in tension with modern liberal conceptions of the public sphere where debates over common good are premised on 'atomistic views of the social agent' and contractually based notions of trust (ibid.: 29). These conceptions of public sphere are also informed by a strict interpretation of the dichotomy between private and public spheres and by the ultimate basing of public reason on private interest,[14] whereas socio-religious discourses and movements primarily base their public reason on practical reason sanctified by religious tradition, however variably interpreted. For these scholars, there is something unique about the 'Islamic public sphere' in that they believe if one can conjure its existence, one can destabilise not only what Nancy Fraser called Habermas's bourgeois presuppositions (Fraser 1992; see also Salvatore and Le Vine 2005)—chief among them secularisation—but also, more broadly, the narrative of the public sphere as an achievement of Western capitalist societies. In other words, a central problem for scholars on Islamic public sphere is that most conceptions of the public sphere, including that of Habermas, consider secularly oriented rationality to be the normative terrain on which public life thrives. Therefore the need to critically explore 'the different means through which social practices inspired by Islam interact and sometimes clash with different forms of secularity as incorporated in the ideologies and practices' (Salvatore and Le Vine 2005: 7). This has had the positive effect of unsettling narrow Eurocentric definitions of civil society and the public sphere as essentially secular and Islam as incompatible with modern democratic processes (Bayat 2007).

At the same time, as Warner (2002) has noted, the idea of the public privileged within the social imaginary of modernity tends to exclude any recognition of the institutional and disciplinary conditions that enable it. For the public to be seen as both autonomous and sovereign with respect to the state, Warner suggests, it must be understood as self-organising, constituted solely by the circulation of its own discourse beyond the reach of any external norms or formal mediations (ibid.: 67–74). Drawing upon the work of Warner, among others, in his study of those involved in producing and listening to cassette sermons in Cairo, Hirschkind (2006) has shown how the public sphere is not limited to the kinds of deliberative practices that many hail as the hallmarks of rational political debate.[15] Analysing what he calls an Islamic 'counterpublic', Hirschkind reveals the equally significant disciplinary mechanisms within the public sphere. Hirschkind states that scholars of the public sphere have tended to dismiss the role of the virtues as inessential or irrelevant to the processes of public debate. For Hirschkind, this way of framing the inquiry reflects, in part, a tendency within liberal thought to view the individual as necessarily in conflict with the community and the forms of collective discipline that undergird it (ibid.: 106).[16] In contrast to a space for the formation of opinion through subjective reason (Habermas 1991 [1989]), this arena is geared to the deployment of the disciplining power of dialogue and debate, a goal that takes public deliberation as one of its modalities.

Drawing on these concerns, Chapter 4 by T. Hashim examines divergent practices of Islam among different traditions of Mappila Muslims in the Kerala public sphere, aimed at deducing a set of rules for religious conduct to guide their members in resolving the mundane issues of daily life. The domain of Islamic/Muslim public sphere of Kerala, over the course of this century, has come to be seen by many Muslims as necessary for the revival and strengthening of the Islamic community (ummah). Emphasis is placed on the cultivation of Islamic/Muslim virtues in the domain of public deliberation and argumentation between religious scholars and their audiences. As such, these emergent practices cannot be simply explained away as a modernising turn towards an increasingly individualised form of rational piety or as the deployment of religion for the task of consolidating national culture. Rather, as Hashim endeavours to show, they need to be analysed within a particular articulation of personal and political virtues in contemporary Islamic discourse. His essay contributes to the debate in the anthropology of Islam that addresses the question as to how Islamic movements with their pluricentric authority and internal contestation over participation in Muslim politics have had varied manifestations and outcomes in different national and regional contexts.

In the study of Islam in British India, Reetz (2006) has used the concept of public sphere to understand the emergence of a large number of Islamic 'groups' in the twentieth century. During this period, different educational as well as revivalist and reformist movements emerged as important actors in the public sphere. They adopted novel ways such as issuing fatwas (religious verdicts) on political matters and using legal means to achieve their religious goals, and the result was a 'disjuncture between public activism and the religious message itself' (ibid.: 311), where participation and prominence in the profane public sphere fractured religious cohesion. According to Reetz, it was also by participating as public actors in the public sphere that the 'closed mind-set' of the religious groups and their 'self-serving religiosity' could be negotiated and moulded according to principles of 'civility of public life' (ibid.: 311–15). From this perspective, the concept of public sphere offered a panacea for accommodating the multitude of Islamic movements to find their space in modular modernity. In a different vein, the concept of civil Islam traces the emergence of democratic and pluralist trends among Muslim groups and analyses the process of 'democratization in the age of religious revitalization', especially how these groups increasingly utilised democratic institutions to check state power, rather than Islamising the state (Hefner 2000: 3). In their later work, Hefner and his colleagues have argued for a similar remaking of Muslim politics and religion. Their approach urges us to shift our analytical gaze from propaganda to the praxis of religious organisations, which amply illustrates that there is no monolithic Muslim public sphere or politics (Hefner 2005). Here, we would like to draw attention to Irfan Ahmad's (2010) fine-grained analysis of the transformation of the Jamaat-e-Islami in India, as the organisation framed its discourse/ideology in the language of democratic rights of the postcolonial political context.

Two essays in this volume demonstrate how significant changes in recent Islamic reform are rooted in the rhetoric and language of civic activism, human welfare as well as Islamic religiosity. The case of the Solidarity Youth Movement (SYM) in Kerala, the youth wing of the Jamaat-e-Islami, and the palliative care movement spearheaded by the Mujahid movement amply illustrate this transformation. In Chapter 5, on the SYM, Shahul Ameen K. T. raises the following questions: Can an offshoot of a minority religious organisation/movement influence religious and civil society discourses of a region? If yes, what explains this influence? How does it remake the concerns and identity of the parent organisation and of the larger society? Drawing on ethnographic research on the SYM, the author shows how the SYM practitioners interpret Islamic scriptural and other traditions—including common usages—as they engage in civic activism. The essay also discusses how the SYM introduces an ethico-religious dimension to public sphere debates as well as civil society activism. By highlighting the practices of the SYM, it underscores the ways in which it widens the political and theological horizons of Jamaat-e-Islami and, thereby, the politics of Islamism.

R. Santhosh, in Chapter 7, addresses the involvement of a Muslim reformist organisation, the Mujahid movement, in the palliative care movement in Kerala. The movement has been at the forefront of a state-wide palliative-care initiative and has been highly successful in facilitating this through its organisational networks in the Muslim-dominated areas of the state. The author explores how multiple narratives of Islamic encounter with secularism are produced in the Indian context, thereby problematising its relation with modernity. These two essays articulate, albeit in different ways, Salvatore and Eickelman's (2004: 94) observation on the public sphere and Islam where the former was not limited to 'modern' societies but was the sphere of contestation over the definition of 'common good' and the virtues, obligations and rights required for realising that common good.[17]

Conclusion

The seven chapters in this volume explore Islam in contemporary India in diverse domains as they remain in conversation with themes in the sociology of Islam outlined in this essay. What connects them is their commitment to an ethnographic approach while paying attention to the historical details. The authors would like to pay their tribute to Professor J. P. S. Uberoi, who commented on the essays when they were presented at a seminar organised at IIT Kanpur. Drawing on his work in Afghanistan, Uberoi raised the signature anthropological question: How does the 'field view' conceptualise the Muslim lifeworld as located in religious precepts, customary practices, public norms and power? Uberoi argued that we need to understand the functioning of social institutions and their interconnections in order to comment on what a 'system of Islam' is. For Uberoi, the purpose is not to document the effects of the religio-legal on life and organisation (the customary) but to unearth their mutual interconnectedness (Uberoi 1971: 399). This anthropological gaze reminds us of Salvatore's (2016: 9–10) notion of Islamic 'ecumene' that understands Islam as an 'extremely mobile set of pattern of normativity and civility' where both the religious and civil dimensions overlap without gravitating on an exclusive centre. In his ethnography of the Andarab region of Afghanistan, Uberoi (1968) has illustrated how the tenets of Islam, contingencies of tribal social structure and a nascent bureaucratic state negotiated to maintain what people considered as 'Islamic'. Here, the method of dispute resolution and governance were delicately balanced between state authorities, the *qazi*'s court, and the cultural expectations of honour and shame (ibid.). Uberoi's work showed how ownership of property, rules of the segmentary lineage system and quranic prescriptions were actualised through local demography, genealogies and gender relations. Committed to the ethnographic lens, the essays in the volume aim to explore the new associational practices, debates in the Islamic public sphere/secularity, and civil society activism. The impact of bureaucratisation of religious governance and personal law in contemporary India and Sufi shrines are the sites where we further investigate this relationship.

A new anthropology of Islam is the insistence that analysis begins by paying attention to the genealogies of discourses (academic, state, 'official', global as well as those of our research subjects and interlocutors), which might become authoritative and normative, and through which politics in Muslim societies is comprehended, experienced, legitimated or contested (Soares and Osella 2009). The essays in this volume explore the many lives of Islam as they negotiate reform, revival and everyday piety in the context of secular democracy. The ideal of secularism rests in uneasy tension with the reality of religion. In this scheme of things, the state is seen as the institution through which religion is administered and secularism is upheld. Both these tasks, as recent history shows, has proved to be much more difficult than imagined. The essays attempt to bring a fresh analysis of the processes through which religion is reconfigured at different sites.

Notes

1. It is matter for a separate enquiry as to how the curious geopolitical notion of religion has truncated the study of Islam in India. Yet, South Asia, as compared to the Arab countries, hosts the second largest number of Muslims in the Islamic world (Reetz 2006: 1–2).
2. In her recent work on low-income group neighbourhoods of Delhi, Das (2015: 248) has echoed this position when she writes that if one cares for the articulation of religiosity, the everyday life of Muslims shows that it is 'neither a story of secularism nor of syncretism but rather one in which the heterogeneity of everyday life allows Hindus and Muslims to receive the claims of each other that have arisen by the sheer fact of proximity, face-to-face relations, and the privileging of aesthetic immediacy of emotions even over the prohibitions emanating from various authoritative discourses of Islam and Hinduism'.
3. Robinson (1986) responded to both Minault and Das, defending himself against the accusations raised by the 'Aunty Sallies'.
4. Though Mines (1975) uses the rural–urban divide, it has nothing in common with Gellner's (1981) *ma'irib* and *mashirik* divides. In short, while the latter stresses the role of 'Islamic blueprint', the former highlights the role of Weberian categories (i.e., party and status) for creating Islamic revival. Evidencing this orientation, Mines published a volume titled *Muslim Merchants: The Economic Behavior of an Indian Muslim Community* (1972).
5. The term 'syncretism' has a particular Western history. It was originally coined in a positive sense by Plutarch in the first century AD [*Moralia* 2.490b] and

acquired overriding negative connotations in the seventeenth century (Stewart 1999: 45). The term was adopted in the mid-nineteenth century by the discipline of history of religion that understood it as the blending of elements from diverse religions into a single doctrine or cult, and used it in largely pejorative terms, since it too saw syncretism as a movement towards a more unified heterogeneity (though not homogeneity); towards a more cosmopolitan and at the same time less polytheistic unification of deities, pieties and rituals; towards pantheism (as opposed to monotheism). This negative view, reflected in the Protestant missionary literature, continued through the nineteenth century and well into the twentieth. Meanwhile, the advent of anthropology shifted the connotation once again from negative to positive, as it came to be associated with cultural and linguistic mixture in general. This opened the floodgates to a huge variety of uses, making the term more or less interchangeable with 'acculturation', 'hybridisation', 'creolisation', 'bricolage', etc. See, for instance, Stewart and Shaw (1994) and Stewart and Ernst (2003). Once again, this raises problems of precision: In each case, questions remain to be answered as to how such mixings occur, whether they vary in time and place, whether they are intentional or unintentional, etc. In the interest of manageability, many scholars—though by no means all—prefer to restrict 'syncretism' to religious interactions. In an important essay, van der Veer (1994) has established that the historical roots of syncretism's semantic association with transdenominational universalism lie in the rise of Protestantism and the decline of the absolute authority of Catholicism. He further argues that syncretism's subsequent identification with cultural relativism accompanied the spread of colonialism and the vigorous, often aggressive, and politically charged contact with alien religious cultures that colonial expansion promoted. Syncretism appears as a term used in Christian theology at least since the seventeenth century. Denoting an 'attempt to sink differences and effect union between sects or philosophical schools' (ibid.: 185), syncretism as a favourable term came into its own with the decline of the Catholic church, which hitherto held complete authority to decide what was absolute truth and condemn all deviations from that truth as heresies; syncretism in a Catholic regime, suggests van der Veer, was associated pejoratively with a 'betrayal of principles ... an attempt to secure unity at the expense of truth' (ibid.: 186).

6. A dargah is a shrine or tomb built over the grave of a revered religious figure, often that of a Sufi saint.
7. Sufi Islam is often perceived and understood in juxtaposition to what is commonly constructed as 'normative Islam'. This understanding emanates from the notion that the Sufi way of life went beyond the tenets of sharia or Islamic law. However, recent studies connect Sufi literature to the greater vehicle of Muslim piety, reminding us of the danger that often lies in talking about Sufism in a different breath from Islamic law or the study of the Hadith. Green (2004: 125), recounting Sufi writing in Persian, cites a work by al-Hujwiri titled *Kashf al-mahjub*, composed in the mid-eleventh century, and its emphasis on *akhlaq* (morality) and *adab* (etiquette), to argue that Sufism was a path to perfecting one's adherence to normative Islam, rather than an alternative to it.

8. The Barelwi movement, one of the most influential modern religious movements among the Muslims in the subcontinent, was initiated by Maulana Ahmad Raza Khan Barelwi (1856–1921), who tried to inculcate in individual Muslims a stricter adherence to the sharia or Islamic law to bring about reform or to engage in *tajdid* (renewal of faith). The importance of Ahmad Raza Khan and the Barelwi movement lay in their efforts to define, within the reforming discourse of the late nineteenth and twentieth centuries, a position stressing Sunnah, the following of the Prophet's path, with the help of saintly intermediaries (for details, see Sanyal 1996).
9. As Osella and Osella (2008: 249–50) have noted, in South Asia as elsewhere (see, for instance, Otayek and Soares 2007), much ethnographic work has largely concentrated on the study of popular religious practices—in particular, Sufism and saints' shrine worship (see, for instance, Ahmad 1981; Ahmad and Reifeld 2004; Roy 2005; Troll 1989; Waseem 2003; Werbner and Basu 1998; see also Bayly 1989; Werbner 2003)—and thus celebrates Sufi-inspired forms of Islam as tolerant, plural, authentic and so on, against a maligned Other of reformist Islam. For notable exceptions on this aspect, see van der Veer (1992), Hansen (1999), Gardner (1995), Ewing (1997), Simpson (2006), Marsden (2005), Blank (2001) and Verkaaik (2004).
10. The dominant concepts being debated in international fora are secularisation and secularism (see, for example, Iqtidar 2011). While secularisation is a concept addressing processes of functional differentiation, religious decline and private practices of religion, secularism refers to the institutional arrangements separating politics/the state and religion as well as their ideological legitimisations. The relationship between secularism and secularisation is often indexed by the term secularity.
11. Nandy's (1990) approach to unpacking religion avows that, one, it is both possible and necessary to draw a dividing line, within religion, between 'religion-as-faith' and 'religion-as-ideology'. By faith, he means 'religion as a way of life, a tradition which is definitionally non-monolithic and operationally plural' (ibid.: 70). By ideology he means religion as a sub-national, national or cross-national identifier of populations contesting for or protecting non-religious, usually political or socio-economic, interests. Such religions-as-ideologies usually get identified with one or more texts which, rather than the ways of life of the believers, then become the final identifiers of the pure forms of the religions (ibid.). 'Religion as faith' or, more particularly, the idea of religious faith is a rich and confusing field. The ground is rendered even more complicated if one stresses the philosophical need to avoid generality and focus instead on particular religious beliefs as they show themselves in the language and actions of believers (Hegde 2000: 462).
12. Casanova (1994: 5) defined deprivatisation in the following way: 'By deprivatization I mean the fact that religious traditions throughout the world are refusing to accept the marginal and privatized role which theories of modernity as well as theories of secularization had reserved for them'.

13. As critics of *The Structural Transformation of the Public Sphere: An Inquiry into a Bourgeois Society* have pointed out, Habermas (1991 [1989]) paid insufficient attention to religion in this early work. Indeed, in his introduction to an influential collection on Habermas and the public sphere, Calhoun (1992 [1978]: 35–36) noted not only Habermas's relative 'neglect of religion' but also, and more forcefully, his 'antireligious assumptions'.
14. Islamic public sphere operates from a different orientation than the liberal or Jacobin European frameworks. Accordingly, the resulting public sphere, Salvatore and Le Vine (2005) argue, can potentially be seen as a positive-sum game, one that reflects a logic quite distinct from the scarcely plastic—if not zero-sum—notions of social justice based on standards of 'pure reason', or, at least, from the zeroing formal culture—the elision of specific cultural and even legal traditions—that often accompanies Western discourses of 'the public'. Such a singular kind of public reason silences other kinds of reason embodied by autonomous social actors, especially those grounded in a religious identity (ibid.: 5).
15. The resultant public is less a sphere of discussion than one of subjection to authority, part of a project aimed at promoting and securing a uniform model of moral behaviour. In short, the public arena constituted by deliberation and argumentation tends to be identified either as a deliberative space of argument and contestation between individuals or as a normative space for education in community-oriented virtue (Hirschkind 2006: 106).
16. Hirschkind (2006) states that scholars of the public sphere have tended to dismiss the role of virtues as inessential or irrelevant to the processes of public debate. To predicate public deliberation and participation on the prior cultivation of a set of virtues, it is argued, only makes sense in the context of an Aristotelian notion that we, human beings, have certain definable ends that those virtues enable us achieve—a notion that has no place in a liberal society committed to value pluralism and individual autonomy (ibid.: 232).
17. Drawing on John Dewey's insights on the 'public', the authors argue that the contemporary Islamic public sphere is grounded in a multitude of associational practices ranging from the publishing business and reading groups to mosque and collective prayer sermons. These sites, along with the media, produce a dynamic public sphere that is not rooted in notions of European rationality. The authors also draw on Casanova who had built on later Habermas to remind us of the role played by the non-conformist sects and other disestablished religion in fighting the 'unjust and sinful state' (Salvatore and Eickelman 2004: 7).

References

Agrama, Hussein Ali. 2012. *Questioning Secularism: Islam, Sovereignty and the Rule of Law in Egypt*. Chicago: University of Chicago Press.

Ahmad, Imtiaz (ed.). 1973. *Caste and Social Stratification among Muslims in India*. New Delhi: Manohar Publications.

——— (ed.). 1976. *Family, Kinship and Marriage among Muslims in India*. New Delhi: Manohar Publications.

——— (ed.). 1981. *Ritual and Religion among Muslims in India*. New Delhi: Manohar Publications.

Ahmad, Imtiaz and Helmut Reifeld (eds). 2004. *Lived Islam in South Asia: Adaptation, Accommodation, and Conflict*. Delhi: Social Science Press.

Ahmad, Irfan. 2010. *Islamism and Democracy in India: The Transformation of Jamaat-e-Islami*. New Delhi: Permanent Black.

Asad, Talal. 2003. *Formations of the Secular: Christianity, Islam and Modernity*. California: Stanford University Press.

———. 2006a. 'Responses', in David Scott and Charles Hirschkind (eds), *Powers of the Secular Modern: Talal Asad and His Interlocutors*, pp. 206–42. Stanford, CA: Stanford University Press.

———. 2006b. 'Trying to Understand French Secularism', in Hent de Vries and Lawrence E. Sullivan (eds), *Political Theologies: Public Religions in a Post-Secular World*, pp. 494–526. New York: Fordham University Press.

Assayag, Jackie. 2004a. *At the Confluence of Two Rivers: Muslims and Hindus in South India*. New Delhi: Manohar Publications.

———. 2004b. 'Can Hindus and Muslims Coexist?', in Imtiaz Ahmad and Helmut Reifeld (eds), *Lived Islam in South Asia: Adaptation, Accommodations and Conflict*, pp. 40–60. Delhi: Social Science Press.

Baubérot, J. 2000. *Histoire de la Laïcité Française* (History of French Secularity). Paris: Presses Universitaires de France.

Bayat, A. 2007. *Making Islam Democratic: Social Movements and the Post-Islamist Turn*. Stanford: Stanford University Press.

Bayly, Susan. 1989. *Saints, Goddesses, and Kings: Muslims and Christians in South Indian Society, 1700–1900*. Cambridge: Cambridge University Press.

Bilgrami, Akeel (ed.). 2006. *The Crisis of Secularism in India*. London: Duke University Press.

Blank, J. 2001. *Mullahs on the Mainframe: Islam and Modernity among the Daudi Bohras*. Chicago, IL: University of Chicago Press.

Calhoun, Craig. 1992 [1978]. 'Introduction', in Craig Calhoun (ed.), *Habermas and the Public Sphere*, pp. 1–48. Cambridge: MIT Press.

Casanova, José. 1994. *Public Religions in the Modern World*. Chicago: University of Chicago Press.

Chakrabarti, Anindita. 2016. 'Democracy as Civil Religion: Reading Alexis De Tocqueville in India', *Journal of Human Values*, 22 (1): 14–25.

———. 2018. *Faith and Social Movements: Religious Reform in Contemporary India*. Cambridge: Cambridge University Press.

Chatterjee, Partha. 2006. 'Fasting for Bin Laden: The Politics of Secularization in Contemporary India', in Charles Hirschkind and David Scott (eds), *Powers of the Secular Modern: Talal Asad and His Interlocutors*, pp. 57–74. Stanford, CA: Stanford University Press.

Connolly, William. 1999. *Why I am Not a Secularist.* Minneapolis: University of Minnesota Press.

Das, Veena. 1984. 'For a Folk Theology and Theological Anthropology of Islam', *Contributions to Indian Sociology,* 18 (2): 293–300.

———. 2015. *Affliction: Health, Disease, Poverty (Forms of Living).* Fordham: Fordham University Press.

Eaton, Richard M. 1978. 'The Profile of Popular Islam in the Pakistani Punjab', *Journal of South Asian and Middle Eastern Studies,* 2 (1): 74–92.

Eickelman, Dale F., and John W. Anderson. 2003. *New Media in the Muslim World: The Emerging Public Sphere.* Indiana: Indiana University Press.

Ewing, Katherine P. 1997. *Arguing Sainthood: Modernity, Psychoanalysis and Islam.* Durham: Duke University Press.

Fazalbhoy, N. 1997. 'Sociology of Muslims in India: A Review', *Economic and Political Weekly,* 32 (26): 1547–51.

Fraser, N. 1992. 'Rethinking the Public Sphere: A Contribution to the Critique of Actually Existing Democracy', *Social Text,* 25 (26): 56–80.

Gardner, K. 1995. *Global Migrants, Local Lives: Travel and Transformation in Rural Bangladesh.* Oxford: Clarendon Press.

Gellner, Ernst. 1981. *Muslim Society.* Cambridge: New Cambridge University Press.

Göle, Nilüfer and Ludwig Amman. 2006. *Islam in Public: Turkey, Iran and Europe.* Istanbul: Bilgi University Press.

Gottschalk, Peter. 2001. *Beyond Hindu and Muslim: Multiple Identities in Narratives of Village India.* New Delhi: Oxford University Press.

Green, Nile. 2004. 'Emerging Approaches to the Sufi Traditions of South Asia: Between Texts, Territories, and the Transcendent', *South Asia Research,* 24 (2): 123–48.

Habermas, Jürgen. 1991 [1989]. *The Structural Transformation of the Public Sphere: An Inquiry into a Bourgeois Society.* Chicago: MIT Press.

Hansen, T. B. 1999. *Wages of Violence: Naming and Identity in Postcolonial Bombay.* Princeton, NJ: Princeton University Press.

Hefner, Robert W. 2000. *Civil Islam: Muslims and Democratization in Indonesia.* Princeton: Princeton University Press.

——— (ed.). 2005. *Remaking Muslim Politics: Pluralism, Contestation, Democratization.* Princeton: Princeton University Press.

Hegde, Sasheej. 2000. 'Always Already Secular: Afterthoughts on the Secular–Communal Question', *Economic and Political Weekly,* 40 (4): 322–34.

Hirschkind, Charles. 2006. *The Ethical Soundscape: Cassette Sermons and Islamic Counterpublics.* Columbia: Columbia University Press.

Iqtidar, Humeira. 2011. *Secularizing Islamists? Jamaat-e-Islami and Jamaat-ud-Dawa in Urban Pakistan.* London: The University of Chicago Press.

Keane, Webb. 2007. *Christian Moderns: Freedom and Fetish in the Mission Encounter.* California: University of California Press.

Launay, R. 1992. *Beyond the Stream: Islam and Society in a West African Town.* Berkeley: University of California Press.

Mahmood, Saba. 2008. 'Secular Imperatives?', *Public Culture*, 20 (3): 461–65.
Mamdani, Mahmood. 2002. 'Good Muslim, Bad Muslim: A Political Perspective on Culture and Terrorism', *American Anthropologist*, 104 (3): 766–75.
Marsden, Magnus. 2005. *Living Islam: Muslim Religious Experience in Pakistan's North-West Frontier*. Cambridge: Cambridge University Press.
Mayaram, Shail. 1997a. *Resisting Regimes: Myth, Memory and the Shaping of a Muslim Identity*. New Delhi: Oxford University Press.
———. 1997b. 'Rethinking Meo Identity: Cultural Faultline, Syncreticism, Hybridity or Liminality', *Comparative Studies of South Asia, Africa and the Middle East*, 17 (2): 35–44.
Minault, Gail. 1984. 'Some Reflections on Islamic Revivalism vs. Assimilation among Muslims in India', *Contributions of Indian Sociology*, 8 (2): 301–05.
Mines, Mattison. 1972. *Muslim Merchants: The Economic Behavior of an Indian Muslim Community*. Michigan: The University of Michigan.
———. 1975. 'Islamisation and Muslim Ethnicity in South India', *Royal Anthropological Institute of Great Britain and Ireland*, 10 (3): 404–18.
Nandy, Ashis. 1990. 'The Politics of Secularism and the Recovery of Religious Tolerance', in Veena Das (ed.), *Mirrors of Violence: Communities, Riots and Survivors in South Asia*, pp. 66–93. New Delhi: Oxford University Press.
Osella, Caroline. 2015. 'Debating Shirk in Keralam, South India: Monotheism between Tradition, Text and Performance', *Open Library of Humanities*, 1 (1): 1–36.
Osella, Filippo and Caroline Osella. 2008. 'Introduction: Islamic Reformism in South Asia', *Modern Asian Studies*, 42 (2/3): 247–57.
Otayek, R., and B. Soares. 2007. 'Introduction: Islam and Muslim Politics in Africa', in B. Soares and R. Otayek (eds), *Islam and Muslim Politics in Africa*, pp. 1–24. Basingstoke: Palgrave Macmillan.
Parkin, D. J. 2000. 'Inside and Outside the Mosque: A Master Trope', in D. J. Parkin and S. C. Headley (eds), *Islamic Prayer across the Indian Ocean: Inside and Outside the Mosque*, pp. 1–22. Richmond, Surrey: Curzon.
Reetz, Dietrich. 2006. *Islam in the Public Sphere: Religious Groups in India, 1900–1947*. London: Oxford University Press.
Robinson, Francis. 1983. 'Islam and Muslim Society in South Asia', *Contributions to Indian Sociology*, 17 (2): 185–203.
———. 1986. 'Islam and Muslim Society in South Asia: A Reply to Das and Minault', *Contributions to Indian Sociology*, 20 (1): 97–104.
Roy, Asim. 2005. 'Thinking over Popular Islam in South Asia: A Search for a Paradigm', in Mushirul Hasan and Asim Roy (eds), *Living Together Separately: Cultural India in History and Politics*, pp. 29–61. New Delhi: Oxford University Press.
Salvatore, Armando. 2007. *The Public Sphere: Liberal Modernity, Catholicism, Islam*. New York: Palgrave Macmillan.
———. 2016. *The Sociology of Islam: Knowledge, Power and Civility*. West Sussex: John Wiley & Sons Ltd.
Salvatore, Armando and Dale F. Eickelman. 2004. *Public Islam and the Common Good*. Leiden: Brill.

Salvatore, Armando and Mark Le Vine. 2005. *Religion, Social Practice, and Contested Hegemonies: Reconstructing the Public Sphere in Muslim Majority Societies*. New York: Palgrave Macmillan.

Sanyal, Usha. 1996. *Devotional Islam and Politics in British India: Ahmad Riza Khan Barelwi and His Movement, 1870–1920*. New Delhi: Yoda Press.

Simpson, E. 2006. *Muslim Society and the Western Indian Ocean: The Seafarers of Kachchh*. New Delhi: Routledge.

Sitharaman, Sudha. 2010. 'Conflict over Worship: A Study of the Sri Guru Dattatreya Swami Bababudhan Dargah in South India', in Gita Dharampal-Frick, Robert Langer and Nils Holger Petersen (eds), *Ritual Dynamics and the Science of Ritual*, pp. 205–33. Wiesbaden: Harrassowitz Verlag.

———. 2013. 'Limits of Syncretism: Bababudhan Dargah in South India as a Paradigm for Overlapping Religious Affiliations and Co-existence', in Herausgegeben von Andreas H. Pries, Laetitia Martzolff, Robert Langer and Claus Ambos (eds), *Rituale als Ausdruck von Kulturkontakt: SynKretismus zwischen Negation und Neudefinition*, pp. 79–110. Wiesbaden: Harrassowitz Verlag.

Soares, Benjamin and Filippo Osella. 2009. 'Islam, Politics, Anthropology', *The Journal of the Royal Anthropological Institute*, 15 (1): 1–23.

Stewart, Charles. 1999. 'Syncretism and its Synonyms: Reflections on Cultural Mixture', *Diacritics*, 29 (3): 40–62.

Stewart, Charles and Rosalind Shaw (eds). 1994. *Syncretism/Anti-syncretism: The Politics of Religious Synthesis*, pp. 196–212. London and New York: Routledge.

Stewart, Tony K., and Carl W. Ernst. 2003. 'Syncreticism', in Peter J. Claus and Margret A. Mills (eds), *South Asian Folklore: An Encyclopaedia*, pp. 586–87. New York: Garland Publishing, Inc.

Sullivan, Winnifred Fallers. 2005. *The Impossibility of Religious Freedom*. Princeton: Princeton University Press.

Taylor, Charles. 2007. *A Secular Age*. Harvard: Harvard University Press.

———. 2011. 'What Does Secularism Mean?', in Charles Taylor (ed.), *Dilemmas and Connections: Selected Essays*, pp. 303–25. Cambridge: Harvard University Press,

Troll, C. W. 1989. *Muslim Shrines in India*. New Delhi: Oxford University Press.

Uberoi, J. P. S. 1968. 'District Administration in the Northern High-lands of Afghanistan', *Sociological Bulletin*, 28 (1): 65–89.

———. 1971. 'Men, Women and Property in Northern Afghanistan', in S. T. Lokhandawala (ed.), *India and Contemporary Islam*, pp. 398–415. Simla: Indian Institute of Advanced Study.

van der Veer, Peter. 1992. 'Playing or Praying: A Sufi Saint's Day in Surat', *The Journal of Asian Studies*, 51 (3): 545–64.

———. 1994. 'Syncretism, Multiculturalism, and the Discourse of Tolerance', in Charles Stewart and Rosalind Shaw (eds), *Syncretism/Anti-syncretism: The Politics of Religious Synthesis*, pp. 185–99. London and New York: Routledge.

Verkaaik, O. 2004. *Migrants and Militants: Fun and Urban Violence in Pakistan*. Princeton: Princeton University Press.

Viswanathan, Gauri. 1998. *Outside the Fold—Conversion, Modernity, and Belief*. Princeton: Princeton University Press.

Warner, Michael. 2002. *Publics and Counterpublics*. New York: Zone Books.

Waseem, M. (ed. and trans.) 2003. *On Becoming an Indian Muslim: French Essays on Aspects of Syncretism*. Delhi: Oxford University Press.

Werbner, P. 2003. *Pilgrims of Love: The Anthropology of a Global Sufi Cult*. Bloomington: Indiana University Press.

Werbner, P., and H. Basu (eds). 1998. *Embodying Charisma: Modernity, Locality and the Performance of Emotion in Sufi Cults*. London: Routledge.

Wohlrab-Sahr, Monica and Marian Burchardt. 2012. 'Multiple Secularities: Religion and Modernity in the Global Age—Introduction', *International Sociology*, 28 (6): 605–11.

1

Muslim Subjectivities, Embedded Identities

Constructions of Secularity in Everyday Life

Aditya Kapoor

This essay illustrates the different ways by which the religious and the secular domains of our everyday life are intertwined. The attempt is to problematise our understanding of the secular as the relegation of religion to the private domain of our lives. Anchored in the observation that the concept of secularism, as a political ideology, is a product of a specific historical context in modern Europe, this essay argues that caution needs to be exercised as we universalise a normative understanding of secularism that erases the other possible frames of interaction between the religious and the secular. Following the work of Talal Asad (1986), I consider religious traditions as discursive traditions, which are constantly shifting and situationally redrawing the boundaries between the religious and the secular. Both the concepts came up in similar historical settings and more importantly they render each other meaningful. Asad (1993) points towards the dialectical relationship between religion and the secular, and argues that the way we understand the notion of religion and the secular has a geographical and temporal signifier of modern Western Europe. It is in this context that the emergence of the notion of secular has constituted the way we understand religion today.

The essay also argues that we need to pay attention to the fact that religious communities are embedded in a specific context (Jairath 2011). The interaction of religion and the secular takes multiple dimensions based on the local context. As Bhargava (1998) and Casanova (2008) have argued, taking the example of continental Europe and America, religion and the secular interact in multiple ways in public life, giving rise to the idea of 'contextual' secularism. Therefore, the historical genealogy of secularism, with its roots in Western political discourses, questions the portrayal of secularism in binary terms of public and secular versus private and religious.

The essay focuses on two issues. First, it looks at how religious ideas and practices shape the complex interaction between the religious and the secular spheres. Second, by focusing on the everyday life of Muslims, the essay traces the fluidity of social boundaries and identities. These interact with other identities, and this dynamism questions the notion of essentialisation (religious identity in this case) as a determinate marker in the social life of people. The essay is based on ethnographic fieldwork amongst a Muslim community in a village named Furfura, located in the Hooghly district of West Bengal. The 16-month fieldwork (October 2010 to February 2013) focused on the domain of the mundane and the ordinary as it exhibits the complexities and ambivalences of everyday life and raised the following questions: How does one be a Muslim in a secular world? How are traditions interpreted and meanings constituted which inform everyday life? In engaging with these question, Soares and Otayek's (2007) concept of Islam *mondain* is helpful in understanding the complexities associated with 'being a Muslim' in everyday life. Islam mondain refers to the various ways of being Muslim in our contemporary world, where no particular way has a precedent over the others. As a concept, it does not privilege Islam over other aspects of everyday life, but attempts to focus on the relational aspect of Islam with other dimensions of everyday life. Islam mondain encompasses the diversity and dynamism related with various modes through which Muslims relate themselves with Islam and other aspects of their everyday life. Giving primacy to the notion of agency and questioning the deterministic role of Islam as the primary source of ethics in the lives of Muslims is, therefore, seen as one among many other sources that may constitute everyday ethics for its adherents. Engaging with the complexities involved in everyday life in a low-income Muslim neighbourhood of Delhi, Das (2010) shows how ethics in everyday life, with their multiple sources and interpretations, contribute to notions of 'being Muslim' rather than prescriptions emanating from authoritative discourses of Islam.

This essay engages with this question by foregrounding the oft-ignored truism that the construction of social identity is a polymorphic process, and therefore we must pay adequate attention towards how different identities are negotiated in accordance with the contingencies of everyday life. Religious dispositions in this perspective can be one among many other sources constituting identity. The essay will demonstrate that any clear demarcation between categories like 'religion-as-faith' and 'religion-as-ideology' blurs when we see them in the background of everyday life.[1] This implies that there are no clear boundaries in everyday life to separate the politics associated with religion with popular devotional forms of religion. In this regard, I argue that the construction of religion as faith or as an ideology is a contextually embedded process with shifting boundaries. Religious practices that may be seen as faith in certain historical situations may, in due course of time, emerge as ideology.[2] In everyday life, this demarcation fails as in specific situations, ideology can also inform and condition some of the religious practices. We need to also explore how social context facilitates continuation, disjunction as well as emergence of certain religious traditions and practices. This exhibits a wide spectrum of interaction of the religious and the secular in our everyday life.

This essay is divided into two sections. The first section deals with how religious ideology and practices are contextually constituted in reciprocity with the wider socio-political context. It shows how the Sufi order that came up in colonial Bengal changed in the context of independent India, and how its practices and ideology underwent shifts. The second section dwells on an account of everyday engagements of Muslims with the question of identity and illustrates the fluid social boundaries through which Muslim subjectivities are constituted. The narratives displace any rigid demarcation between the religious and the secular aspects of everyday life.

The Contextual Understanding of Ideology and Practice

Furfura is famous for the shrine of Abu Bakr Siddique (d. 1939). He was initiated in four Sufi *silsilas* (orders)—Chistiya, Qaderiya, Naaqshbandiya and Mujjaddediya. He introduced his own Sufi silsila, named Furfura Shareif. He was also a religious reformer of the Hanafi sect and a pir in undivided Bengal. For his reformist activities, he was known popularly as *mujjadded-e-zaman*—the one who renewed the faith in his time. The endeavours of Abu Bakr Siddique were not restricted to religious activities. He was also active in the contemporary politics of his times. He was active in some of the Muslim socio-political organisations in the early nineteenth century, and later supported the Muslim League.[3] After his death in 1939, a shrine was built at his grave at Furfura, and today the shrine is one of the most important religious sites for Muslims in eastern India. Anyone visiting the shrine of Abu Bakr Siddique will notice quite a few unique features. At the entrance of the shrine, certain written instructions are given to the devotees—for instance, kissing or touching the grave; doing *sajda* (prostration) in front of grave; lighting candles or scented sticks; or offering rosewater, flowers or *chadors* (coverings) on the grave are strictly prohibited. Other activities generally popular at other Sufi shrines, like music in the form of qawwali or any other use of musical instruments, are also prohibited. The shrine is open only to men; women are not allowed inside, not even inside the premises of the shrine. There is no annual urs[4] (festival) celebration and there is no tradition of *gaddinashin*[5] in this shrine. Instead of the annual urs, at this shrine, *isale swahab*—transferring of rewards to the dead and reciting the Quran for the dead—is conducted every year on the 21st, 22nd and 23rd days of the Falgun month of the Bengali calendar. In most Sufi shrines in the South Asian region, pirs or other officials of the shrine are present inside the shrine complex to intercede on behalf of the devotees who visit the shrine. But in the shrine of Abu Bakr Siddique, except for the devotees, no one is present inside the shrine to pray on behalf of the devotees. Even the pirs are not present inside the shrine, and they sit in their respective *gaddis* (offices), situated outside the boundaries of the shrine. Interestingly, Hindus do not frequent this shrine, which is common with other Sufi shrines of this region.

All the activities that are proscribed and prescribed for the devotees are based on the reformist ideology of Abu Bakr Siddique, which is outlined in his *wasiyatnama* (will). The wasiyatnama contains instructions that act like a guide for Abu Bakr Siddique's devotees and the custodians of the shrine to manage their everyday life in accordance with the rules of the silsila Furfura Sahreif. According to his wasiyatnama, apart from religious instructions to save Muslims from committing shirk and bida,[6] Abu Bakr also advises Muslims to reconstitute their everyday life on the model of the Quran and the Hadith. It means that it is not sufficient on the part of Muslims to pray five times a day, fast during the month of Ramzan or perform pious acts—it is equally important for Muslims to behave like 'proper' Muslims in their everyday life. According to the wasiyatnama, this can be done only by following the sharia and modelling one's life on the Sunnah (traditions) of the Prophet. Therefore, to be a Muslim signifies drawing boundaries between what constitutes the Islamic and the un-Islamic. Abu Bakr starts the wasiyatnama by attacking the popular religious practices of Muslims of this region like shrine veneration, celebrating urs and celebrations associated with Milad-un-Nabi (the day Prophet Muhammad was born). His concern with the everyday life of Muslims allows him to focus extensively on what constitutes halal (prescribed) and haram (proscribed). He instructs Muslims to avoid usury, to choose an occupation that is permissible in sharia, not to hear popular music[7] and not to participate in *taziya*[8] processions on the day of Muharram. Moreover, one had to be concerned about halal food.

Abu Bakr also emphasised community markers to be strictly followed by Muslims. Therefore, he asked Muslim men to keep a beard, wear long kurtas unlike those that are worn by Hindus in this region and Muslim women to observe purdah. Muslims had to pray five times a day and fast during the month of Ramzan. Abu Bakr also advised his followers not to attend *jatras* and *kirtans*[9] of Hindus, which are frequent in rural Bengal (influenced by Vaishnavism), not to sell products like milk or flowers to Hindus for their puja (worship), not have sweets and other products made by Hindus, not to participate in Hindu festivals, not to beat drums and listen to music, not to burst firecrackers on Milad-un-Nabi, not allow music and other local customs in marriages, not play games like football and be aware of what constitutes proper Islamic conduct in their everyday life. Finally, the wasiyatnama elaborates Abu Bakr's views regarding other sects in Islam. Distinguishing his Sufi order from other Sufi orders, he asked his followers to avoid those Sufi orders that do not pay adequate emphasis on sharia and focus only on the philosophical aspects of Islam. He was against other Islamic sects that were against any of the four schools of jurisprudence of Sunni Islam and those who did not follow the *sahaba* (companions of Prophets). In this regard, he advised his followers to maintain distance from other Islamic sects like Shias, Qadiyanis, Kharijis, Wahhabis and Ahle Hadiths.

After his death in 1939, Abu Bakr Siddique's five sons, popularly known as *paanch pir kebla*,[10] built a shrine on his grave. The views expressed in the wasiyatnama became the guiding principles of the order influencing the practices centring the shrine. To understand the reformist views of Abu Bakr Siddique and his attempts to construct an exclusivist ideology, we need to locate his views in the socio-political context of that time, which revolves around the background of partition of Bengal in 1905. Ahmed (1981) has shown how the first census in 1871 played an important role in the communal politics of Bengal, where in due course of time, Muslim elites, based on their numerical superiority in eastern Bengal, demanded bifurcation of the province. This demand was based on the demographic profile of the eastern part of the province, where Muslims were in the majority. The division of Bengal in 1905 further escalated the tensions between the Hindu and the Muslim communities when Hindu bhadralok,[11] as part of Indian National Congress, opposed the partition. This political tension led to communal riots in several parts of Bengal. The construction of an exclusive Muslim identity by the early twentieth century took its root in this region. Similar socio-religious processes were at work among Hindus. Hindu reform movements tried to construct a homogeneous Hindu community.[12] In the case of Muslims in Bengal, as Ahmed (1981), Chakraborty (2002), Sarkar (2002) and Roy (2008) have pointed out, the religious elite played the role of cultural mediators between the urban-based community elite and their rural counterparts in a politically charged environment. By doing this, they tried to bridge the gap between the Urdu-speaking urban Muslim elite, the middle class and the rural Bengali-speaking Muslims who constituted the majority. The role of Abu Bakr Siddique can be seen as that of one such cultural mediator who was instrumental in the construction of a corporate and exclusivist identity among Muslims in Bengal.

After Independence, the five sons of Abu Bakr Siddique continued the reformist activities, but in the new socio-political context of independent India, the separatist attitude and the focus on Muslim exclusivity ware toned down in favour of an inclusive rhetoric of religious preaching. For example, the wasiyatnama mentions how his followers should maintain relationships with Hindus. But in later editions of the wasiyatnama, the word 'Hindu' was replaced by the more neutral word 'non-Muslims'. Other activities of the Sufi order include inter-religious dialogues organised by some of the pirs of Furfura Shareif at Kolkata every year during the Durga Puja festival and distribution of clothes among the poor in several districts of West Bengal. At present, 32 grandsons of Abu Bakr Siddique are the custodians of the shrine. This shift in the activities and teachings of Furfura Shareif is evident from the regular periodicals and religious books that Abu Bakr's successors have published to propagate their message.[13] Most importantly, the activities of Furfura Shareif are not just restricted to the everyday life of Muslim practices. In due course of time, the pirs of Furfura Shareif ventured actively into political and economic spheres, which necessitate placing their everyday activities within the socio-political and economic context of the region. For example, the pirs of Furfura Shareif are in diverse business activities ranging from boutiques and real estate to owning commercial complexes. They also sell amulets, sacred water of the shrine and CDs of their sermons delivered at various places, locally known as *jalsa*. They have invested in educational institutions where modern secular education is imparted along with religious education. Some of the pirs of Furfura Shareif are also very active in the electoral politics of West Bengal. Leaders of different political parties visit the shrine to seek their support, and the pirs in turn support leaders from different political parties and campaign for them during the elections. To show off their political strength, the pirs organise dharnas (protests) at Kolkata to press for their demands, which generally revolve around socio-political and economic interests of Muslims living in West Bengal. The instrumental use of the public sphere to address concerns of the Muslim community gives them the legitimacy to claim themselves as spokespersons of the community. In this pursuit, they are approached by different political parties of West Bengal who negotiate with them for electoral support.

The preceding discussion illustrates how the socio-political context of late nineteenth-century colonial Bengal facilitated the emergence of reformist tendencies among Muslims, which came up in opposition to prevalent religious practices that Roy (1983) has termed as syncretic and inclusive. The ideology of Abu Bakr was one among various other Muslim reformist views of this period. But I would like to draw attention to the fact that in the changed socio-political context after Independence, the exclusivist ideology of the Furfura order changed and paved the way for a different set of practices and engagement with wider society. Rachik (2009), analysing such shifts in religious practices in a different context of north-west Africa, argues for a contextual understanding of the emergence and proliferation of religious ideologies and practices. He argues that religious ideology emerges because of the failure of traditional forms of religious life to address the needs of the people. This necessitates the reconfiguration of ideas and practices, which further creates the conditions where the role of the religious elite becomes important. Rachik places the religious elite between an engineer and a bricoleur,[14] where the ideologue like an engineer uses techniques to revisit the intellectual store of scripture and like a bricoleur works with limited tools, motivated by the logic of the situation. This highlights the importance of the creative potential of human agency and the context in which certain ideas and practices emerge and undergo shifts.

Abu Bakr wanted to reform the Muslim community by advocating his fellow Muslims to eradicate locally accreted practices. But many of the contemporary practices promoted by his descendants in present times are influenced by popular Sufi practices. For example, while the present custodians of Furfura Shareif claim to follow the reformist message of Abu Bakr, they also sell amulets, *panipoda* (sacred water) and *telpoda* (sacred oil) with divine medicinal properties. These objects are generally associated with other Sufi shrines in popular imagination, but they were not advocated by Abu Bakr Siddique. In his wasiyatnama, Abu Bakr Siddique attempted to create awareness among his followers regarding what he considered as correct Islamic practices but keeping in mind the contemporary reality. On the one hand, he laid emphasis on sharia as a guide for Muslims, and on the other, he encouraged his followers to study English or modern subjects, though not at the expense of religious education. He encouraged Muslims to educate their girl-children by sending them to schools or madrasahs, provided they maintained strict purdah. In his wasiyatnama, he advises his followers to maintain distance from those pirs who promote superstitions in the name of Sufism. He explicitly mentions that no pir can alleviate anyone out of distress, as the job of the pir is only to guide a person to the right path. The selling of amulets and other religious objects by the present custodians of the shrine are in contradiction with the guidelines of the wasiyatnama. On this issue, one of the pirs of Furfura Shareif narrated the following in a personal conversation:

> In principle, they [pirs] are opposed to selling amulets or other religious objects, but such practices are prevalent because people demand it. Ordinary Muslims are still not aware of the true message of Islam and resort to these popular practices. For them, going to a Sufi shrine is a means to get rid of the everyday problems of life. But we always emphasise the reformist message of the order of Furfura Sahreif. Not everyone who comes to the shrine can be initiated. We cannot motivate them to abandon such practices in one day. In order to reach them and propagate the reformist message, we provide them

with amulets and other religious objects, but we do not promote such practices.

We see how the idea of reformation provides a new form and continuity to the existing religious practices. Religious reformation can be the recuperation of existing religious practices that are refracted through contemporary social and political conditions. In this regard, it is interesting to see how local idioms and imageries like use of local folklore of paanch pir and celebrating isale swahab in the month of Falgun exhibit the contextual nature of this Sufi order. The term 'isale swahab' is used by the pirs of Furfura Shareif to distinguish their annual festival from urs, but Muslims who visit the shrine do not use the term 'isale swahab' in their everyday parlance. The grandeur associated with isale swahab makes it something similar to urs. In my fieldwork, I found that Muslim devotees in their conversations never use the term 'isale swahab' but rather refer to it as *bado* jalsa (grand jalsa). Although the practices associated with isale swahab are unique, the grandeur associated with it in its annual celebration and the range of activities surrounding it—like the community kitchen during the festival, the way the shrine is decorated and the number of makeshift shops that come up during that time selling dresses, books, toys, jewellery, household utensils, eateries and other items—give the feel of a village fair, which is similar to the urs festival in case of other Sufi shrines. Ricci's (2011) analysis of the Islamisation of Java provides us with an important insight to understand this phenomenon. Ricci focuses on how the Arabic language underwent changes in terms of spelling, pronunciation and meaning to construct a local Islamic imagery appealing to the natives. The local idioms provide a base for any external ideas to harbour. There is a dialectical relation involved in this process, whereby both the local and the external vocabularies and the meaning associated with them change not only in terms of form, but also in terms of sensibilities. This analytical framework can help us understand the shifts and accommodations that any religious tradition undergoes in the course of time in interaction with other social conditions. Thus, focusing on the contemporary practices surrounding this shrine, we see how ideas associated with Islamic reformation are shaped and changed by its local context. It is important here to understand that Islamic reformation is not a break from existing practices. In fact, Islamic reformation intrinsically acquires its vocabulary by appropriating local and popular devotional practices. This blurs any rigid boundary between Sufism and Islamic reformation that is generally understood in terms of a binary between local and global Islam. Instead of looking at Sufism and Islamic reformation as homogeneous blocks that exist in terms of a binary, we need to explore how ideas emanating from different streams of devotional practices interact, influence and manifest within a social context in which such interaction takes place.

Everyday Life and Construction of Polymorphous Identities

This section deals with the everyday life of Muslims in Furfura. The focus is on the multiple ways by which they construct their sense of 'being Muslim'. This section seeks to highlight two important issues. First, it seeks to answer how the question of 'being Muslim' draws from multiple registers of everyday life, where religious identity is one among many markers that influence the ontological status of 'being Muslim'. Second, it questions the stereotypes associated with Muslim subjectivity, which essentialise Muslim identity as homogeneously constituted. The notions of being Muslim are not independent from the cultural aspects of everyday life. In this background, culture should not be understood narrowly as the carrier of any civilisational essence with a continuous historical lineage that can explain the subjectivities and everyday lives of people (Mamdani 2004: 17). Instead, culture should be understood as a process that is open to be determined by multiple social and historical factors, constantly influencing and shaping its form in any given social context.

The term 'beyond Islam' has been used by Zubaida (2011) to understand the de-sacralised nature of everyday lives in Middle-Eastern societies. Understanding Muslims beyond Islam rests on two important presuppositions. Muslims in their everyday lives do many things that have nothing to do with Islam. On the other hand, there exist diverse interpretative registers. Therefore, what constitutes the Islamic is relational and can undergo historical shifts. Zubaida (2011) is critical of the use of the adjective 'Islamic' in understanding Muslims. He is instead interested in showing how cultural notions attached with social categories like ulema and certain cultural traits like Islamic finance or the use of alcohol in Islam have undergone historic shifts in Muslim societies. He points out that 'Islam' is not the only signifier that determines the everyday life of Muslims. I use the term 'beyond Islam' to focus on the everyday religious practices of Muslims to show how their everyday religious practices are shaped by multiple socio-cultural factors.

Soares and Otayek (2007) and Osella and Soares (2010) have extended the scope of this question by pointing to the multiple possibilities of 'being a Muslim' in the secular spheres of everyday life. They put forward the concept of Islam mondain to explain the efforts taken by Muslims to produce themselves as religious yet modern subjects within the context of the uncertain political and economic situation of contemporary times (ibid.). As a concept, Islam mondain points to two important dimensions of the everyday life of Muslims. It focuses on everyday life and acknowledges the diverse ways of being Muslim, and it emphasises the local context in which such religious subjectivities are formed and articulated. To consider Muslims as active agents of their lives is an important aspect in understanding how they produce themselves as Muslims in the contemporary world. Marsden and Retsikas (2013) engage with this issue by formulating the notion of systematicity and articulation. Systematicity refers to the efforts undertaken by Muslims to evoke Islam within a particular social context. Articulation, on the other hand, refers to the ways in which Islam is produced, reproduced or transformed in any particular social context (ibid.: 2–3). The notion of systematicity and articulation emphasise the agentive role played by Muslims in their everyday life to evoke Islam, and it considers the diverse ways through which Islam is produced amidst the contingencies of everyday life. By underlining the importance of social context, it attempts to address the problems associated with treating Muslims as a homogeneous and static community. The fluidity involved in everyday practices where Islam overlaps with other dimensions of life is an important arena for studying Muslim subjectivities and their varying relationship with Islam.

During fieldwork, I found that my Muslim respondents acknowledge that many of their religious and ritualistic practices are influenced by sources other than Islam. But they do not see these practices in tension with Islamic tenets. Their subjectivities are constituted through practices in terms of *farz*, *niyom* and *parampara*. Farz means duty—it is a set of religious instructions that are obligatory in nature, such as praying five times a day or not indulging in usury. These duties cannot be compromised or negotiated. Niyom consists of a set of practices and rituals that are informed by scriptures. Most of the constituting elements of niyom are informed by the Hadith, and the traditions of the Prophet or Sunnah. They are desirable to be followed to be a good Muslim, but they may not be obligatory. Parampara means local traditions; it has cultural underpinnings. These are practices that are followed by Muslims by virtue of being from a particular region. A good number of constituting elements of parampara consist of practices that are influenced by local Hindu rituals. It has shaped the way Islam is followed in this region. For example, offering *sinni* (a sweet made of wheat-flour and sugar, usually offered to Lord Krishna by Hindus) at the shrines of dead Muslim saints or any inanimate object like a rock or a tree considered as a pir is a widespread practice among the Muslims of this region.[15] Parampara, in general, has nothing much to do with Islamic scriptures, but in certain cases, it can articulate Islamic idioms. Parampara does not figure in any authoritative scripture like the Quran or the Hadith. Nonetheless, it plays an important part in the construction of an embedded worldview and uses a variety of other sources. Rituals like applying turmeric paste on the body of the bride before marriage or the celebration of *olima*[16] have nothing specifically to do with Islam, but such practices are part of the everyday life of Muslims, indicating their embedded character in any cultural and geographical context. In spite of constant opposition from the pirs of Furfura Shareif, such practices are followed in everyday life.

Let me elaborate this point by citing another example. In a conversation with a madrasah student, I was informed that Muslims in West Bengal consider Thursday to be an auspicious day and do not slaughter animals on that day. Interestingly, he said that Thursday being *lakkhibar*[17] is auspicious. When I asked him to explain this, he was unable to provide any reasonable answer, but he insisted that, 'there is nothing as such in niyom, but we consider it as auspicious as it is part of our parampara'. After a pause, he elaborated:

> Even if a person dies on Thursday, we consider it to be gracious. In Islam, we believe that life does not end after death. Even a dead body has feelings as the soul does not leave the body just after death, and the body feels pain after death in the grave for the sins the person has committed in his lifetime. The *farista* [angel] takes the soul out of body only on Friday, on the day of *juma*. So, if a person dies on Thursday, then the duration of suffering in the grave will be less and the soul will part the body on Friday.

Here we see how beliefs, like those associated with lakkhibar, are defined as parampara or tradition and they coexist in harmony with scriptural religious tenets. Moreover, local Muslims are not ignorant of the scriptures, but the way they construct a tripartite division between farz, niyom and parampara is reflective of the diverse sources of their religious and ritualistic practices. Therefore, being a Muslim can be seen as a dynamic process, as Muslims acknowledge the Hindu roots of certain custormary practices, but they do not see them in contradiction with Islam. In a conversation on this matter, a villager informed:

> We follow many practices, which have nothing to do with niyom. They are our parampara and they are *aanchalik* [pertaining to a particular region] in nature. These practices are part of the cultural environment of this region, and not all of them are exclusively Hindu. There is nothing wrong in practising them as one cannot eliminate the local influences of the region on our religious practices, provided it does not violate the core of Islam.

This narrative highlights how the local and the 'religious' are perceived and articulated. They are aware of being a Muslim and a Bengali, with their rituals and practices being conditioned by multiple sources. Textual traditions are not the only source that constitute their identity. Muslims negotiate these categories according to their pragmatic concerns. The case of Furfura corroborates to an understanding of everyday ethics in the Foucauldian sense, where the processes of subjectivation (self-formation) takes place in a field that has multiple sources of constitutive moral spaces, religion being one of them.

At the same time, I noted an increasing awareness among Muslims regarding what constitutes proper Islamic conduct. The heightened consciousness about correct ways of being a Muslim corresponds to the objectification of Muslim consciousness (Eickelman and Piscatori 1996: 37–45). The objectification of Muslim consciousness as a process is a product of several factors like modern Islamic reform movements, new communication technology, print media, rising literacy levels and the emergence of the public sphere that facilitates open discussion and debate on topics related to what constitutes the Islamic or the un-Islamic in the everyday life of Muslims. These factors have facilitated the emergence of multiple voices that speak for Islam and compete to be heard. The proliferation of multiple voices has created a situation where the religious practices of a community in any regional setting are simultaneously influenced by a number of competing discourses. Communicated through the print and electronic media, multiple authoritative voices engage with the believers as they make sense of what is considered as Islamic practice. Seen from the point of view of the practitioner, the coherent tags of syncretism and reformism irrevocably break down.

Locating the multiple registers that influence and condition the religious consciousness of Muslims is important to understand the fluidity of their subjectivities. Let me explain this by another example. In a group conversation, Abu, a young madrasah graduate from Furfura madrasah and a follower of the silsila, questioned some of the activities of the present pirs of Furfura Sahreif as deviation from the ideology laid by Abu Bakr Siddique. Abu and his friends questioned a number of practices of some of the pirs such as their extravagant lifestyle, political activities in the village and their nexus with the political leaders of the state. In doing so, they questioned the spiritual authority of the pirs of Furfura Shareif. They said that a pir is a person who leads a simple life; he is the one who is filled with humility and serves God without engaging in this mundane world. For them, the present custodians of the shrine fail to live up to this standard. Abu elaborated further by pointing out that in contemporary times, Muslims who have turned religious shrines into seats of business have corrupted Sufism. He quoted the views of Zakir Naik and Delawar Hussain Saidi,[18] whose recorded sermons he has watched on CDs, to support his views. I questioned him about his reference to Zakir Naik and Delawar Hussain Saidi, as they are strongly opposed on theological grounds by the present pirs of Furfura Shareif. He replied:

> It is true that pirs of the Furfura order oppose Zakir Naik and Delawar Hussain Saidi on *maslaki* [theological] grounds, but whatever these scholars [referring to Naik and Saidi] say is not wrong as they quote from the scriptures. Islam is a rational religion; there is no scope of ambiguity as everything in Islam is written. One can read the scripture oneself and decide what is right and what is wrong!

As we see in the preceding narrative, Abu constructs an ideal definition of a pir, and based on that, he evaluates the pirs of Furfura Shareif. He also presents Islam as a rational religion, clear in its message, which anyone can read and understand. The act of choosing one set of discourse over another and understanding Islam in a coherent way, its portrayal in simplistic terms by eradicating the ambiguities involved in its scriptures and its reading without delving into its philosophical history corresponds to the objectification of Muslim consciousness. At times, the sources of objectification of Muslim consciousness may appear mismatched. Nevertheless, it is important to understand that irrespective of sectarian affiliations, Muslims actively engage with other discourses and ways of being Muslim. In this respect, the process of objectification of Muslim consciousness comes close to the concept of Islam mondain, whereby different agencies and situations facilitate Muslims to explore different ways of being Muslim. The active engagement of Muslims with diverse aspects of everyday life to produce themselves as Muslims further blurs any rigid boundary between the religious and the secular aspects of their lives.

Conclusion

Sufism is generally understood in the background of syncretic and composite culture of India. The syncretic dimension associated with Sufism underscores the indigenisation of exogenous Islamic traditions in the Indian context. On the other hand, Islamic reformation is seen as a scriptural and orthodox response to syncretic Sufi traditions. This essay questions the binary understanding of Sufism and Islamic reformism. Everyday practices like the tripartite division between farz, niyom and parampara may be articulated as regionally influenced practices, but they are understood within the discursive frame of Islam. These practices are followed with an awareness that they do not contradict the basic tenets of Islam. Recent debates have problematised the binary understanding of Sufism as syncretic tradition and reformism as Islamic orthodoxy. Scholars have paid attention to the semantic field in which discourses of syncretic traditions are understood. Everyday practices that are labelled as syncretic may be understood as 'dynamically translated' (Stewart 2010: 381–83) by Muslim respondents in a given context, whereby Muslims expand the semantic domain of locally available ideational realm, and place regionally influenced practices within the discursive field of Islam. The interplay between Islamic traditions and the regional context may allow different features of culture, at times with disjunctive systems of discourses, to operate, yet no single mode of discourse can account for the variety of lived experiences with which people operate in everyday life. Similarly, van der Veer (2005) argues that syncretic practices may encompass other religious traditions, but instead of understanding it in a descriptive way, the focus should be on how 'other' religious traditions are understood and incorporated in the worldview of the people. His ethnographic study of a Sufi shrine in Gujarat suggests that people from different religious communities apply different semantic fields to participate in common rituals. Further, there exists a hierarchy in the worldview of the people whereby 'other' religious traditions are understood and expressed.

This essay also illustrates the blurred boundaries between the religious and secular domains of everyday life. To this end, by engaging with a Muslim community in rural West Bengal, I argue that there is a need to de-exceptionalise and contextualise the study of Muslim communities, and go beyond conceptualising neat binaries that compartmentalise our understanding. As we have seen in the case of the Sufi order of Furfura Shareif, it was established in the early twentieth century within the socio-political background of pre-Independence India, where Sufi ethos was creatively fused with the ideas of Islamic reformation. It is also interesting to see how, after the death of Abu Bakr Siddique, the custodians of the shrine toned down their earlier emphasis on Muslim exclusivity, and with the changing socio-political context after Independence, they deployed local cultural imageries for wider acceptance of the Sufi order among the Muslims in the region. It shows how social processes in a certain historical context can transform the nature of religious authority and open up space for reflexive deliberation and debate. Islam emerges as an interpretative resource that influences Muslim subjectivities and their notions of identity. On the other hand, we also see that Islam is neither the blueprint of their social life, nor does it have an overarching precedence over other social factors in the determination of ways of being Muslim. This necessitates us to focus on the socio-political context and ascertain how certain aspects of our social life acquire a sacred character in a certain context, whereas accepted religious practices get detangled from their traditional spheres. We can understand this by the dialectical interaction between text and context. Religious texts may be interpreted in multiple ways in different contexts, but texts may also influence the semantic field in which they are understood. As the changing practices of the Sufi shrine in this essay suggest, a better way to understand this dimension is by focusing the polymorphic processes between the religious and secular domains of everyday life.

Notes

1. The terms 'religion as faith' and 'religion as ideology' have been used by Nandy (1985, 1998). Nandy refutes the notion of secularism that confines religion to the private space of life and draws a distinction between these two terms to point that in modern times it is 'religion as ideology' that has the potential to create communal problems.
2. The classic study on this issue is E. E. Evans-Pritchard's *The Sanusi of Cyrenica* (1949). Recently, Rachik (2009) has also dealt with this issue.

3. Historians like Ahmed (1981), Sumit Sarkar (2002), Chakraborty (2002) and Mahua Sarkar (2008) have pointed the political activities of Abu Bakr Siddique in their works.
4. Urs is an Arabic word, meaning wedding. It is the annual festival centring any Sufi shrine. It is the date on which the Sufi pir died, and it takes the form of a celebration because after death, the pir is believed to be in union with God.
5. Gaddinashin is a tradition popular in Sufi shrines where after the death of the Sufi pir, the senior-most disciple becomes the spiritual head of the shrine. Generally, in practice, this position is hereditary, where the eldest son of the deceased Sufi pir becomes the spiritual head of the shrine.
6. Shirk means attributing divine qualities to any worldly being or objects. Bida refers to innovations that are un-Islamic in nature. Both shirk and bida are the prime concerns of Muslim reform movements, which consider them as un-Islamic.
7. However, he allows Islamic ghazals, by which he means couplets in praise of God alone, sung without any musical instruments. These should be sung for a religious purpose, not for entertainment and without any presence of women.
8. A miniature mausoleum signifying the tomb of Ali, the grandson of Prophet Muhammad, and his sons, Hasan and Husayn.
9. Jatra is a traditional theatrical performance of local artists in rural Bengal. It is still popular in rural parts of West Bengal. The motif of jatras can be any religious or popular story based on everyday life. Kirtans are devotional songs generally sung in groups on festive occasions.
10. In his wasiyatnama, Abu Bakr Siddique points that after his death, he expects his five sons to take forward his reformist message and the Sufi order that he started. The phrase 'paanch pir kebla' is, however, not mentioned by him anywhere in the wasiyatnama. I think the phrase became popular after the death of Abu Bakr Siddique, when the next generation had an urgency to legitimise its authority and popularise itself by popular local folklore. Paanch pir, which literary means five pirs, has an important genealogy in medieval Bengal. Eaton (1997) points that people in lower Bengal worship five clay mounds in the Noakhali district of Bangladesh as paanch pir. There is no evidence that these mounds are graves of pirs, but it is popularly believed that these pirs protect boatmen from dangers in their voyages.
11. Bhadralok can be roughly translated as 'gentlefolk'. As a social category, it emerged in colonial Bengal, comprising the landed elite mainly from the upper-caste Bengali Hindu community.
12. For details, refer to Sharma (2013) for an in-depth analysis of how Vivekananda tried to construct a masculine robust majoritarian nationalism. Also see Sarkar (2002) for an analysis of how the Bengali bhadralok community tried to construct a homogeneous identity by experimenting with caste consolidation and by limiting mobilisation by the lower castes. For details on subaltern caste mobilisation in Bengal, refer to Bandyopadhyay (2004).
13. The communal politics of Abu Bakr Siddique and the role of periodicals and political pamphlets in propagating his message are discussed by Ahmed (1981),

Sumit Sarkar (2002), Mahua Sarkar (2008) and Chakraborty (2002). This can be contrasted with the sermon recordings and various books and pamphlets written by the sons and grandsons of Abu Bakr Siddique, which emphasise less on Muslim exclusivity and more on sectarian identity, illustrating how to be a 'good' Muslim according to the order of Furfura Shareif.

14. The concept of bricoleur was introduced by Lévi-Strauss in his book *The Savage Mind* (1966). *Bricolage* is a French word that means the process of improvisation. Lévi-Strauss uses the term 'bricoleur' in studying myths, where he draws an analogy between a mythical thought and a bricoleur, who improvises things to solve any immediate problem by using available resources in opposition to an engineer, who is governed by the means–end rational thinking.
15. In Bengal, objects like a stone or a tree can be venerated as a pir by Muslims. For details, please refer to Roy (1983) and Eaton (1997). Roy (1983) mentions that, historically, the cultural environment of the Bengal region has been influenced by multiple religious practices like animism, Buddhism, Nathism, Tantric Hinduism and Vaishnavism. Islam came into Bengal in the medieval times. This diversity negates any unidimensional understanding or influence of any particular religious doctrine or practice over others among the people of this region.
16. Olima is also known as *valima* among Muslims in northern India. It is a ritual to be performed after marriage, on the day of the nuptial night.
17. Lakkhibar means day of Goddess Lakkhi (Lakshmi in Hindi), who is a Hindu deity of wealth. On this day, Hindus worship the deity and generally avoid non-vegetarian food.
18. Zakir Naik is a Muslim televangelist based in Mumbai. Delawar Hussain Saidi is a prominent leader of Jamaat-e-Islami Bangladesh. Both of them are prominent speakers on Islam, and books and CDs containing their sermons are easily available at bookstores selling Islamic books in West Bengal. Jamaat-e-Islami is an Islamist party that opposes Sufism or any type of saint veneration. Naik's attempt has been to project Islam as a scientific and rational religion, free of any type of superstition. The pirs of the Furfura order oppose both of them on theological grounds, and on several occasions, publicly and in personal conversation with me, have labelled Naik and the jamaatis as heretic. Irrespective of the opposition, books and CDs containing the thoughts and sermons of Naik and Saidi are sold in bookstores at Furfura.
19. The term 'sacralisation' has been taken from Madan (2011) and the term 'de-sacralisation' from Zubaida (2011).

References

Ahmed, Rafiuddin. 1981. *The Bengal Muslims 1871–1906: A Quest for Identity*. New Delhi: Oxford University Press.

Asad, Talal. 1986. 'The Idea of an Anthropology of Islam', Occasional Paper Series, Centre for Contemporary Arab Studies, Georgetown University.

———. 1993. *Genealogies of Religion: Discipline and Reasons of Power in Christianity and Islam*. Baltimore, MD: John Hopkins University Press.

Bandyopadhyay, Sekhar. 2004. *From Plassey to Partition: A History of Modern India*. New Delhi: Orient BlackSwan.

Bhargava, Rajeev. 1998. 'Introduction', in Rajeev Bhargava (ed.), *Secularism and Its Critics*, pp. 1–30. New Delhi: Oxford University Press.

Casanova, José. 2008. 'Public Religion Revisited', in Hent de Varies (ed.), *Religion: Beyond the Concept*, pp. 101–19. New York: Fordham University Press.

Chakraborty, Ashoke Kumar. 2002. *Bengali Muslim Literati and the Development of Muslim Community in Bengal*. Shimla: Indian Institute of Advanced Study.

Das, Veena. 2010. 'Moral and Spiritual Striving in the Everyday: To Be a Muslim in Contemporary India', in Anand Pandian and Daud Ali (eds), *Ethical Life in South Asia*, pp. 232–52. New Delhi: Oxford University Press.

Eaton, Richard. 1997. *The Rise of Islam and the Bengal Frontier, 1204–1760*. New Delhi: Oxford University Press.

Eickelman, D. F., and James Piscatori. 1996. *Muslim Politics*. Princeton: Princeton University Press.

Evans-Pritchard, E. E. 1949. *The Sanusi of Cyrenaica*. Oxford: Oxford University Press.

Jairath, Vinod K. 2011. 'Introduction: Towards a Framework', in Vinod K. Jairath (ed.), *Frontiers of Embedded Muslim Communities in India*, pp. 1–28. New Delhi: Routledge.

Lévi-Strauss, Claude. 1966. *The Savage Mind*. London: Weidenfeld and Nicolson.

———. 2011. *Modern Myths, Locked Minds: Secularism and Fundamentalism in India*. New Delhi: Oxford University Press.

Madan, T. N. 2011. *Modern Myths, Locked Minds: Secularism and Fundamentalism in India*. New Delhi: Oxford University Press.

Mamdani, Mahmood. 2004. *Good Muslim, Bad Muslim: Islam, the USA and the Global War Against Terror*. New Delhi: Permanent Black.

Marsden, Magnus and Konstantinos Retsikas (eds). 2013. 'Introduction', in *Articulating Islam: Anthropological Approaches to Muslim World*, pp. 1–32. Dordecht: Springer.

Nandy, Ashis. 1985. 'Anti-secularist Manifesto', *India International Centre Quarterly*, 22 (1): 35–64.

———. 1998. 'The Politics of Secularism and the Recovery of Religious Toleration', in Rajeev Bhargava (ed.), *Secularism and Its Critics*, pp. 321–44. New Delhi: Oxford University Press.

Osella, Filippo and Benjamin Soares (eds). 2010. 'Islam, Politics, Anthropology', in *Islam, Politics, Anthropology*, pp. 1–22. Sussex, UK: Wiley Blackwell.

Rachik, Hassan. 2009. 'How Religion Turns into Ideology', *The Journal of North African Studies*, 4 (3): 347–58.

Ricci, Ronit. 2011. *Islam Translated: Literature, Conversion, and the Arabic Cosmopolis of South and Southeast Asia*. Ranikhet: Permanent Black.

Roy, Asim. 1983. *The Islamic Syncretistic Tradition in Bengal*. New Jersey: Princeton University Press.

Roy, Asim. 2008. 'Impact of Islamic Revival and Reform in Colonial Bengal and Bengal Muslim Identity: A Revisit', in Asim Roy (ed.), *Islam in History and Politics*, pp. 47–87. New Delhi: Oxford University Press.

Sarkar, Mahua. 2008. *Visible Histories, Disappearing Women: Producing Muslim Womanhood in Late Colonial Bengal*. Durham and London: Duke University Press.

Sarkar, Sumit. 2002. *Beyond Nationalist Frames: Relocating Post Modernism, Hindutva, History*. New Delhi: Permanent Black.

Sharma, Jyotirmay. 2013. *Cosmic Love and Human Apathy: Swami Vivekananda's Restatement of Religion*. New Delhi: HarperCollins.

Soares, Benjamin and René Otayek (eds). 2007. 'Introduction: Islam and Muslim Politics in Africa', in *Islam and Muslim Politics in Africa*, pp. 1–26. New York: Palgrave Macmillan.

Stewart, Tony K. 2010. 'In Search of Equivalence: Conceiving the Muslim–Hindu Encounter through Translation Theory', in Richard M. Eaton (ed.), *India's Islamic Tradition, 711–1750*, pp. 363–92. New Delhi: Oxford University Press.

van der Veer, Peter. 2005. 'Syncretism, Multiculturalism and the Discourse of Tolerance', in Charles Stewart and Rosalind Shaw (eds), *Syncretism/Anti-syncretism: The Politics of Religious Synthesis*, pp. 185–99. London: Routledge.

Zubaida, Sami. 2011. *Beyond Islam: A New Understanding of the Middle East*. London: I. B. Tauris.

2

State and Legal Reform

A Study of the Matrilineal Mappila Muslims of Malabar

Aleena Sebastian*

This essay attempts to explore the legal shifts that have taken place over the years in colonial and postcolonial Malabar[1] with regard to the matrilineal practices of the Mappilas.[2] The study foregrounds the 'courtroom' as a site where the court of law enters into dialogue with the socio-cultural pluralities in colonial Malabar. The dichotomy created by the colonial state between the codified customary law and the practices of the people led to the redefinition of the Mappila tharavad.[3] The colonial state failed to understand the

* I am grateful to Prof. Vinod K. Jairath, Prof. Aparna Rayaprol, Dr Pushpesh Kumar (Department of Sociology, University of Hyderabad) and Dr Salah P. (Centre for Regional Studies, University of Hyderabad) for their important suggestions. I also thank the University Grants Commission, New Delhi, for the financial assistance to carry out the field study and archival research.

strategic roles people enter into to sustain the co-existence of the 'supposedly antithetical' religious and cultural elements in their social organisation and inheritance pattern. This inability of the colonial state negated the possibility of the co-existence of religious and customary elements, dismissing it as a 'piebald system' in the courtrooms.

The twentieth century witnessed legal interventions by the colonial and the postcolonial state, which resulted in new forms of familial relations and the creation of a uniform law for Muslims in matters relating to family, marriage, inheritance and succession (Kottakkunnummal 2014: 1–12; Kumari 2003: 332). This historical shift can be looked at as a form of contestation posed to the practice of matriliny as also to the changing power relations in the matrilineal tharavad[4] and the socio-economic aspirations of the Mappilas. The legislative alteration was informed by the Islamic reformist intervention in the legal sphere in colonial and postcolonial Malabar.

Irrespective of the legal interventions by the state, which are viewed as detrimental to the existence of matrilineal elements, Mappila women (especially in the coastal belt of Kozhikode in the south Malabar region), ignoring the opposition from the menfolk, employed strategic means to sustain these practices in contemporary times. The conversion of the matrilineal tharavad into waqf property is one such means. In recent times, the ways in which this continuity in the practices is maintained invokes the possibility of a sociological analysis of the engagement of Mappila women with the legal shift in colonial and postcolonial periods.

This study, with the aid of ethnographic sources and a reading of court cases and legislative interventions in colonial and postcolonial Malabar, initiates a context-specific historical analysis of legal pluralities through the contestations and negotiations between the state, religion and customary practices. The essay is divided into five sections. In the first section, the matrilineal social organisation in pre-colonial Malabar is described to understand how Islam is reconstituted in a matrilineal society and how matriliny, in turn, is reconstituted by Islam. The second section looks at the attempts of the colonial judiciary to codify customary practices, which have led to the creation of the dichotomy between codified law and the practices of the people.

The refashioning of Mappila tharavad by legislative interventions in the first half of the twentieth century is discussed in the third section. Foregrounding the contestations raised in the Madras Legislative Assembly over the Mappila Marumakkathayam Bill of Khan Bahadur Mahamad Schamnad Sahib in 1937, this section attempts to show how legislative reforms were also informed by reformist interventions in the legal sphere in colonial Malabar. The fourth section explores the debates over the validity of customary and religious practices that came to be questioned in the postcolonial period, with the formation of the Indian Constitution Act. It shows how irrespective of the challenges posed and the transformations initiated by historically specific factors at various moments in the history of Malabar, Mappila women employ strategic means to continue with matrilineal practices. The strategic role played by these women, by converting tharavad into waqf property, is discussed in the fifth section of the essay. Their engagement with legal reforms is explored through their narratives.

Matrilineal Social Organisation in Pre-colonial Malabar

The Marumakkathayam or matrilineal system of inheritance is an important aspect of social organisation in Malabar since the pre-colonial times. The communities governed by the customs and usages of this system assumed succession through nephews, and this pattern of inheritance is also referred to as Aliyasanthana in South Canara (Aiyar 1922). Various communities governed by the Marumakkathayam practice in Malabar include the Nayars, Thiyyas, Payyannur Brahmins, the Kurichiya tribes of Wayanad, and the Mappila Muslims in the coastal belt of north and south Malabar such as the Koyas of Kozhikode, Keyis of Thalassery and the Arackal royal family of Kannur (Aiyappan and Mahadevan 1990; Balakrishnan 1981; Logan 2000: 153–56). Elements of matriliny are also observed in certain pockets of Cochin and Travancore among Muslims, Nayars, Ezhavas, Christians and Nanjinad Vellalas (Ali 1933: 96; Jeffrey: 1994; Puthenkalam 1977: *vi*; Saradamoni 1999). A distinct political economy, regional specificities and ecological factors have led to the persistence of matriliny as a heterogeneous practice since the pre-colonial times.

The tharavad is the social unit of the communities that are governed by the Marumakkathayam practice. When the tharavad fails to accommodate all members, *tavazhis* (branches) are formed in the female line, and the members of a matrilineal tharavad are related to each other either through *mudal sambandham* or *pula sambandham* (Ali 1933: 53).

> Usually the members of the Tarawad live in the family house and also own family property, in which case the relation of the members is summed up in the expression *'Mudal Sambandham'* and *'Pula Sambandham'* [emphasis added]. The former means community of property, and the latter community of pollution (i.e., it indicates the necessity of the members having a common interest to observe birth and death ceremonials). Where there is no property relation between the parties, they are usually said to have only community pollution. (ibid.)

While the right to have a common interest in the ancestral property forms the basis for mudal sambandham ties, pula sambandham does not bind its members to a 'community of property' but to the observance of birth- and death-related ceremonies of its members. Pula sambandham is nothing but the observance of pollution where there is no property relation between its members. In the case of the matrilineal Hindus of Malabar, Aiyar (1922: 1–6) argues that the Malabar law that deals with customs and usages does not hold anything in common with the Hindu law (which is based on the Mitakshara law) that can be found amongst other segments of the south Indian Hindu population.

The Mappila Muslims in the coastal belt of north Malabar and south Malabar follow matrilineal practices. Matrilineal elements can also be observed in the social organisation of Lakshadweep and Sri Lankan Muslims of South Asia under 'the rubric of Islam' (Dube 1994; McGilvray 2014). The adherence to Islam by matrilineal communities opens up an interesting window to study the customary practices vis-à-vis Islamic personal law, as the general assumption about Islam is that it is patrilineal in nature.

Matrilineal practices among the Mappilas do not indicate a uniform pattern throughout the Malabar region. For example, most of the south Malabar Mappilas follow Makkathayam—the patrilineal system of inheritance with succession through sons. However, exceptions to this can be seen among the Koyas of Kozhikode and the Tangals[5] of Ponnani. Matrilocality among the Koyas and matrilineal succession to religious positions among the Tangals of Ponnani (for example, religious *stanam* [position] of the Valiya Tangal of Ponnani) are marked by the presence of matrilineal elements (Innes 1951: 193; Sebastian 2013).

In contrast to the south Malabar Mappilas, the majority of the north Malabar Mappilas are followers of matrilineal practices. The matrilineal social organisation forms a predominant pattern among the people throughout the north Malabar region irrespective of their religious backgrounds. Trade and agriculture constituted an important aspect of the political economy of the south Malabar Mappilas in colonial and pre-colonial times.

The consolidation of British power in the nineteenth century transformed the socio-economic organisation in Malabar, and even the pre-colonial legal sphere was not left unaffected. Colonial intervention in customary practices dissociated colonial law from the everyday practices of the people. This issue seemed much more complex in the case of the Mappilas as the Malabar law of the Mappilas was a combination of the Muhammadan law and the Marumakkathayam (Kumari 2003: 331).

Codification of Mappila Custom and Usage in Colonial Malabar: The Case of the Judiciary

The co-existence of the matrilineal system of inheritance and the Muhammadan law in matters related to family, marriage, inheritance, succession, dower and gift deeds posed many challenges to the colonial judiciary in terms of dealing with the socio-cultural pluralities of nineteenth-century Malabar. According to Moore (1905: 323–25), the Sudder Courts[6] refused to accept the Marumakkathayam among the Mappilas of north Malabar in the early decades of the nineteenth century. The court judgements of this period often referred to the arguments put forward by Logan (cited in Moore 1905: 323–25) that the Muhammadan law is the original law and that the Marumakkathayam system of inheritance is a later adoption. Moore (1905: 325) disagrees with Logan and opines that the Mappilas were followers of matrilineal practices even before they embraced Islam.

The local usage among the Mappilas was eventually recognised by the lower courts in the second half of the nineteenth century. In its attempt to deal with the supposedly antithetical religious and customary practices, the colonial state codified the Marumakkathayam customs and usages. The dichotomy created by the colonial state between the codified law and the actual practices of the people led to the redefinition of the Mappila tharavad. The colonial state failed to understand how the communities perceived and aimed to preserve the religious and cultural elements in their social organisation and inheritance pattern. This inability of the colonial state negated the possibility of the co-existence of customary and religious forms of inheritance, as it was dismissed as a 'piebald system of descent' in the courtrooms (Moore 1905: 326; Wigram 1882: 152). Holloway used the term 'piebald system of descent' first in 1861 (Case A. S. 110 of 1861, cited in Wigram 1882: 152) to refer to the existence of two different laws of inheritance within the same household. This property pattern arises when a woman who is governed by the Marumakkathayam law of inheritance enters into marital alliance with a man who is a follower of the ordinary Muhammadan law or vice versa. The dilemma of the colonial court to decide the manner of devolution of property in such a situation of double descent is what is implied through Holloway's remark.

In the context of the transformation of matrilineal tharavads of the Nayars in colonial Malabar, Arunima (2003: 36) argues that the colonial state redefined the Nayar tharavad as 'an *impartible* and *corporate unit* with *inalienable rights* in land' (emphasis added). The legal reform consolidated the managerial power of the tharavad in the hands of the *karnavar*[7] by altering the internal structure of the matrilineal Nayar tharavad. The judicial proceedings point out that similar attempts have been carried out by the colonial state in the case of the matrilineal Mappilas as well. This essay, therefore, alludes to the view that in the nineteenth century, the Mappila tharavad came to be conceptualised as an indivisible corporate unit with the legal recognition of the jointly held property as impartible. The various aspects of the Mappila tharavad that have come to be modified through codification are discussed subsequently. With the aid of court judgements on deeds related to matrilineal tharavads, an attempt is made to show how disjunction is created between codified law and everyday practices.

On disputes related to property, questions over the devolution of self-acquisitions of a Marumakkathayee (follower of the Marumakkathayam system of inheritance) posed challenges to the colonial judiciary in the classification and conceptualisation of different kinds of property. What one could infer from the court judgements of the late nineteenth century and the early decades of the twentieth century is that the concept of impartibility was extended to bring the self-acquired property of Marumakkathayees under the purview of the indivisible tharavad. During this period, self-acquired property and ancestral property were not considered as two different types of property by the colonial courts. Both types of property followed a single rule of devolution (Kumari 2003: 342–44). Hence, self-acquisition by a member of the matrilineal tharavad merged into the main tharavad at his/her death. In *Kunhimbi Umma versus Kandy Moithin*,[8] the appellate civil court comes to the conclusion that the self-acquired property of the person who dies intestate would merge into the main tharavad as the property of the main tharavad. If the parties are governed by the Muhammadan law instead of the matrilineal law, the devolution of the estate could be in accordance with the Muhammadan law.

In addition to the matters concerning the inheritance and succession in a matrilineal tharavad of Mappila Muslims, institutions such as family and marriage also came to be tied to the concept of impartibility in the colonial legal system. In *P. K. Pakrichi versus P. K. Kunhacha*,[9] the court concluded that a gift made to the husband of a Mappila girl at the time of her marriage does not revert to her tharavad after her death or divorce if she is a follower of the Muhammadan law and not the Marumakkathayam law. Under the Muhammadan law, the patrilocal residence of the girl after her marriage keeps her natal family free from the obligation to maintain her. The case remains so even if she is divorced. Hence, the gift made to her husband at the time of marriage does not become the property of her natal family in the long run. However, the property will be reverted to her tharavad if she is governed by the Marumakkathayam system of inheritance.

Yet another important issue during this period was the existence of two systems of inheritance in the same household in relation to the devolution of ancestral property, self-acquisitions, gift deeds and dower. On suits related to multiple inheritance patterns, the customary usages to which the parties belonged by birth played the decisive factor in the judgement. For example, in the case of the Mappilas who were Muhammadans by religion and matrilineal by custom, the query raised was whether the parties concerned were governed by the Marumakkathayam or the Muhammadan law. In *Kunhambi versus Kalanthar,*[10] the appellate civil court opines that

> the law applicable to a suit is the law to which parties as a matter of fact by their custom and usages have adopted, not the law which the Courts by a consideration of the historical circumstances relating to the parties or of their religious books or otherwise consider to be the law that they ought to have adopted.

The Madras Civil Courts Act 1873, Section 16, is referred to validate this point. According to the Civil Courts Act, Muhammadans should be governed by the Muhammadan law and the Hindus by the Hindu law in questions regarding marriage, succession, inheritance, caste and any religious usage or institution. Nevertheless, if any custom having the force of law exists among Muhammadans and Hindus, it shall form the basis for the rule of decision. The co-existence of customary and religious elements was not given adequate attention by the colonial courts. The codification of customary practices ruled out the possibility of the co-existence of both the elements in the social organisation of the Mappila tharavad. Any attempts by successive generations to alter these practices were also dismissed by the colonial courts.

The codification of matrilineal practices had certain gender implications and consequences for women's right to property management. It consolidated the managerial power of the ancestral property in the hands of the karnavar (Arunima 2003: 72–105). The restructuring of the tharavad along the gendered hierarchy of power and property relations is another important aspect of the disjunction between the codified law and everyday practices in the colonial period. In *Kottal*

Kinhali Umma versus Chettiankandayil Kannan and Kottal Avuja Haji,[11] the court comes to the conclusion that

> in theory, senior women are the proprietors of lands belonging to the matrilineal *tharavads*. However, it is observed that in practice, the *karnavar* or the eldest male manages the *tharavad* properties. According to the matrilineal law of Malabar, the managerial power is vested exclusively with him and not in any female members.

A similar judgement was given in the case of *Vengadan Kuttiali versus Alakadan Kunhi Kutti and Others.*[12] Women's claim over the right to property ownership and management was discarded by the colonial courts as an unknown custom.

The dichotomy which set in through the codification of customary law neglected women's rights by legally vesting the control of property in the hands of men. The gap between the codified frozen custom and the actual practices of the people left out certain kinds of property relations such as *strisothu* unarticulated. Strisothu or *henummula* is a custom of settling property with females and their female descendants, which can be observed in the case of the matrilineal Hindus and the Mappilas of Malabar.

The redefinition of the tharavad in the nineteenth century as an indivisible unit with equal rights to the ancestral property by its male and female members challenged the provision of holding a portion of the property exclusively by a group of female members. In *Muhammad Kunhi versus Pakrichi Umma,*[13] the appellate civil full bench, while stating that property cannot be settled as strisothu to the exclusion of its male members, chose to remain silent on giving its opinions on the existence of matrilineal tharavads under the managerial power of the *karnoti* (the eldest female member in the tharavad). The custom where males had no rights to management in the tharavad affairs was pushed aside as an invented custom.

The custom of settling property on females seemed much more complex in the case of gift deeds executed in the colonial period. In *Mooriyat Peetikayil Kunhamina versus Mooriyat Kunhambi,*[14] both the district munsif court and the appellate civil court stated that the creation of a perpetual succession through a gift deed excluding the male members is unknown to the Marumakkathayam law or the Muhammadan law and thus stands invalid. In *Kypreth Moithiyan Kutty versus Natukandy Puthiyapurayil Ayissa,*[15] a gift deed was executed by a member of the Marumakkathayam tharavad to his wife and children, though she had children from a previous marriage. The question raised is whether the donees inherit the plaint property with the incidents of tharavad property, or as ordinary donees, with each entitled to an equal share as tenants in common to the exclusion of children from the earlier marriage. Justice Venkatasubba Rao and Justice Reilly made the point that no man has any right to create a corporate unit by his own act, which is unknown to the law. According to the appellate civil court, in this case, a tavazhi cannot be constituted by a mother and some of her children alone, excluding the children born to her in a former relationship.

In *Kunhacha Umma versus Kutti Mammi Hajee,*[16] it is laid out that when a member of the matrilineal tharavad executes a gift deed in favour of his wife and children without proper details by the donor as to the way it should be enjoyed, the tavazhi formed by the mother and children through the gift deed would inherit the property with all the incidents of a tharavad property (that is, coparcenary rights and impartibility). It will not become their absolute property. The property becomes the *putravakasam* property, that is, an estate acquired by the members of a tavazhi by way of gifts from their fathers (Ali 1933: 53; Joseph 1918: 227).

The legal transformations, set in through the codification of Mappila custom and usage, bound various aspects of the tharavad to the concept of impartibility or inseparability. In this context, both the ancestral property and the self-acquired property followed a single rule of devolution (Kumari 2003: 342–44). On the one hand, the legal intervention of the colonial state created a dichotomy between the codified law and the local custom and practices of people, and, on the other, it posed the Muhammadan law and the matrilineal practices as binaries, neglecting the various ways in which custom and religion interact and intersect through a process of accommodation, negotiation and contestation in the everyday life of Mappilas (Sebastian 2012, 2013). The colonial state failed to understand the ways in which Islam is reconstituted in a matrilineal society and how matriliny is reconstituted, in turn, by Islam. The reorganisation of the intra-affairs of the tharavad and its economic relations had certain consequences for women. The gap created between codified law and practice in property ownership and management by the colonial state had detrimental effects on the economic rights of matrilineal Mappila women in the northern part of Malabar where, by custom, women inherited landed properties and the matrilineal tharavad.

Refashioning of Mappila Tharavads in the Twentieth Century

The legal recognition of the ancestral property and the self-acquired property as two types of property constituting two laws of inheritance (that is, the Muhammadan law for the self-acquired property of the individuals and the Marumakkathayam law for the ancestral property) is one of the major transformations that occurred in the first half of the twentieth century.[17] We need to view this in the context of the socio-economic changes that were brought in with the advent of colonial rule in Malabar. The younger male members contested the managerial power of the karnavar in the matrilineal tharavad through the machinery set up by the colonial legal system at the turn of the nineteenth century. In the Original Suit No. 322 of 1889,[18] a senior *anandravan* (nephew) of a Mappila tharavad accused the karnavar of misappropriation of the tharavad property to the advantage of his wife and children. According to the anandravan, this was an act detrimental to the common interest of the tharavad. The court makes the decree in favour of the anandravan, demanding a speedy recovery of the sued property to the tharavad from the karnavar.

In their attempt for autonomy and self-identity, demands were raised by the younger generation to transfer the self-acquired property to one's own children instead of transferring it to their matrilineal heirs. The legislative modifications that followed in the first half of the twentieth century favoured the devolution of self-acquired property to one's own children. These new economic relations under the colonial bureaucracy provided avenues for the younger male members from the affluent Mappila tharavads to acquire private property. While the entry into salaried jobs facilitated the acquisition of individual property by the younger male members, the downfall of trade and the transformation of market relations under the colonial rule reduced the profits that one earned from the ancestral property. An increase in the self-acquisition of properties by the junior members was followed by a decrease in the ancestral property. Under the new economic conditions created by colonial rule, twentieth-century Malabar witnessed the redefinition of familial relations, which strengthened patrilineal–patrilocal and conjugal ties over matrilineal–matrilocal ties.

The enactment of the Mappila Succession Act of 1918 and the Mappila Wills Act of 1928 refashioned the matrilineal tharavad in accordance with the changing aspirations of its people. The Mappila Succession Act of 1918, applicable to the Mappilas domiciled in the Madras Presidency, enabled the transfer of the self-acquisitions of a person who died intestate or without any testamentary disposition according to the rules of Muhammadan law. The act included those Mappilas who were governed by the Marumakkathayam or the Aliyasanthana law of inheritance. With the enactment of the Mappila Succession Act, the colonial state entered into another period of legal reform. The concept of impartibility fostered through earlier legislations, such as the Malabar Wills Act of 1898, obtained a new turn by the second decade of the twentieth century. Even as the Malabar Wills Act of 1898 provided provisions to gift away property through the execution of a will, questions regarding intestate succession remained ambiguous till the endorsement of the Mappila Succession Act in 1918. According to Kottakkunnummal (2014: 3), the history of the Wills Act steered the emergence of the concept of self-acquired property.

The Mappila Wills Act, which came into being in 1928, was extended to the whole of the Madras Presidency to include the Mappilas who were governed by the Marumakkathayam or the Aliyasantana law of inheritance. This act enabled the devolution of the testamentary dispositions by the Mappilas in accordance with the provisions of the Mappila Succession Act of 1918. Repealing the Malabar Wills Act of 1898 allowed the transfer of self-acquired property according to the Muhammadan law.

These legislative reforms were also informed by the Islamic reformist intervention in the legal sphere. The reformist movement was initiated by Sayyid Sanaullah Makhti Tangal, Chalilakattu Kunjahmad Haji, Hamadani Sheikh and Vakkom Moulavi in the early decades of the nineteenth and the twentieth centuries (Kareem 1981: 513–16; Kurup and Ismail 2008: 245–310; Samad 1998). The reformists contested the prevailing local practices among the Muslim communities such as Chandanakkudom (urs), Nercha (anniversaries of saints), moulid (an 'antiphonal reading' of the life events of the Prophet or a saint) and *rathib* (a ceremonial practice conducted in the name of a saint) (Samad 1998: 18–19). These practices were perceived by the reformers as 'local accretions' or 'un-Islamic and unlawful innovations'. The reformers challenged various aspects of matriliny such as descent in the female line, matrilocality and the acceptance of the maternal uncle as the guardian of children instead of the father (Lindberg 2009: 90; Sebastian 2012, 2013: 80).

> Islamic reformism is one of the strongest influences at work in the critique of matriliny. Reformists argue that the *tharavadu* system fosters a lack of responsibility in men, since wives and children are accommodated in the matrilineal home, where mothers and brothers will see that women and their children will never starve, even if a woman's husband is feckless. (Osella 2012: 11)

Legal interventions to revoke matrilineal practices among the Mappilas of Malabar were demanded by the Islamic reformers in the first half of the twentieth century. The opinions received by the select committee on the Mappila Marumakkathayam Bill proposed by Khan Bahadur Mahamad Schamnad Sahib in 1937 needs to be analysed in the context of the Islamic reformist intervention in the legal sphere. According to C. P. Mohideen Kutty[19] (president, Village Congress Committee, Ch. Palliprom, Valapad, South Malabar), considering the total population of Malabar, the Mappilas who follow the Marumakkathayam law form only a 'microscopic minority'. This law stands contradictory to the Islamic law and should be repealed. Matrilineal practice among

Muslims as an un-Islamic custom surfaced in the bill as one of the major issues. According to K. P. Muhammad Mahajir, the

> Marumakkathayam system of inheritance happened to be copied by a section of the Mappila Muslims of Malabar as a necessary evil in the early days. Though a purely non-Muslim institution, it has served many families towards prosperity, for decades in the past. It could have been reformed into a healthier institution by ruin of many Mappila families in Malabar ... It is nothing but an anomaly to see the Mappilas of North Malabar who in all other respects follow the Islamic (law of Shariat) have adopted this law of inheritance for a very long time. This may be due to their close contact with Hindu families from which they have embraced Islam.[20]

Various religious associations such as Salahul Islam Sangham (Calicut), Muslim Association (Paravanna, south Malabar) and Young Men's Muslim Association (Baliapatam) urged for the removal of the Marumakkathayam law, which according to them was an unnatural law that needed to be replaced with the Islamic law.[21] The opinions received on the bill point out the socio-economic concerns of the time such as the economic bankruptcy of the matrilineal Mappila communities under colonial rule, the desire of the younger male members to be economically independent and to transfer their self-acquired property to their own children instead of devolving it into the matrilineal property, and the assumption of Marumakkathayam usage as bida or an unlawful innovation (Sebastian 2016: 88). With the enactment of the Mappila Marumakkathayam Act in 1939, provisions were provided for individuals to claim partition of the tharavad and dwell as nuclear families.

The inter-play of socio-economic and religious factors eventually led to the partial revoking of the matrilineal form of inheritance through the enactment of the Shariat Act in 1937. Thus, the attempt of the colonial state to deal with the legal pluralities in the matrilineal practices of the Mappilas eventually led to the creation of a uniform law for Muslims. The nature of the trajectory of colonial legal intervention since the early decades of the twentieth century till the mid-twentieth century in Malabar has reshaped the social organisation on the basis of patrilineal inheritance, patrilocality and conjugal ties.

Law, Custom and Religion: The Postcolonial Situation

The debates over matrilineal practices among the Mappila Muslims of Malabar entered into a new phase in the postcolonial period. The validity of both customary and religious practices came to be questioned with the formation of the Indian Constitution Act. The Shariat Act of 1937 and the Mappila Marumakkathayam Act of 1939 were amended in 1949 and 1954, respectively. The nature of interaction between sharia (Muslim personal law), the Marumakkathayam law and the postcolonial state law brings forth the ways in which people avail of multiple legal provisions, strategically and contextually.

For an in-depth analysis of this engagement with the legal pluralities in the postcolonial context, Case No. 41 of 1954,[22] Puthiyapurayil Abdurahiman (karnavar and manager of the tavazhi tharavad) and *Avookar versus Thayath Kacheentavida Avoomma and Others* is referred to as a case in study. The suit was referred by the district munsif of Cannanore (Kannur) to the Madras High Court. It came before the court for hearing on 12 October 1955 for the decision of the high court to the question, 'whether the Madras Shariat (Amendment) Act (Act XVIII of 1949) is Ultravires of Section 19, Clause (1) (f) of the Constitution Act'. The extent of applicability of the Madras Shariat Amendment Act as a decisive factor on people's right to property, while the Indian Constitution Act on property rights is extant, was brought to debate through this case. The defendants relied on the provisions of the Constitution Act to protect their customary rights against Islamic law on which the plaintiffs depended. It is interesting to note how the litigants selectively choose legal provisions to their benefit.

An intriguing situation arose in the suit filed by the widow of Abdulla Kalpa for partition and separate possession of the plaint property. Abdulla belonged to a tharavad governed by Marumakkathayam. His main tharavad entered into a *karar*[23] on 30 October 1918. As per the karar, the main tharavad was divided into three branches or tavazhis. The terms of the karar also mentioned that if one of the branches became extinct, then the properties belonging to it would lapse into the possession of other branches. Abdulla belonged to the third branch. He was the only surviving member of his tharavad, and he passed away on 10 January 1952. The first branch also soon became extinct. The ambiguity posed in this case was whether the property of his branch would lapse into the remaining branch, that is, the first tavazhi, or whether his widow and children could inherit it according to the Muslim Shariat Act. Thayath Kacheentavida Avvomma, the widow of Abdulla Kalpa and the plaintiff in this suit, demanded the transfer of the property, based on the provisions of the Madras Shariat (Amendment) Act of 1949.

Puthiyapurayil Abdurahim, the karnavar of the tharavad and one of the defendants in the suit, contended that according to the provisions of Article 19, Clause (1) (f) of the Constitution Act, the Madras Shariat Amendment Act should be considered invalid. Litigations of a similar nature were referred to the high court. The question that was posed was whether the Madras Shariat Amendment Act aimed to repeal the customary Marumakkathayam law in matters related to family, marriage, succession and inheritance. As per the observations made by the high court in the light of the earlier colonial enactments on will, succession and the Marumakkathayam practice, both the Shariat Act of 1937 and the Madras Shariat (Amendment) Act of 1949 did not abolish the rights and incidents of a Mappila matrilineal tharavad. However, the postcolonial courts witnessed the emergence of divergent views.

> For it cannot be denied that the object of the Muslim Personal Law (Shariat) Application Act was to put an end to all anti-Islamic customs and rules that had obtained the force of law and in their stead to apply the original principles of Islamic law itself. (Basheer Ahmed Sayeed, cited in Case No. 41 of 1954: 15)

In a certain sense, the postcolonial state continued to engage with the colonial construction of impartibility of the matrilineal tharavad in judicial proceedings. It can be inferred from the legal shift that has taken place since the colonial period that certain aspects of the matrilineal tharavad, such as joint property, were excluded from reform with certain decrees. The observation made by the judge in *Puthiyapurayil Abdurahiman versus Thayath Kacheentavida Avoomma* was that no member of the Mappila tharavad has a share in the property of the tharavad till its partition. Hence, any claim for an intestate succession of the 'impartible' property remains void. According to Justice P. V. Rajamannar and Justice Panchapakesa Ayyar,

> it is not correct to say that when a junior member of a *tharavad* dies "his share" devolves to the other members of *tharavad*. The correct legal position is that the property is owned by the *tharavad* as a composite entity, the members of which fluctuate, i.e., the members increase or decrease. (Ibid.: 20–21)

The court, in this case, came to the conclusion that the question of constitutional validity of the Madras Act XVIII of 1949 cannot be raised and the judgement went in favour of the tharavad.

The nature of postcolonial legal reform needs to be read in continuity with its colonial past. The trajectory it has followed since the colonial period carries in it the conceptualisation of the matrilineal tharavad as an undivided corporate unit. One can see this assumption persisting in the engagement of legal pluralities in the postcolonial period. The drift towards the creation of a uniform law for Muslims is initiated by a simultaneous adherence to the concept of impartibility. The interaction between matrilineal customary law, religious law and state law entails dimensions of contestation, negotiation and accommodation.

The implications of the newly amended acts abrogating matrilineal practices remained partial, but the legislative reforms in the case of the matrilineal Hindus in Malabar came to a closure with the abolition of matriliny in 1976 under the Joint Family Abolition Act. The distinctiveness of legal reform in the case of the matrilineal Muslims of Malabar is that no enactment has been passed so far for the complete abolition of matriliny. Muslims of Malabar are permitted to be governed by the Marumakkathayam law in the absence of evidence to the contrary.[24] Even when the existing matrilineal properties are allowed to be inherited according to the Marumakkathayam law, the formation of new branches is out of the question. In a way, the matrilineal law is valid only till the cessation of the existing ancestral properties.

The implications of the legal reforms for the matrilineal Mappila tharavads need to be read along with the socio-economic transformations that the Mappila tharavad has undergone in the context of the post-1960s land reforms and the post-1970s gulf migration. The legal reforms and socio-economic changes together contributed to the modification of certain practices, thereby setting forth a trend towards patrilineality.

Under the postcolonial land reforms, the first communist government in Kerala predominantly acquired the ancestral landed properties of Mappila landlords in the north Malabar region. The redistribution of this property among the tenants modified the landlord–tenant relations in Malabar. The extension of sharia to agricultural land in the 1960s had detrimental effects on the social position of the north Malabar matrilineal Mappila women who held inheritance rights over the landed properties. As per the Mappila Marumakkathayam Amendment Act of Kerala Act No. 32 of 1963, the share that any member of the Mappila tharavad received in partition would devolve according to sharia (Agarwal 1994: 232–33). Finally, the economic conditions brought in by the gulf migration in the 1970s led to the emergence of nuclear families in large numbers, and they began to replace matrilineal ties with new forms of familial relations such as conjugality (Osella and Osella 2008: 322; Riedel 2013: 43).

The new forms of familial relations became visible since the early decades of the twentieth century. In the context of the reformation of the public sphere in colonial Kerala, Devika (2006: 47; 2007: 72–76) argues that the social trend seemed to favour monogamous marital unions through the creation of modern domesticity and conjugality. The reorganisation of marital relations through legislative intervention also followed the same path. The acceptance of the husband as the breadwinner relegated women to the domestic sphere, placing upon them a sense of moral responsibility towards their husband and children.

Irrespective of the socio-economic, religious and legislative challenges, the community employed various means to sustain their customary practices. It is important to explore the legal strategies exercised by women to sustain the matrilineal practices in the context of the emergence of patrilineal forms of familial and property relations.

Women's Strategy: Conversion of Matrilineal Tharavad as Waqf Property

The wider economic and political processes that take place within a society have varied consequences for the social position of women (Ganesh and Risseeuw 1998: 11–46; Risseeuw and Palriwala 1996: 16), and women are not passive receptors of these changes. They exercise strategic decisions through acts of negotiation and accommodation. The intercession of the colonial and the postcolonial state in the legal sphere, the historically specific social and economic transformations, and the advent of Islamic reformism in the twentieth century altered the social position of matrilineal Mappila women in Malabar.

The refashioning of the matrilineal tharavad through the codification of colonial law in the nineteenth century reconstituted the internal structure, furthering the gendered hierarchy of power relations related to property rights and management. The codified matrilineal customs entailed a set of rigid criteria and the matrilineal customary practices evolved as a 'frozen category' under the colonial state. According to this formulation of the colonial state, matriliny and patriliny came to be understood as opposites in the structure of the social organisation. The presence of one assumed the total absence of the other (Kodoth 2007: 222) and the co-existence of both the elements within the community seemed irrelevant to the colonial judiciary. The hidden patriarchal structures within the matrilineal tharavad were not only discounted by the colonial state but also reinforced through the consolidation of managerial power under the senior male head of the tharavad. Existence of women's exclusive property rights in the form of strisothu or henummula was also either not recognised or denied by the colonial state.

The changes that have been taking place in Malabar in the twentieth century had varied consequences for the internal kinship relations of these communities. Women were put into a disadvantaged position in the tharavads, while the male members continued to control the tharavad as managers. Consequently, alienation of the tharavad by male members began to take place in the colonial period, posing a threat to the matrilocal residence of its female members. The misappropriation of the tharavad property and the alienation of the jointly held property to one's own wives and children by the male members in the first half of the twentieth century impacted the socio-economic position of matrilineal Mappila women. The advent of Islamic reformism in this period challenged the practice of matriliny as an un-Islamic custom. According to the reformists, sharia was against matrilineal inheritance and the matrilocal system. Matrilineage, matrilocal residence of married women and the legal guardianship of children by maternal uncles instead of their fathers were unacceptable to the reformists. As mentioned in the earlier sections of this essay, the legislative and Islamic reformist interventions induced by social, economic and religious factors modified matriliny along the lines of patriliny. At this juncture, the challenging task for women was to negotiate with the un-Islamic nature of matriliny in order to sustain matrilineal practices.

The strategic conversion of the matrilineal tharavad as a waqf property enabled Mappila women (especially in the coastal belt of Calicut, south Malabar) to negotiate with the challenges posed by Islamic reformist trends.[25] The contestations raised by the Islamic reformers were strategically solved by drawing from concepts located in the religious sphere itself.

The word 'waqf' means 'detention' or 'stoppage'. Waqf is 'the detention of a thing in the implied ownership of the Almighty God, in such a way that its profits may be applied for the benefit of human beings, and the detention when once made, is absolute so that the thing dedicated can neither be sold, nor given nor inherited' (Abu Yusuf, cited in Gupta and Sarkar 1983: 89). According to the Muslim Waqf Act of 1954, '"*waqf*" means the permanent dedication by a person professing Islam of any movable or immovable property for any purpose recognized by the Muslim Law as pious, religious or charitable'.

Twentieth-century Malabar witnessed the conversion of the matrilineal tharavad into waqf property. Such conversion helped women secure property rights from the manipulative sale of their property by the menfolk. Even today, a number of such properties can be observed among the matrilineal Koyas along the coasts of Kozhikode (Calicut) as the dedication of a property as waqf is permanent, after which such property cannot be sold, partitioned or mortgaged. This characteristic of waqf property was extended to the matrilineal Mappila tharavad to sustain matrilineal practices such as matrilocality. Karnoti or the eldest female member of the tharavad is the trustee of the waqf property, which is often the tharavad. The combination of waqf and matrilocality allows a unique pattern of residence, wherein the property does not go to the religious authorities until the death of the last female member of the matrilineal Mappila tharavad. This provision secures women the right to have a permanent claim on the tharavad house. At the death of the last female member, the tharavad would be handed over to the religious authorities to build a mosque or school. However, this has often led to disputes between the surviving male members of the tharavad and the authorities to whom the property is to be handed over, as can be seen from the following narrative.

> My neighbour's tharavad is a waqf property. There has been conflict arising frequently between the male and female members to own this property. Last year, the only surviving female member in the matrilineal line also passed away. As per the rule, the property now should be handed over to the religious authorities to build a school. But, the male members refused to give away the property. They filed a suit in the court. The legal battle is still going on. This is not an isolated incident. You may come across similar cases in this locality. A small piece of land along the coastal line is expensive. Hence, nobody wants to give it away on charity. In some cases, the male members do not go to the court. They seek alternative ways to procure the property. They negotiate with the religious authorities by finding a different plot outside the locality for waqf and secure the tharavad in their possession. This is an internal adjustment. (Abdullah Koya, age 66)

Apart from the disputes over property ownership between male and female members, conflict arises between the female members who are residing in the waqf tharavad. Though it is customary for women to be entitled to the heirship on a seniority basis, the economically well-to-do elder sister moves away to a neo-local residence, leaving the tharavad to her economically weaker younger sister. However, this is not the case always, and it leads to disagreements, especially when the senior female member's right over the property becomes vulnerable if she has no female children. The concept of waqf has brought forth an interesting dimension of power relations between the female members of the matrilineal tharavad. However, it is also interesting to note that women hold different views on the practice of waqf, depending on their social class. While the conversion of a joint household as waqf property secures women's residential rights, women also hold divergent views on this practice in relation to their class position. This can be inferred from the following narrative:

> Ours is a waqf property. It is high time that we renovate it. But there is no money. Some sections of the tharavad have already fallen. Hence, we occupy only a small portion near the kitchen. The well-to-do members have already moved out neo-locally. The possibility of a partition and procuring one's individual share is also out of question as this is a waqf property. The land value is high in this area. If we could get the individual share then it would have been sufficient enough to dwell in a better place. (Khadija, a lower-middle class Koya woman, age 53)

As the preceding conversation indicates, land value is high along the coastal belt of Kozhikode. According to lower-middle class Koya women, the conversion of tharavad into waqf has taken away the possibility of selling the property. They neither have the money to renovate the fallen roof of the tharavad nor the legal right to alienate the property for sale. However, in the context of manipulative sale by male members, one cannot discount the advantage that the waqf offers to women to have ownership over property, as can be seen from Raziya's narrative.

> In one way, waqf is good. In the earlier days, women in our community were illiterate. Even if they studied, they studied till the fourth standard. It was rare that they studied beyond this level. As they were illiterate, they were often cheated by the male members who manipulated and sold the tharavad and ancestral properties. If the tharavad property was in the name of women, it couldn't be sold off.

> Even in my case, our previous generations were well-to-do members. In the long run, men destroyed everything. We are fortunate that our tharavad house is waqf. What would have been the situation otherwise? We would have been on the streets. After my eldest sister, this property will be inherited by my middle sister. After her, this tharavad will belong to me. Though the tharavad belongs to my eldest sister, she does not stay here. She resides in a separate house with her husband and children. Currently, my middle sister and I stay in the tharavad. I do not have to go separate as she doesn't have children, but I have four boys. A waqf property will not go to male members. So, after my death, this property will go to my eldest sister's daughter. Hence the tharavad doesn't perish you see. (Raziya, a middle-class Koya woman, age 43)

The strategic conversion of tharavad into waqf implies two things. First, it contests the widely held assumption of Islam as patrilineal in nature and its persistence in complete opposition to the matrilineal customary practices. A study of the kinship practices of the matrilineal Mappilas indicates a creative combination of Islam and matriliny. Second, it necessitates a probe into the important ways in which women employ strategies to sustain matrilineal practices by drawing upon the elements of two supposedly antithetical systems of inheritance.

The modifications in the Malabar law relating to the matrilineal Mappila Muslims at various moments in the history of Malabar brought forth several changes:

1. In an attempt to create a uniform law, the state, through its colonial and postcolonial political and socio-economic manifestations, transformed matrilineal inheritance on the lines of patrilineal inheritance, thereby subsuming the diversity embedded in its empirical form.
2. The legal intervention in the ancestral properties remained partial in comparison to the self-acquired property, and the colonial construction of impartibility continued to thrive as a key factor in defining tharavad even in the postcolonial period.
3. The Muslim communities of Malabar witnessed the separation of self-acquired property of the individual from the domain of

> ancestral property in the early part of the twentieth century, as self-acquisitions were brought under the purview of the Muhammadan law. This could be one of the reasons why a complete abolition of the matrilineal system of inheritance was not required in the 1970s in the case of the Mappilas, while other matrilineal non-Muslim communities were moving towards a complete legal revocation of the matrilineal system of inheritance.

The study of the nature of the legal shift that has been taking place among the matrilineal Mappilas also needs to be analysed in the context of similar attempts by the colonial and the postcolonial state to transform matrilineal practices among the non-Muslim matrilineal communities of Malabar and the impact of socio-economic, political and religious factors on matrilineal practices.

Conclusion

Exploration of matrilineal practices among the Muslim communities of Malabar enables one to understand how Islamic principles of family law are negotiated in a matrilineal society and how matriliny, in turn, is reconstituted by Islam. The existence of matrilineal practices in the kinship rules of the Mappilas raised challenges for the judiciary in the colonial period, in settling disputes over matters related to family, marriage, inheritance, succession, dower and gift deeds. This essay has attempted to foreground the courtroom as a site where the court of law enters into dialogue with the socio-cultural pluralities in Malabar. The court proceedings on Mappila Marumakkathayam tharavad can be looked at as a constant form of engagement of the colonial and the postcolonial state, seeking ways to accommodate matrilineal and religious elements within the purview of the Malabar law. In their attempt to codify practices, the colonial judiciary created a dichotomy between the codified law and the practices of the people, which limited the judiciary from an in-depth engagement with the customs and usages as practised by the Mappilas in their everyday life in colonial Malabar.

The nature of the legal shift that has taken place in the case of the matrilineal Mappilas of Malabar needs to be understood as an outcome of the inter-play of various context-specific factors. The emergence of new economic conditions under the colonial rule modified the power relations in the matrilineal Mappila tharavads. Market reforms led to the downfall of trading endeavours of the Mappilas and the subsequent deterioration of the tharavads. During this period, the younger male members, who were mostly from the well-to-do tharavads, entered the colonial bureaucracy, acquired properties and opposed the merging of their self-acquired property with the ancestral property. Demands were raised by them for the recognition of conjugality over matrilineality, which resulted in legal reforms fostering new forms of familial relations in conciliation with the demands of the younger male members.

Apart from this, the interventions of Islamic reformers into the legal sphere like the matrilineal bill of Khan Mahamad Schamnad Sahib had important consequences for the Mappila tharavad. And finally, one cannot discount the impact of postcolonial land reforms, the gulf migration in the 1970s and the economic conditions created by it in the mushrooming of nuclear families, which replaced matrilineal ties.

The trajectory of legal reform in Malabar and in the colonial and the postcolonial contexts foregrounds the changing socio-economic aspirations of its people. This shift can be understood as a form of contestation posed to the practice of matriliny and as paving the way for the creation of a uniform law for Muslims, discounting the lived aspects of religion and kinship. The socio-economic and legal transformation of the Mappila tharavad in colonial and postcolonial Malabar had certain consequences for the women in terms of property ownership and management rights. As pointed out by Devika (2006: 47), the reformation of the public sphere in colonial Malabar led to the strengthening of 'conjugality' and 'modern domesticity', by relegating women to the domestic sphere. Despite the challenges, Mappila women employ strategic means to continue with their customary practices by negotiating between religious and customary practices. The conversion of tharavad into waqf property among the Koyas of Kozhikode is one such instance.

The analysis of legal reform of the Mappila tharavad enables one to understand the ways in which colonial and postcolonial courts engage with the socio-cultural pluralities of Malabar. The trajectory followed by legal reform at different moments in the history of Malabar allows one to understand the legal reform of the Mappila tharavad as an outcome of the historically specific interaction of various factors such as socio-economic transformations, Islamic reformist trends and the public sphere.

Notes

1. Malabar, Travancore and Cochin formed the three political divisions in pre-colonial Kerala (Lakshmi 2012: 33).
2. Kerala Muslims are generally referred to as the 'Mappilas'. According to Miller (1992: 31), the offspring of foreign husbands and indigenous wives are called 'Mappila'. The word 'Mappila' was substituted by the word 'Muslim' through the enactment of the Mappila Marumakkathayam (Amendment) Act, Kerala Act No. 32 of 1963 (Agarwal 1994: 233). Nevertheless, the term 'Mappila' continues to be used in academic writings on Kerala Muslims even today.
3. The term 'redefinition of *tharavad*' is used by Arunima (2003: 36) in the context of the transformation of the matrilineal Nayar tharavad in colonial Malabar. The present study borrows the term from this work (ibid.) in the analysis of the legal reform of the matrilineal Mappila tharavad.
4. According to Ali (1933: 51), tharavad is the social unit among the people who are governed by the Marumakkathayam system of inheritance. A tharavad comprises a group of individuals who claim descent in the female line from a common female ancestress.
5. Tangals are considered superior in status to other Muslims in Kerala, as they are believed to be the descendants of the Prophet.
6. Courts of revenue in British India.
7. The senior-most male member in a matrilineal tharavad.
8. Indian Law Reports 1904, Volume 27, pp. 77–79, Tellicherry Revenue Reference Library.
9. Indian Law Reports 1913, Volume 36, pp. 385–86, Tellicherry Revenue Reference Library.
10. Indian Law Reports 1915, Volume 38, pp. 1052–63, Tellicherry Revenue Reference Library.
11. Original Suit No. 432 of 1898 in List 1, Volume 1, Serial No. 810, Tellicherry Court Records, Kozhikode Regional Archives.
12. Original Suit No. 522 of 1898 in List I, Volume 1, Serial No. 815, Tellicherry Court Records, Kozhikode Regional Archives.
13. Indian Law Reports 1923, Volume 46, pp. 650–59, Tellicherry Revenue Reference Library.
14. Indian Law Reports 1909, Volume 32, pp. 315–18, Tellicherry Revenue Reference Library.

15. Indian Law Reports 1928, Volume 51, pp. 574–84, Tellicherry Revenue Reference Library.
16. Indian Law Reports 1893, Volume 16, pp. 201–07, Tellicherry Revenue Reference Library.
17. Property is of two types in the case of the matrilineal Muslims of Lakshadweep as well. The ancestral property is termed 'Velliarcha' or Friday property, the alienation of which is not permitted without the consent of members. The self-acquired property of an individual is called 'Thingalarcha' or Monday property. Inheritance of ancestral property is governed by customary usages, while individual property devolves according to Islamic law (Dube 1994: 1275–77).
18. Volume 1, List 2, Serial No. 861, Tellicherry Court Records, Kozhikode Regional Archives.
19. Cited in *'Opinions Received' by the Select Committee on the Mappila Marumakkathayam Bill of Khan Bahadur Mahamad Schamnad Sahib* 1938, p. 81.
20. Cited in *'Opinions Received'*, pp. 9–10.
21. Cited in *'Opinions Received'*, pp. 50–77.
22. Tellicherry Court Records, Kozhikode Regional Archives.
23. Deed or consensus that is arrived between contesting parties.
24. *Mariyomma versus Aayissa* cited in *Kerala Law Times* (2000: 465).
25. The Mappila men and women along the coastal belt of Calicut are now very much part of the Mujahid reformist movement. While negotiating between religious and cultural practices, they are still deeply connected to the reformist movement. To understand this dimension, one needs to have a much more nuanced understanding of reformist movements.

References

Primary Sources

Acts

The Malabar Wills Act, Madras Act No. III of 1898.
The Mappila Marumakkathayam Act, Madras Act No. XVII of 1939.
The Mappila Succession Act 1918, Madras Acts for 1915–1918.
The Mappila Wills Act, [Tamil Nadu] Act No. VII of 1928.
The Madras Marumakkathayam Act, Act No. XXII of 1933.
The Muslim Personal Law (Shariat) Applications Act, Act No. XXVI of 1937.
The Muslim Wakf Act, Act No. 29 of 1954.

Other Primary Sources

Arakkal Records: *'Opinions Received' by the Select Committee on the Mappila Marumakkathayam Bill of Khan Bahadur Mahamad Schamnad Sahib*. 1938. Madras: Government Press.

Indian Law Reports, Madras Series, Volumes 10–54 (1887–1931), Revenue Reference Library, Tellicherry.

Innes, C. A. 1951. *Madras District Gazetteer* (edited by F. B. Evans, I. C. S). Madras: The Superintendent Press.

Kerala Law Times. 2000. 3: 465–72.

Logan, William. 2000. *Malabar Manual*, Volume 1. Trivandrum: Kerala Gazetteers Department.

Madras Records, Various Department Files (1880–56), Kozhikode Regional Archives.

Madras Records, Law Department Files (1921–55), Kozhikode Regional Archives.

Moore, Lewis. 1905. *Malabar Law and Custom*. Madras: Higginbotham & Co.

Tellicherry Court Records, List I & II, Volumes 1–4 (1870–1900, 1955), Kozhikode Regional Archives.

Secondary Sources

Agarwal, Bina. 1994. *A Field of One's Own: Gender and Land Rights in South Asia*. New York: Cambridge University Press.

Aiyappan, A., and K. Mahadevan. 1990. *Ecology, Economy, Matriliny and Fertility of Kurichiyas*. Delhi: B. R. Publishing Corporation.

Aiyar, P. R. Sundara. 1922. *Treatise on Malabar and Aliyasanthana Law*. Madras: The Madras Law Journal Office.

Ali, Hamid. 1933. *Custom and Law in Anglo-Muslim Jurisprudence*. Calcutta: Thacker, Spink & Co.

Arunima, G. 2003. *There Comes Papa: Colonialism and the Transformation of Matriliny in Kerala, Malabar c. 1850–1940*. New Delhi: Orient Longman.

Balakrishnan, P. V. 1981. *Matrilineal System in Malabar*. Cannanore: The Satyavani Prakashan.

Devika, J. 2006. 'Negotiating Women's Social Space: Public Debates on Gender in Early Modern Kerala, India', *Inter-Asia Cultural Studies*, 7 (1): 43–61.

———. 2007. *En-Gendering Individuals: The Language of Re-forming in Twentieth Century Keralam*. New Delhi: Orient Longman.

Dube, Leela. 1994. 'Conflict and Compromise: Devolution and Disposal of Property in a Matrilineal Muslim Society', *Economic and Political Weekly*, 29 (21): 1273–77, 1279–83.

Ganesh, Kamala and Carla Risseeuw. 1998. 'Introduction: Gendered Change in Marriage and Family: A Policy Concern', in Kamala Ganesh and Carla Risseeuw (eds), *Negotiation and Space: A Gendered Analysis of Changing Kin and Security Networks in South Asia and Sub-Saharan Africa*, pp. 11–46. New Delhi: Sage Publications.

Gupta, R. K., and S. C. Sarkar 1983. *An Overview of Muslim Law*. New Delhi: Surjeet Publications.

Jeffrey, Robin. 1994. *The Decline of Nair Dominance: Society and Politics in Travancore, 1847–1908*. New Delhi: Manohar.

Joseph, Modayil Pothen. 1918. *The Principles of Marumakkathayam Law with a Commentary on the Nair Regulation of 1088*. Kottayam: The Church Missionary's Society's Press.

Kareem, K. K. Muhamed Abdul. 1981. *Makthi Thangalude Sampoorna Krithikal* (in Malayalam). Calicut: Vachanam Books.

Kodoth, Praveena. 2007. 'Framing Custom, Directing Practices: Authority, Property and Matriliny under Colonial Law in Nineteenth-century Malabar', in Shail Mayaram, M. S. S. Pandian and Ajay Skaria (eds), *Muslims, Dalits and the Fabrications of History*, pp. 188–223. New Delhi: Permanent Black & Ravi Dayal Publisher.

Kottakkunnummal, Manaf. 2014. 'Indigenous Customs and Colonial Law: Contestations in Religion, Gender and Family among Matrilineal Muslims in Colonial Malabar, Kerala, c. 1910–1928', *Sage Open*, January–March: 1–12.

Kumari, C. V. 2003. 'State and Social Change—The Role of Judiciary: A Case Study of Malabar 1792–1940', Ph.D. dissertation, University of Calicut, India.

Kurup, K. K. N., and E. Ismail. 2008. *Emergence of Islam in Kerala in Twentieth Century*. New Delhi: Standard Publishers.

Lakshmi, L. R. S. 2012. *The Malabar Muslims: A Different Perspective*. New Delhi: Cambridge University Press.

Lindberg, Anna. 2009. 'Islamisation, Modernisation, or Globalisation? Changed Gender Relations among South Indian Muslims', *South Asia: Journal of South Asian Studies*, 32 (1): 86–109.

McGilvray, Dennis B. 2014. 'A Matrilineal Sufi Shaykh in Sri Lanka', *South Asian History and Culture*, 5 (2): 246–61.

Miller, Roland E. 1992. *Mappila Muslims of Kerala*. Madras: Orient Longman.

Osella, Caroline. 2012. 'Desires under Reform: Contemporary Reconfigurations of Family, Marriage, Love and Gendering in a Transnational South Indian Matrilineal Muslim Community', *Culture and Religion*, 13 (2): 1–39.

Osella, Filippo and Caroline Osella. 2008. 'Islamism and Social Reform in Kerala, South India', *Modern Asian Studies*, 42 (2–3): 317–46.

Puthenkalam, J. 1977. *Marriage and the Family in Kerala (with Special Reference to Matrilineal Castes)*. New Delhi: Printaid.

Riedel, Barbara. 2013. 'Cosmopolitanism at Work on the Malabar Coast of South India: A Study with Muslim Students in Kozhikode', *Transcience*, 4 (2): 36–49.

Risseeuw, Carla and Rajni Palriwala. 1996. 'Introduction: Shifting Circles of Support', in Rajni Palriwala and Carla Risseeuw (eds), *Shifting Circles of Support: Contextualising Gender and Kinship in South Asia and Sub-Saharan Africa*, pp. 15–47. New Delhi: Sage Publications.

Samad, M. Abdul. 1998. *Islam in Kerala: Groups and Movements in the Twentieth Century*. Kollam: Laurel Publications.

Saradamoni, K. 1999. *Matriliny Transformed: Family, Law and Ideology in Twentieth Century Travancore*. New Delhi: Sage Publications.

Sebastian, Aleena. 2012. 'Matrilineal Practices among Muslims: A Comparative Analysis of Matrilineal Practices among Koyas of Kozhikode and Minangkabau of West Sumatra', unpublished M.Phil. dissertation, University of Hyderabad, India.

———. 2013. 'Matrilineal Practices among Koyas of Kozhikode', *Journal of South Asian Studies*, 1 (1): 66–82.

———. 2016. 'Matrilineal Practices along the Coasts of Malabar', *Sociological Bulletin*, 65 (1): 89–106.

Wigram, H. M. A. 1882. *A Commentary on Malabar Law and Custom*. Madras: Granes, Cookson and Co., Scottish Press.

3

Religion, Secularity and Law

The Case of Bababudhan Dargah in South India

Sudha Sitharaman

In India today, there is a general consensus that freedom of religion and the right to preservation and practice of different religions are essential in a society as diverse as India. There is also a widespread consensus internationally that a neutral secular state is required to safeguard these rights. However, unlike the Western state that pursues a policy of 'non-interference',[1] the Indian state seeks to actively interfere in religion, leading scholars to remark on its distinctiveness (Bhargava 2007, cited in Srikantan 2012: 3) or inconsistency (Madan 1998, cited in Srikantan 2012: 3). The legal enforcement of religious rights flows from the Indian Constitution itself, which guarantees freedom of religious belief and practice under Article 25, the autonomy of religious institutions under Article 26, along with other significant rights such as the provisions for religious denominations to establish and maintain institutions for religious and charitable purposes (such as educational institutions) under Article 30. Despite the legal recognition of these rights and the constitutional framework that enshrines religious pluralism, there has been considerable dissatisfaction over the manner in which religious freedom is legally enforced. Many a time, elements of religiosity that reflect a commitment to a practice as much as a commitment to a belief have come into contradiction with one another and the right to practise religion of one has infringed upon the rights of another, rather than being, for the most parts, a collision of incompatible religious practices themselves. However, the state cannot abrogate its responsibility to generate stable, equitable relationships between the state and heterogeneous communities. This seemingly obvious and neutral right of religious liberty has yielded mutually contradictory and often discriminatory results, especially when religious freedom, which is foundational to liberal political rule, is shot through with tensions generating its own peculiar set of problems. The religious–political ambiguities are expressions of deeper indeterminacies that are at the very foundation of secular power.

All the same, political secularism as a project of the state is upheld by liberals and right-wingers alike, albeit in different ways, as both assume that this particular socio-political arrangement is the best way to ward off the dangers of religious strife. On the contrary, I want to suggest that the modern state and political secularism, particularly the modern state's production and regulation of religious differences, have played a far more decisive role in transforming pre-existing religious differences, thereby producing new forms of communal polarisations and making religion more rather than less salient to Hindus and Muslims alike. In order to substantiate my argument, I will consider the legal and political contestations around the case of Bababudhan dargah[2] in the state of Karnataka, south India, to illustrate how the exercise of sovereign power of the liberal modern state tends to give rise to continual conflict and how this has long been and is increasingly fraught with an irrevocable indeterminacy, therefore being, at best, only precariously secular. Religious freedom has emerged as a highly contentious and charged issue.

The Dispute

In the wild, beautiful location set midway up the Bababudhan hills in the Chickmagalur district of Karnataka, south India, in the village called Dattatripit, stands the *khanqah* (hospice) of Dada Hayath Meer Qalandar, popularly known as Bababudhan dargah, in a cave. The cave houses an altar or a seat, which is believed to be the *chillah*[3] of Dada Hayath Meer Qalandar. While many see it as a *peetha* (rostrum or seat) of Swamy Dattatreya, others believe that Dada Hayath Meer Qalandar and Swamy Dattatreya are two forms of the same divinity. According to the Hindu Puranas, Dattatreya is a protean figure who has been appropriated by a wide range of traditions from Tantric to Sufism,[4] and Dada, as legend has it, was a close associate of Prophet Muhammad who travelled to India to preach Islam. It is believed that Syed Shah Jamaluddin Maghribi, a native of Baghdad and popularly called Bababudhan, came to Chickmagalur in the sixteenth century via Yemen and continued this spiritual lineage, and it is his successors who are now the *sajjadah nashins* (custodians) of the dargah. For centuries, both Muslims and non-Muslims have venerated the saints at the shrine.[5] The Bababudhan dargah, a 'multi-religious' centre with a complex array of religiosities, has today become a single set of mutually exclusive categories of self-identification, exclusion and tensions between Hindus, Muslims and secular activists. The Guru Dattatreya Peetha Samvardhana Samiti (Committee for the Development of Datta Peetha, hereafter Samiti), an outfit floated by the Vishwa Hindu Parishad (World Hindu Council or VHP) along with the Bajrang Dal, vows to liberate the shrine from, what they claim is, 'Muslim control' and re-establish what they believe are Hindu entitlements over the peetha. Towards this end and since the late 1980s, they have been organising what is popularly called the Datta Jayanthi[6] in the month of December, claiming that the chillah of Dada Hayat Meer Qalandar is originally a peetha of Lord Dattatreya. They demand that Agamic[7] forms of worship be introduced in place of those that are being practised and that a Hindu *archaka* (priest) be appointed in place of the *mujawar* (the person who performs the rituals in the dargah). Countering them, the Karnataka Komu Souharda Vedike (Forum for Communal Harmony, Karnataka, hereafter Vedike) demand that the syncretic character of the shrine be retained through the practice of celebrating urs,[8] while calling for a hold on Datta Jayanthi. They argue that 'new' rituals, if introduced, will tantamount to 'conversion' of the shrine, which goes against the Places of Worship (Special Provisions) Act 1991.[9] The conflict between these two sets of claims and the constitutional provisions of ensuring religious freedom has produced a substantial volume of case law and legal scholarship. And the media tends to project this schism as a product of primordial conflict (among Hindus and Muslims) that characterises the Indian political landscape, Hindutva's (Hinduness) inherent intolerance and/or growing *salafiya*[10] attempts at reform among Muslims. However, even those critical of this interpretation nonetheless worry that the religious diversity that characterised the region for centuries may vanish. In this essay, I attempt to challenge this manner of conceptualising the conflict—as one between secular necessity (tolerant, progressive left) and religious threat (intolerant, conservative right).

The conflict over the Bababudhan dargah is a violation of contesting claimants' right to religious freedom, a core commitment of liberal democratic governance, where the state cannot abrogate the secular principle of neutrality, that is, equality towards all religions. Accordingly, the Vedike (secular organisations) urge that the central tenets of secularism be followed more assiduously and judiciously in the context of the state having come to espouse a particular religious position that has resulted in privileging majoritarian religious norms and threatens to dissolve the state's claim to religious neutrality. On the other hand, the Samiti (Hindu claimants) argues that the principle of religious freedom be made more resilient in practice by granting religious freedom to all and not just some, and that all religions be allowed equal space and voice in the shrine, as it ought to be within liberal societies. This leads to the argument that secularism is not first and foremost about the freedoms associated with it but rather about governance. The resolution to this incommensurable divide between the religious and the secular cannot be addressed without paying adequate attention to how political secularism has transformed identity and inter-faith relations.

Secularism, as we all know, has been the subject of much theorising.[11] This has been, in part, an attempt to give a picture of secularism that better fits the actual practices of secular states and also allows for the important differences between them. These newer approaches have, in an effort to trace the processes of power by which these normative standards were fashioned, effected a separation between secularism's normative standards and the analytic categories used to understand them. Taking the arguments beyond a scale of secularity (which facilitates notions of partial, precarious or complete success), and collapsing the normative with the analytic, I wish to instead bring attention more securely to what secularism does.

Following Asad's (2006) interrogation of French secularism, I conceptualise political secularism as the modern state's sovereign power to reorganise the substantive features of religious life, stipulating what religion is or ought to be, assigning its proper content and disseminating concomitant subjectivities, ethical frameworks and quotidian practices. This understanding highlights that as a process of defining, managing and intervening in religious life and sensibility, secularism has been historically, and remains till today, an expression of the state's sovereign power. I shall apply this idea to argue that as a feature of the modern state's growing regulatory capacity, political secularism has long been, and is increasingly, fraught with an irrevocable indeterminacy. I hope to show that it is erroneous to resolve the Bababudhan dispute within the framework of the right to religious freedom and the principle of state neutrality. For the peculiar intractability of secularism lies not only in the normativity of its categories, but also, significantly, in the indeterminacies it provokes. This claim may appear counter-intuitive to many who believe that secularism is a solution to the problem of religious strife rather than a force in its creation. In what follows, the focus is on the ways in which religious beliefs and practices associated with them have developed in the disputed site and how they have come to shape and invoke communities in new ways. Modern secular governance, I argue, has contributed to the exacerbation of religious tensions, hardening inter-faith boundaries and polarising religious differences. Political secularism, as I hope to show, has sought to reshape the form religion takes, the practices it redeems as truly (versus superficially) spiritual, the kind of subjectivity it endorses, the particular relationship to history that it prescribes, and its effectiveness, which inevitably depends upon transforming the religious domain through numerous reforms and state injunctions.

The Failure of Categories

The central question to the Bababudhan dispute revolves around the ascertainment of 'ownership' of the shrine, as to whether it should rest with the Hindus (Hindu endowments) or the Muslims (Waqf Board), undergirding which is an understanding of the nature of practices in the shrine and, therefore, its identification with a particular religion. The Waqf Act was passed in 1954. The enlisting of the *awqaf*[12] (plural of waqf) properties began in Karnataka in 1964, and in 1973, the Government of Karnataka issued an order[13] stating that all that was notified as Muzrai[14] Muslim Waqf should come under the administration of a single entity—the Waqf Board.[15] In 1975, the deputy commissioner of Chickmagalur consulted the government for guidance with regard to classifying the Bababudhan shrine, which is revered by both Muslims and non-Muslims. The dargah, which had so far been under the administration of a sajjadah nashin and enlisted as a Muzrai institution, was transferred to the Waqf Board in the same year. In effect, the shrine, which was neither exclusively Muslim nor Hindu, was unilaterally declared an Islamic institution. Following the order, the government issued a gazette notification declaring the property as waqf and appointed a *mutavalli* (manager, trustee or governor) for the waqf.

In 1976, a controversy arose over the transfer of the dargah to the Waqf Board. On learning of the actions of the government, certain Hindu devotees appealed to the district court, pleading that the dargah should not be transferred to the Waqf Board as it affects the 'rights' and 'interests' of the Hindu devotees of the shrine. Several cases and counter-cases were registered in the courts, which ruled that the shrine is a unique institution where both Hindus and Muhammadans offer prayers to a common deity, but in different names. Interestingly, the Muslim custodian of the shrine supported the Muzrai Department's stand arguing against the Waqf Board's claim on the grounds that the shrine was not exclusively for Muslims as both Hindus and Muslims venerated it. The Waqf Board went on appeal to the High Court of Karnataka, which reiterated the findings of the lower court, stating that the property could not be considered waqf,[16] and dismissed the petition. The high court restored the management to the Muzrai Department from the Waqf Board in 1980. With this court order, the proprietary status of the shrine, that is, of it belonging to the Hindu Religious Institutions and Charitable Endowments was considered settled, following which the Waqf Board appealed to the Supreme Court in 1991, which was also dismissed.

A parallel litigation against the custodial rights of the sajjadah nashin initiated in the early 1980s resulted in the charitable endowments commissioner conducting a public hearing to determine the practices prevalent prior to 1975.[17] It was imperative to do so to ascertain if the shrine was a Hindu or a Muslim place of worship. The public hearing conclusively showed that the practices could not be identified as either Hindu or Muslim, and so in 1989, after the public hearing, the state ruled that the dargah is under the jurisdiction of the Muzrai Department and not the Waqf Board, that the Muslim sajjadah nashin is the sole administrator of the dargah, and that the rituals that have traditionally been conducted be continued and not tampered with.

However, in another listing of institutions under the Karnataka Hindu Religious Institutions and Charitable Endowments Act 1997, the shrine was brought under Hindu endowments, where the disputed site was described as 'Sri Guru Dattatreya Devasthana' or 'temple', thereby trying to project it as a Hindu place of worship. This listing, under the category of temple in the Endowments Act 1997, was, however, struck down by the High Court of Karnataka, and the notification became redundant.

Contestation over the nature of practices at the shrine through legal means continued unabated. In 2000, a suit was filed by the Samiti in the High Court of Karnataka, alleging that the dargah was actually an ancient cave temple in which Guru Dattatreya Swamy performed penance. The Samiti further alleged that the institution passed on to Muslim hands during the regime of Hyder Ali who ruled Mysore between the period 1761 and 1782 and when Ismail Shah Qadri, a fakir who was residing at Srirangapatna (near Mysore), was appointed as the manager. Thus, the Samiti claims that the shrine lost trace of its Hindu practices. Earlier, in 2000, the newly anointed sajjadah nashin was dismissed by the government on charges of misappropriation of funds and restricted his rights only to the performance of rituals. It also constituted a 19-member committee under the chairmanship of the district commissioner to look after the affairs of the shrine.[18] This government order was challenged by the sajjadah nashin in the high court as also by one Bandagi Hussain Shahkadri, who claimed to be the rightful successor as sajjadah nashin of the dargah.[19] The High Court of Karnataka, responding to all the three petitions, passed a common order on 14 February 2007, dismissing the petitions of the sajjadah nashin and Bandagi Hussain Shahkadri,[20] and directing the government to constitute a committee that would hold an enquiry to identify an eligible person who could be appointed as the sajjadah nashin. The court allowed the claim of the Samiti[21] in part by quashing the order that listed practices in the shrine (dated 25 February 1989) and directing the endowment commissioner to pass a fresh order after holding another enquiry as regards to the religious nature of the shrine prior to Hyder Ali's period. This order was challenged by the state[22] and also by the sajjadah nashin[23] in the division bench of the high court, which was dismissed on 4 August 2008, with a direction to the endowment commissioner to carry out the single-judge order of 14 February 2007.

In 2007, the high court held that the Samiti's grievances, that is, of not being allowed to observe rituals and religious practices, such as offering puja and the appointment of archaka, needs to be verified by ascertaining the nature of practices that prevailed from time immemorial. Therefore, an order was passed to conduct a further enquiry by the endowment commissioner to ascertain the nature of practices, whether Hindu or Islamic, prior to the time of Hyder Ali, so that the Samiti could perform such practices as established by the commissioner. In December 2008, the Supreme Court passed an interim order stating that 'status quo be maintained at the shrine'.[24] At this juncture, the commissioner of endowments was asked to submit a report after making an enquiry into the claims and counter-claims of the contending parties. As per the directions of the Supreme Court, the commissioner heard the matter and filed the report in 2010. Finally, as matters stand today, the Supreme Court, in its final order of 3 September 2015, entrusted the Karnataka state cabinet with the responsibility of settling the dispute on the religious nature of 'Sri Guru Dattatreya Bababudanswamy Dargah'. However, the court kept open the 'recourse to legal remedies in case any of the contesting parties had any grievance against the decision of the state government.

The recording of the shrine under the modern classificatory scheme, initially as dargah and, therefore, to come under Muzrai, and then in 1975 as property of the Waqf Board, that is, Islamic, and again brought back under the Hindu endowments, and then again as *devasthana* (temple), and now again as dargah under the Hindu endowments is, I contend, a failure of categories. What are the practices in 'Sri Guru Dattatreya Bababudanswamy Dargah'? Are these practices Hindu or Islamic? What kind of 'religious' institution is the shrine? Can the answer be found within the framework of the following questions: Is it a dargah, peetha or a devasthana? What is the place of the dargah in the Hindu and/or Islamic religious imaginary? With whom should the property of the dargah rest, the Hindu endowments or the Waqf Board? Is the sajjadah nashin a religious or an administrative head of the dargah? In whom is embodied the religious and the secular authority of the shrine? What practices do they authorise? What is the lineage of those powers—is it hereditary or is it one of selection and/or succession? How are we to understand the differences between distinct communities and between radically different groups such as the Samiti and the Vedike and/or their political agenda? Where do we or us (or ours) stop and they or others (or them) begin? One is a logical negation of the other in each of these questions. However, what should a liberal state do in such a situation when the choices confronting it are logically exclusive? What are the choices open to the liberal state if it wants to remain neutral and secular?

The constitutive feature of liberal secularism is the liberal ideal of legal and political equality for all citizens in relation to religious differences, namely, the claim that all people ought to be treated equally regardless of religious affiliation—a *normative* principle of state neutrality. Nonetheless, the manner in which these questions are settled remains the prerogative of the sovereign state, which inevitably must make normative judgements about what religion is or ought to be and its proper place in the social life of a polity. My argument is that the right to religious freedom is beset with questions and conundrums, and the processes and practices by which the essences of the religious and the secular are continually defined and redefined need to be understood. But it is by no means an attempt to 'unmask' secularism, to show it up as a myth and thus a kind of religion that has its own articles of faith.[25] Neither is my point simply to say that the secular and the religious mutually inter-penetrate. For all of these positions presuppose, in one way or other, normative conceptions of the secular and the religious, as if they each had distinct, trans-historical essences. All the same, it is often presumed that religious liberty is universally valid and can be objectively assessed as a social fact. The impossibility of its realisation should not blind us to its power, its ongoing promise and its constitutive contradictions.

Secularism and Law

In India, legal debates on the regulation of religion have centred on the lack of coherence in judicial decisions determining the demarcation of the religious as against the secular.[26] This is despite the evolution of the criterion for determining such a demarcation in the form of 'essential practices test'.[27] The courts are frequently asked upon to decide what constitutes an 'essential part of religion', thereby being off limits for state intervention, and what is 'extraneous or unessential', and, therefore, permissible for the state to interfere in (Sen 2009: 86). Dhavan (1987) has elucidated on the inconsistency and incoherence in the judicial application of the essential practices test. He shows how legal decision-making renders every aspect of human life as 'religious', including the carrying of daggers, photography of women, parental custody, and requirements of dress and diet (ibid.: 221). Dhavan expresses dissatisfaction with the imprecise manner in which the essential practices test has been used by the courts and comments that the 'intelligibility of religion' as a legal category is due to the defective interpretation by the courts and their failure to lay down adequate guidelines for the proper implementation of such a test.[28] Dhavan's assessment of the legal regulation of religion appears to be true if one presumes that correct interpretation of law is to depend on judges and local practices. There is a kind of legal formalism that undergirds the argument in that it assumes that the force of law resides not in its normative precepts but in its application. However, such an understanding of law has been challenged by a range of legal and political theorists (for example, Carl Schmitt) who argue that the law cannot be understood merely as rules, but needs to be understood as a theoretical framework that generates, in this case, legal definitions of religion. The Bababudhan dispute begs the question: What makes a discourse and/or a practice 'Hindu' or 'Islamic'? What makes an act or performance essentially religious and consequently distinctive without being confused with caste, sect, family, traditions or culture? Is religion self-evident and identifiable? In view of this, the right to religious liberty if implemented assiduously would treat Hindu and Muslim rights neutrally, as has been the claim of the contesting parties to the dispute. The state's authority to draw a line, and to define the spaces and sensibilities appropriate to religion, are typically vested within the rule of law—in courts, the codes, the constitutions and judicial authority. What may be referred to as the 'active principle of secularism' (Agrama 2006)[29] is the principle that the state has the power and authority to decide what should count as essentially religious and what scope it can have in social life. Drawing on the critique of legal formalism, I would like to argue that one needs to move away from the abstract and neutral understanding of law to understand the grammar of political secularism in its organising structure that generates such descriptions, that is, religion as a discourse and practice. My argument is not that religion has an essential core and if one stripped the appearances one would see that some apparently secular institutions were really religious. On the contrary, there is neither anything essentially religious nor any universal essence that defines 'sacred language' or 'sacred experience' (Asad 2003: 25). This process always involves often-unarticulated understandings about what religion in the abstract is or ought to be. What claims can and cannot be made regarding religion, personhood and freedom?

As I shall endeavour to show subsequently, there were breaks between Hindu/Islam and secular life in which words and practices were rearranged, and new discursive grammars (Wittgenstein 1965) replaced previous ones, and we need to understand the implications of those shifts. It is a matter of showing how contingencies relate to changes in the grammar of concepts, that is, how the changes in concepts articulate changes in practices. Secularism, in this understanding, is not simply the organising structure for what are regularly taken to be *a priori* elements of social organisation—private, public, political and religious—but a discursive operation of a power that generates these very spheres, establishes their boundaries and suffuses them with content, such that they come to acquire a natural quality for those living with its terms (Mahmood 2016: 3). In other words, the state's sovereign power to define religion is neither monolithic nor predetermined. It is shot through with a generative contradiction.

I shall start by recounting the story of reform of law, that is, the gradual restriction of the scope of religious law and tensions involved in the simultaneous search for Indian agency and of imperialist imposition. I see the reform of law neither as a story of progressive liberalisation (Baird 2005) nor as a reflection of a continuing failure to modernise properly, but rather as a dimension of secularisation and, in particular, of how secularisation reflects changing connections between state power, legal institutions, moral norms and religious authority. I would like to argue that the discursive grammar imposed through these legal structures determines much of the discourse on the conflict as exemplified by the Bababudhan dispute.

First, the co-definition of property and the public is a neglected dimension in the history of religious modernisation in the Indian subcontinent, one that can also be seen to be animating the efforts of Hindus and Muslims to gain control over religious institutions, which I shall advert in what follows. Let me begin with my schematic account. One of the central planks of colonial sociology was the codification of diverse practices across the geographical and social landscape of India as a single coherent whole, turning 'religion' into an analytical category. In the case of Hinduism, it was not conceived of as a unified 'religion' until colonial times (Hansen 1999; Kaviraj 2007; van der Veer 2001). Yet, until recently, a similar analysis had not been extended to Islam (apart from few exceptions, for instance, Kasturi 2010 and Kugle 2001), and the dramatic deconstruction of it during colonial times has not been adequately recognised.

A series of legislative acts was promulgated in the various regions of India under British control with the aim of providing guidelines for the governance of temples and a uniform code of law that applied to all 'public' religious and charitable institutions (Mudaliar 1976; Varadachari 2006). In the Mufassal Regulations 1772, formally enacted as the Regulations of 1780 (Fyzee 1963: 412), Warren Hastings stated that in all suits regarding inheritance, marriage, caste and religious institutions, 'the laws of the Koran with respect to the Mahomedans, and those of the Shaster with respect to the Gentoos' shall be adhered to (quoted in Acharyya 1914). An underlying assumption was that the multiplicity of cultural and religious traditions in India could be reducible to a dichotomy: Hindu and Muslim. Despite a plethora of secular legislations that was applicable to religious institutions, the early twentieth century saw the modern categories of the waqf and the Hindu endowments come into being.

While it is not my contention that waqf did not exist till then as the history of waqf in India dates back to twelfth century,[30] what is of interest to me here is the establishment of waqf as an institution. A waqf (plural awqaf) grant is an endowment of land established by wealthy families to support religious, charitable or educational institutions, and the revenue from waqf land can also pass on to heirs of the *waqif* (grantee). An individual who was childless, writes Kozlowski (1985), and without close relatives might have created a waqf, which sustained only religious and charitable activities. However, most endowments were not devoted purely to one purpose or the other. They were mixed. The tendency to distinguish sharply between the apparently selfish and the seemingly altruistic was in large measure the result of the examination and criticism of the institution in colonial legal and political contexts (ibid.: 60). The British interpreted 'private' awqaf as a way to subvert the Islamic laws of inheritance, which, because they are in the Quran, must be immutable, rigorous and sacred. On that basis, they argued that 'private' awqaf were later innovations, corruptions of the original law, which ought to be excised. British administrators also saw 'private' awqaf as a tax-dodging mechanism but argued against them on a scriptural basis. The Privy Council conversely declared family waqf grants to be void. Regulation Number XIX of 1810 gave company officials the right to enforce 'good management' of any public trust, including 'public' awqaf. The Musalman Wakf Validating Act 1913 provided for the recognition of the waqf as an institution. Various acts followed such as the Mussalman Wakf Act 1923, which provided for the public accountability of such waqfs by requiring the mutavalli (manager) of every waqf (except family waqf) to furnish details of the property's income, revenue and expenditure to the district judge. This subsumed the regulation of religious institutions within the larger goal of regulating charitable institutions, with the main aim of making these institutions publicly accountable. Thus, public awqaf, because of their public nature, came to be managed by state officials. Several other local enactments such as the Bihar and Orissa Mussalman Wakf Act of 1926, the Bengal Wakf Act of 1934, the Bombay Mussalman Wakf Act of 1935 and the United Provinces Muslim Wakf Act of 1936 were enacted, making provisions for rendering accounts. In the words of Kozlowski (1985), the institution did not lend itself to facile distinctions between 'private' and 'pious' interest. The new conception of waqf as public charity and the Waqf Board as an overseer of waqf properties made them accountable to the 'public', and the mutavalli was given the responsibility of ensuring public accountability of the institution. The waqf, which as Islamic property was neither public nor private,[31] now came to be regarded as a 'public institution'.

A similar story followed in the case of Hindu endowments. One of the first enactments was the Madras Hindu Endowments Enactment Act of 1925, followed by the Mysore Religious and Charitable Regulation of 1927. And, it was in 1930 that *The Mysore Muzrai Manual* was drafted. A perusal of the *Muzrai Manual* of the nineteenth century reveals a classification of religious places into categories including but not limited to *chattrams* or *musafirkhanas*, feeding houses that provided free food to travellers, *mathas* (Hindu monastic establishments), temples and Muhammadan institutions (once again divided into masjids, *ashurkhanas* (place of mourning for Shia Muslims) and dargahs [Rao 1934]). Despite being described differently (they were seen as being set up by Hindus and Muhammadans respectively), they were subject to the same set of regulations.[32] Muhammadan institutions, were further classified into four kinds: masjid or daily place of worship and *idgah* or occasional place of worship; tombs (*mokhabara, makan, gumbaz* and dargah), where the remains of the members of a royal family, sages, saints and religious men are consigned; ashurkhana or the place where mourning services are held during Muharram; and *takhia* or the residence of fakirs and saints, which is generally in a secluded corner of the *qabarstan* or the common burial ground of Muhammadans (ibid.: 552). There is also a description of the kinds of services offered, with elaborate narrations of the duties to be performed by the inhabitants of those spaces, such as religious (namaz), subsidiary (service of food and water), official (management), burial, educational and communal (the qazi performing dispute-resolution services) as also descriptions of these activities (ibid.: 553–77).[33] Muhammadan institutions in this framework are characterised by their *function* and *activity* and not their *purpose* as in the present framework of waqf law that characterises any institution as being a waqf on the grounds of it having been dedicated by a Muslim for religious or charitable purposes. One can also see that certain *forms of activity* could be characterised as religious. This is, however, different from modern waqf law wherein the institution of the waqf itself has a religious purpose and all the activities need to be justified as religious or charitable. There is a central enactment that is known as the Wakf Act 1995, which governs all matters relating to waqfs.[34] This enactment defines waqf in Section 2 (r) of the act as permanent dedication of a property recognised by the Muslim law as *pious, religious* or *charitable*.

The administration of the waqf comes under the Waqf Board, which governs all places of worship related to Muslims such as mosques and other places, and which includes dargahs as well. A framework of Hindu Religious and Charitable Endowments enactments govern Hindu places of worship (that are similarly defined as being dedicated for purposes that are religious or charitable) and are separate for each state. The point that is emphasised here is the centrality of the legal institutions of the state—in directing and shaping the process of secularisation in colonial and modern societies. The legislation articulated waqf very differently from how it had been classically elaborated within the Islamic jurisprudence. It is now articulated as a legal practice connected to the protection of *public interest* and for *religious purposes*. As a result, one might say that pre-modern Islamic/ Hindu concepts of governance have rearticulated and transmogrified the principles, concepts and institutions of political secularism, thereby giving them a specific form.

Defining purposes that are religious or charitable takes us into realms of internal (psychological) states, that is, of its motive and desire or intentionality. It requires an inquiry into aspects of justiciable behaviour that are 'interior', that is, as indices of the inner intentional states. In this case, internal (psychological) states become part of, and are framed within, a complex of motives, will and desire. There is a constant attempt to unmask ulterior motives of material interest and worldly power behind a range of otherwise ordinary (in either case Hindu or Muslim) practices and expressions of belief in order to defend those freedoms, especially religious freedom, which are seen as constitutive of the ways of life the state is supposed to guarantee (Agrama 2015: 306). Notably, the law does not see religious freedom as simply a right to believe what one wants. It also includes maintaining the conditions under which religious belief can be sustained and cultivated, that is, the conditions under which it can flourish. To the extent that this complex expresses material interests or drives towards worldly power, it becomes suspect. Agrama (2012) calls this a distinctive structure of legalised suspicion. According to Agrama, the process by which the state judges a belief (religious or otherwise) to be worthy of protection entails a range of criteria, key among them its ability to distinguish whether the belief in question is sincere or deployed instrumentally to gain a material advantage (ibid.). It becomes imperative to determine whether acts or expressions of belief are genuinely religiously motivated. This distinction rests on a separation between the realm of material power and the realm of belief, a separation that the state is obligated to parse out and investigate, intervening and probing into the very realm of privacy that it is supposed to protect (ibid.: 150). What is interesting, for Agrama, is that it brings together two tenets under the pretext of religious freedom: first, a vigilance against power and its abuse—a fundamentally liberal tenet, and second, a desire to draw a line between religion and material power—an ostensibly secular tenet (ibid.). This suggests that the suspicion of religion is the flip side of the freedom of religious belief. Both find their pronounced expression and promotion as part of the law. Thus, in determining religious and charitable purposes is the distinction between and reconnection of outer religious expression and private conviction through motive and desire and how the law brings them back together again in the context of a defence of religious freedom. But whether it is preferable for the court to actually investigate sincerity or simply attribute its existence or lack thereof without investigation has been historically difficult to decide.

It is important to recognise the distinction made between outer religious expression and private conviction, as sometimes, the issue is less about having one's religious practices and performances recognised as religion and more about having religious activities recognised as non-religion. Perhaps, one can see this in the listing of customs and practices that are followed in the dargah in accordance with the 1989 order, which lists about six of them—many everyday rituals and those that are performed annually (Sitharaman 2010), the details of which need not concern us here. The government has prevented anything other than the prescribed six practices from being performed at the dargah. For instance, the 19-member committee (eight members each from the Hindu and the Muslim community), set up in 2000 to manage the shrine under the chairmanship of the deputy commissioner, initiated a series of injunctions that complied with all the demands made by the Hindu members, such as permanent hoisting of the saffron flag beside the green one, no animal sacrifice to be done or to be cooked/eaten, no non-vegetarian food to be served on the hill and disallowing of the *mazar*s (tombs) to be covered by *gilaf/chador* (tomb covering). Following these developments, all the eight Muslim members of the committee submitted their resignations. Thus, in the listing of practices at the shrine, religion is understood to be an abstract category of beliefs and doctrines, and in this a secularised conception, religious phenomenal forms—its rituals and observances—are linked only contingently to religious truth. The emphasis remains on individual conscience and experience as the proper locus of religiosity and in the relative diminution of the phenomenal forms of the religion (rites, rituals and other bodily comportments). Now often noted under the rubric of secularity,[35] its predicates are not only found in states edicts and policies but also in culture at large where they are disseminated, reproduced and embodied as sensibilities. In addition, the state took on the role of a theologian in determining when the urs should be held, which was the prerogative of the sajjadah nashin. The Samiti now interprets the urs, which once brought in devotees and pilgrims belonging to various communities, as an exclusive Islamic practice and demands that the district administration set aside half of the total proceeds collected as ground rent for its use and to set up stalls at the time of urs as also other revenues of the shrine, as the shrine belongs to Hindus too.

As Agrama (2015) argues, inasmuch as any nation state is obliged to define a basic set of values around which a national consensus is constructed, minority sensibilities, beliefs and practices always sit at odds with the majoritarian culture that defines these values. The values of the minority in any polity are, therefore, always more subject to the hermeneutics of suspicion, the question always open as to whether their beliefs are sincere or merely instrumental. This is not the result of the failure of the state to be adequately neutral with regard to the beliefs of its citizens but, as Agrama (2015: 311) concludes, is 'built into the historical grammar of secularism and the consequences that follow from it'. Thus, government injunctions rearticulate 'religion' in a manner that is commensurate with modern sensibilities and modes of governance, which is invariably a modular conception of religiosity. Once religious truth is shorn of its manifest forms and divinity of its worldly presence, embodied practices come to be read for their symbolic element (within identity formation). Within the framework of the secularisation narrative, this is part of the differentiation of social spheres and the parsing of religion away into its own separate domain—a process that renders religion increasingly irrelevant within social life. No matter how minimally we define religion (as conscience, belief or experience), it has implications for how collective religious life and identity are lived and practised. And, therefore, even a highly individualised and privatised conception of religion entails a substantive and prescriptive notion of self, sociality and collectivity, which remains unaccounted for in the right to religious liberty.

Accordingly, waqf/Hindu endowments came to be attached to liberal legal concepts by relegating religion to the private sphere. The court's use of Islamic or Hindu concepts may seem expansive at first for bringing in substantive religious content into the neutral language of the secular law. But it is this normative conception of religion that informs law, which privileges belief and conscience at the expense of practices, rights and rituals. This conception of religion, as argued by many scholars (for instance, Keane 2007), owes its emergence to Protestant Christianity (how best to institute the distinction between the transcendent world of abstract concepts and ideas and the material reality of this world)[36] that does not comport with other religious traditions, Islam or Hinduism, particularly the ineluctable relationships that many traditions draw between religious belief and its phenomenal forms.

Structures of Modern Secular Governance

It has been clearly held by the state that the Bababudhan dargah cannot be considered waqf. According to Srikantan (2012: 18):

> Although the attempt has been made by the state to notify the institution as Hindu under the relevant enactment (which becomes redundant due to the repeal of the enactment) its position appears ambivalent as it needs to find out "the true practices" in the shrine and thus ascertain whether a "Hindu religion" exists.

As a result, it systematically compels the Hindus to prove that a particular practice was founded in the orthodox religious texts of Hinduism. Two central criteria for determining the genuine religiosity of acts and expressions in the Indian jurisprudence have been, one, whether or not such acts or expressions were sincerely held to be essential to one's religion, and, two, whether these acts and expressions were authorised and mandated by orthodox religious texts. This being the case, the liberal state can decide on a practice only if it can be demonstrated that it belongs to the realm of religion. In doing so, it assumes that there are authentic 'Hindu practices' that can be found and revived. In other words, it assumes that there are orthodox texts of a religion that determine the nature of these practices, thus bringing in the demand that the Hindu practices be circumscribed in accordance with the Agamas and an archaka be appointed to carry out the rituals in the shrine. Now, this does not necessarily mean that the state can decide on matters of religious doctrine but that it can decide what about doctrine is essentially a religious matter; it also decides which authoritative texts are relevant to making such a determination such as the Agamas. The question of who can interpret the doctrines as 'true' necessitates bringing in the concept of the public, which aggravates the conflict as the idea of what constitutes public has different implications under the Hindu endowments and the waqf as they are bound with mapping the dominion of God. Let me illustrate this point by discussing legal scholarship, exemplified through cases arising in situations where disputed properties are dedicated to God.

Waqf and its plural form awqaf are derived from the Arabic root verb, *waqafa,* which has the basic meaning of 'to stop' or 'to hold'. When the word is employed in a legal sense with regard to a piece of land or a building, it signifies that henceforth that 'property' is 'stopped'. In theory, it can never again change hands by inheritance, sale or seizure. An individual creating a waqf, known in Arabic as the waqif, divests himself or herself of the formal rights of possession, but he/she retains the power to appoint a custodian, mutavalli (literally, 'one who is trusted'), who manages the property that has been dedicated. Founders of awqaf also have the power to distribute the income that the property generates for any purpose they wish, provided that the purpose is meritorious by 'Islamic' standards. The legal definition of waqf is elucidated in *Vidya Varuthi versus Balusami Ayyar,*[37] as 'the tying up of property in the ownership of God, the Almighty and the devotion of the profits for the benefit of human beings' (Bruckner et al. 2004: 45). In the words of Fyzee (2008 [1949]), the real nature of waqf can be well understood by contrasting it with the notion of trust in modern law, that is, when such a dedication is done, the right of the wakif (the grantee) is extinguished and the ownership is transferred to the Almighty. Once a particular property is declared waqf, or any such expression is used so as to imply waqf, or the tenure of the document shows that it is dedicated to pious and charitable purposes, the right of the wakif is extinguished and the ownership is transferred to the Almighty. The donor may name any meritorious purpose to benefit (ibid.: 228). Basically, there is nothing in Islam's religious structure that can be 'identified' with a form or a person.[38] Not even Prophet Muhammad.[39] So, the courts seem to have come to the conclusion that the religious context does not warrant a juristic person argument in Islam as found in the context of Hindu endowments.[40]

According to Mukherjea and Sen (2010), a Hindu idol is recognised as a 'juristic entity' by the court of law. It has a juridical status and is invested with the power to sue and be sued. Its interests are attended to by the person who is in charge of the deity and who in law is its manager, with all the powers which would, in such circumstances, on analogy, be given to the manager of the estate of an infant heir (ibid.: 158). The ideal personality of the idol is, in the nature of things, linked up with the natural personality of the *shebait* (manager) or *dharmakartha*, who, as a person entrusted with the custody and worship of the idol, is obliged and empowered to do what may be required for the service of the idol and for the benefit and preservation of its property.[41]

Primarily, the property is vested in the deity, though the shebait may create derivative tenure and estates conformable to usage. However, in the case of the waqf, human agency in the form of the human representative in charge of managing the property is subordinate to God. In the case of the idol, it actively seeks human agency as it cannot act for itself and has to do so through the shebait. Human agency takes predominance and 'acts' on behalf of the idol. The role of the shebait is different from the role of the mutavalli, whose task is to manage the property. In the case of the mutavalli, God's purposes are embodied in the doctrines of Islam itself. Therefore, it is imperative that dedication is complete and not partial, and that it shows no sign of being linked to human agency.

The legal act of dedication must be understood as mapping the dominion of God as the question of the ownership of property is essentially a theological problem. This can be observed in the contrasting nature of the claims involved in the Bababudhan controversy, where the claims of the Muslims that the shrine be treated as waqf property and transferred to the Waqf Board are based on modern property law, while the Samiti makes a historical claim that what was originally Hindu became Muslim during the reign of Hyder Ali. What is the reason for this contrast? As noted earlier, in dedicating the shrine property to God and divesting oneself of possession as in the case of the waqf, one seeks to affirm the nature of one's relationship with God, which is that of his servant. This allows for clarity with regard to the managerial and representational aspects of property ownership as in the role of the mutavalli. However, for the Hindu, the introduction of such a concept permits any devotee to become a party, allowing organisations such as the Samiti to come into existence merely for this purpose.[42]

In the case of Bababudhan, this gets more complicated by the role of the sajjadah nashin whose duty was to ensure proper management of the shrine, but wherein now one has to ascertain whether the shrine is a public institution (the waqf being a 'public' institution) or whether the sajjadah nashin has proprietorial rights over the shrine or not. The aforementioned proposition leads us to examine the inescapable quality of secularism, in part, emanating from the structure of the modern liberal state that promises to rout out pre-modern forms of hierarchy in order to create a polity where all citizens are formally equal in the eyes of law. The public temple is thus founded on the belief that worshippers of all castes and creeds must be allowed to have access to God, which was the basis for the temple-entry legislation. How did temple-entry legislations emerge? Appadurai (1981) is among the few scholars who attempted to answer the question: What is a south Indian temple? According to him, the term 'temple' as a general category is unable to express the complexities of the institution in the different historical periods and the 'cultural entity' of the temple has continued without any significant changes except in the administrative or managerial aspect of the temple organisation in the colonial and postcolonial period. Historical specificities that constitute the temple space in the pre-modern as against the modern period are fundamentally different, and one of the most significant change that has marked the modern 'Hindu temple' is that it has opened its doors to the non–upper castes. This change has been brought about by the ideas of a 'Hindu public', which is a foundational element of the 'Hindu temple'. And both the 'Hindu community' and the 'Hindu public' are products of many large processes bound up with questions of governance within the modern state (ibid.: 18–19). Beyond the tradition–modern binary, Hindu temples are socially constituted as modern institutions.

The Samiti's historical claim, which has no connection to property law, complicates the question of who can represent it. And once again, it is the concept of the public that dictates this. In declaring the shrine as a public temple, one is bound to allow any Hindu the right of worship. Such a right of worship involves the right to sue on behalf of the idol in order to protect its interest. What is the basis for this? The right of any believer to have access to God in a public temple is essentially an issue of civil rights. More concretely, the state is authorised to distinguish between the 'civil' and 'religious' dimensions of an act(ion) and on that basis decide whether the act is enforceable, punishable, or otherwise deserving of protection or exemption under the law. And that process always involves often-unarticulated understandings about what religion in the abstract is or ought to be.

In the context of the nature of the claims of the two parties being completely different, the question arises as to whether the principle of equal treatment and neutrality can be made applicable. This gives rise to another question, that is, how does the secular state determine such equal treatment? It determines such equal treatment through secular law. Now in the case of Bababudhan, the modern property law framework becomes essential to determine religious rights, and, as we have seen, such a framework is biased towards Semitic religions. In such a case, the secular state is placed in an awkward position, that is, it cannot remain neutral and, therefore, attempts to articulate the legal claims of Hindus in a form that can be fitted into the modern property law framework. It further distorts the issue of who can claim the property rights by making it available to 'the public', thus resulting in competing claims between the various parties representing Hindus (the Hindu devotees who began the dispute and now the Samiti), which has further prolonged the conflict. Such a conception of the public does not have the same implications in Islam as it has one identifiable entity, which is the Waqf Board.

While contrasting conceptions of religion provide an important window into the Bababudhan controversy, to characterise the two as fundamentally opposed does not do justice to how they are both inflected, albeit in different ways, by a secular episteme. Hindus are not alone in appealing to historical accuracy regarding the shrine. The secularist's response to the Hindus is a refutation of historical facts, which they claim that the Hindus have misrepresented, including the role of Hyder Ali in Mysore. Indeed, the degree to which the issue of historical veracity is crucial to both sides of the debate is striking. This, I suggest, is emblematic of the inordinate weight secular conceptions of history and temporality command in religious narratives today—as the way Hindus, secular claimants and courts understand historical events as those located in empty, homogenous time. And it is this secular conception of temporality and history that entangles the Hindus, the courts and the secularists in the same epistemological world. This is not so surprising perhaps because in so much as secularity is constitutive of the modern condition, its normative assumptions also seed the lifeworld of those who seek to challenge its legitimacy. It is this positivist conception of history and the understanding of facts as being crucial for elucidating the present and for correcting misapprehension of the past that distort human relations. Note that despite their disagreements, both Hindu devotees who sought legal intervention and the courts themselves purport to describe ecumenical events in calendrical (linear, empty, homogenous) rather than sacred time, and each posits a distinction between events as they 'really happened' and their narrative meaning. This distinction is part of the history of secularisation of religion, one in which both religionists and the secular (anti-religionists) came to accept the independence of metaphysical truth (transcendent) from the empirical nature of this world (immanent).[43] Both the Hindu and the secular occupy this interpretative space, which is a measure of their common secularity that has become so naturalised that they are unable to recognise it in each other's arguments.

Conclusion

Promoting the normative and practical aspects of religion, defining the spaces it should inhabit, authorising the sensibilities proper to it and then working towards disciplining actual religious traditions—so as to conform to this abstract notion, to fit into those spaces and to express those sensibilities—underscores the centrality of the modern state, especially its legal power to promote secularism. The fact that the modern state apparatus came to define the Bababudhan dargah in accordance with a certain index of practice meant that it was, by definition, unable to recognise the ritual differences that provoked the dispute in the first place. In short, the right of worship became a right that could be claimed through one's status as 'Muslim/Hindu', a status that while acknowledging religious difference at one level (propositional belief) occludes religious difference at other levels (ritual practice), which has made scholars like Galanter (1971: 479) remark, 'No secular state is or can be merely neutral or impartial among religions, for the state defines the boundaries within which neutrality must operate.' For secularism, we must understand, as a historical phenomenon, establishes its truth by rendering questionable its foundational concepts and norms and introduces a fundamental indeterminacy into the very structure—an indeterminacy that does not undermine secularism, but consolidates it by extending the state's sovereign power of decision over social life. However, it would be erroneous to come to the conclusion that secularism as an ideal is a failure if it is unable to deliver on its promise of religious freedom. The impossibility of its realisation should not blind us to its power, its ongoing promise and its constitutive contradictions. In sum, the formidable challenge that awaits the still underdeveloped philosophical project of making sense of normative secularity in the secular age—where religion is not special—is difficult and complex, yet worth pursuing.

Notes

1. Scholars have contested the doctrinal separation that secularism institutes between operations of the state and church, between politics and religion time and again. They argue that even though a number of contemporary democratic or totalitarian regimes abide by the doctrinal separation of religion and state, they also routinely intervene to restrict people's ability to practise their faith. Asad (2006), in his recent interrogation of French secularism, suggests that the secular liberal state's ongoing regulation of religious life should be understood not so much as an exception to the norm of liberal rule, but rather as an exception in the Schmittian sense: as an exercise of sovereign power, that is, the state retains the exclusive authority to define the exception. See also Mahmood (2006, 2016).

2. Dargah is a shrine or tomb (or by extension a lodge) built over the grave of a revered religious figure, often that of a Sufi saint.
3. A place of 40-days' retreat, involving religious seclusion and meditation.
4. Dattatreya, the deity, is the three-headed reincarnation of Brahma, Vishnu and Maheshwara, and is accompanied by four dogs. In fact, a triadic iconography of Dattatreya, combining aspects of the deities Brahma, Vishnu and Shiva emerged during the fourteenth century (Rigopoulos 1998: 116).
5. That dargahs are places of convergence of people (identities), practice (rituals) and/or a shared worldview (myths and doctrines) assumes relevance against the backdrop of the larger debate as to whether the two communities, Hindu and Muslim, were/are separate and exclusive.
6. Datta Jayanti commemorates the birth of Dattatreya.
7. The Agamas are sectarian and monotheistic texts dedicated to Vishnu, Shiva and Devi, which determine the procedures of worship of the deities. Here, 'Agamic forms of worship' refers to a ritual manual of worshipping Dattatreya, who is considered by some to be an avatar of Lord Vishnu, and by others of Lord Shiva.
8. In the Indian subcontinent, dargahs are often sites of festivals, a kind of carnival that is held in honour of the deceased saint on his urs, which is a day dedicated to the saint, usually his death anniversary.
9. An act of Parliament was passed in 1991 in the context of Babri Masjid imbroglio, to prohibit the conversion of any place of worship and to provide for the maintenance of the religious character as it existed on 15 August 1947.
10. Movements urging Muslims to return to the religion's origins and the practices of the first generations of Muslims.
11. See, for instance, Asad (2003, 2006), Bilgrami (2006), Connolly (1999) and Agrama (2010).
12. Waqf is an endowment made by a Muslim to a religious, educational or charitable cause.
13. RD 26 CWF 67, dated 6 April 1973.
14. Muzrai is the general overseer of Hindu religious and charitable endowments in the state, which came into being through the Muzrai Act of 1927.
15. 'As it is desirable that all endowments belonging to the Muslim community be administered under the provisions of the Waqf Act 1954, the government of Mysore is pleased to order that the supervision and control over all Muslim Muzrai institutions (Muzrai Waqfs) in the Mysore state be transferred to the Board of Waqfs, with immediate effect, subject to the following conditions' (RD 26 CWF 67, dated 6 April 1973).
16. *Karnataka Board of Wakfs versus B. C. Nagaraja Rao and Others*, AIR 1991 Kant 400.
17. WP 2294/84.
18. GO Dt. 25.11.2000.
19. WP No. 4262/2002.

20. WP 38148 and WP4262.
21. WP 43621.
22. WA 886/2007.
23. WA 2202/2007.
24. The Supreme Court passed an interim order on 1 December 2008 as follows: 'status quo to be maintained in terms of the order dated 25-2-1989 passed by the Commissioner of Religious and Charitable Endowments in Karnataka. But the commissioner will proceed to hear the parties in the matter as directed by the High Court. Instead of passing any order he shall submit his report to this Court.'
25. See, for instance, Balagangadhara and Roover (2007).
26. For a discussion on this issue, see, for instance, Baird (2005), Sen (2009) and Dhavan (1987).
27. The test was formulated in the Commissioner, Hindu Religious Endowments, *Madras versus Sri Lakshmindira Thirtha Swamiar of Shirur Mutt* (AIR 1954SC 282). The court has used the essential practices test to decide a variety of cases. These can broadly be classified under a few heads. First, the court has taken recourse to this test to decide which religious practices are eligible for constitutional protection. Second, the court has used the test to adjudicate the legitimacy of legislation for managing religious institutions. Finally, the court has employed this doctrine to judge the extent of independence that can be enjoyed by religious denominations (Sen 2009: 87).
28. The role of the court in determining what constitutes religion and essential religious practice has remained undiminished since the formative years of this test. Subsequent rulings have built on case law but hardly ever reconsidered the doctrine of essential practices (ibid.: 58).
29. 'The "active principle" of secular power' is, for Agrama (2006: 30–31), less a deviation from secularism than a demonstration, at once, of how secular power both 'works to entangle social life in the question of religion and politics' and 'enables the assertion of the state's sovereign capacity into broader and more intimate domains of social life'.
30. The earliest recorded waqf in the subcontinent dated from the last years of the twelfth century AD. Muhammad Ibn-sam, one of the Ghurid sultans, set aside the revenue of a single village to support a mosque in the city of Multan (Kozlowski 1985: 22).
31. Euro-American legal lexicons do not supply a single technical term that is exactly equivalent to waqf. Sometimes a waqf serves as a 'trust', suggesting some 'public' religious or charitable institution. At other times, a waqf's provisions resemble those of a 'will' or 'entitlement' and, therefore, have a 'private' dimension (ibid.: 2)
32. Temples and mathas had a different set of regulations based on the perceptions of the British administrators (the wealthy temple was subject to a high degree of regulation, whereas there was an entirely different concern with mathas—that of successorship).

33. The regulations of religious and caste processions and the care of ancient monuments also fell under the ambit of the Muzrai Department.
34. The Central Wakf Council of India is an Indian statutory body established in 1964 by Government of India under the Wakf Act 1954 (now a sub-section of the Wakf Act 1995) for the purpose of advising on matters pertaining to working of the state Wakf Boards and proper administration of the wakfs in the country. The act has seen a few amendments in 2013.
35. Secularity entails a certain judgement on, and appreciation for, what religion should be in the modern world.
36. The Protestant missionaries came armed with the Enlightenment critique of ecclesiastical authority, espousing a privatised conception of religion whose proper locus was the individual, his conscience and personnel experience (Mahmood 2016: 44).
37. 1921 8 I.A. 302.
38. The sharia, in contrast, rejects the idea that the moral subject is completely sovereign (Kant's [1960: 173] 'conscience needs no guide; to have a conscience suffices'). Islamic jurists certainly recognised that a Muslim's relation to God cannot be the object of a judge's (qazi's) verdict. This is not because they thought that the matter was practically inaccessible, but simply that being set doctrinally outside the jurisdiction of an earthly court of law, they regarded it as legally inviolable.
39. The use of God's 99 names (*al-asma al-husna*) should not be seen as pointing to divine things but rather as seeking to draw humans to a divinely ordained life. The Quran, as God's word, requires *waqar* (reverential behaviour) from humans but not *ibada* (worship), as only God can be worshipped. But it possesses a quality that makes it more than the medium of a message. The question posed by the use of these names by Muslims is not whether they are correct representations of Him; it is whether they engage in the right bodily and spiritual attitude, and if so, how. These remarks on Islam are intended as a warning that social ontology directly based on a specific theological claim is not useful for the comparative study of religion.
40. Sikh theology and Hindu theology and religious strictures differ. Although Guru Nanak did affirm the centrality of the Formless as the worshippable God, Guru Gobind added a twist by installing Sri Guru Granth Sahib as a worshipable Guru, as a true representative of God.
41. In the case of Hindu endowments, the dispute with regard to the question as to whether the deity as symbolised and personified by an idol can be a sentient (responsive) being, and as such an owner of property, arises very early in Indian legal history. The courts of India as well as the Privy Council have held uniformly that the Hindu idol is a juristic person in whom the dedicated property vests. For instance, the Supreme Court of India has dealt with this question in the case of *Deokinandan versus Muralidhar*, where T. Venkarama Ayyar J. held that the idol, though a juristic person capable of holding property, is not the

beneficial owner of the endowed property and that only in an 'ideal sense' is the deity the owner of endowed property. Here, we find a clear statement, and in legal terms, that the property dedicated to an idol vests in it.

42. Sufi shrines should be syncretic and more cultural as Hinduism is assumed to be universal already.
43. As Frei (1974: 5) argues, in the pre-modern world, the question of factuality of revelation was not distinguishable from its meaning, but as the eighteenth century progressed, the two came to be epistemologically and interpretatively separated. It was no longer possible to treat the Bible as a figural narrative within which one's own life was situated; its spiritual meaning was to be distinguished from its historical context, on the one hand, and the imminence of one's life, on the other. This separation between 'reality' and 'meaning' was crucial to those who sought to establish the factual validity of biblical events and for the sceptics who used its factual fallibility to cast doubt on divine agency and revelation (quoted in Mahmood 2016: 197).

References

Acharyya, Kisore B. 1914. *Codification in British India: 1914.* Cornell: Cornell University Library.

Agrama, Hussein Ali. 2006. 'Asking the Right Question: Two Engagements with Islam and Modernity', *Political Theory*, 35 (4): 647–56.

———. 2010. 'Ethics, Authority, Tradition: Towards an Anthropology of the Fatwa', *American Ethnologist*, 37 (1): 2–18.

———. 2012. *Questioning Secularism: Islam, Sovereignty and the Rule of Law in Egypt.* Chicago: University of Chicago Press.

———. 2015. 'Religious Freedom and the Bind of Suspicion in Contemporary Secularity', in Winnifred Fallers Sullivan, Elizabeth Shakman Hurd, Saba Mahmood and Peter G. Danchin (eds), *Politics of Religious Freedom*, pp. 301–12. Chicago: University of Chicago Press.

Appadurai, Arjun. 1981. *Worship and Conflict under Colonial Rule: A South Indian Case.* Cambridge: Cambridge University Press.

Asad, Talal. 2003. *Formation of the Secular: Christianity, Islam, Modernity.* California: Stanford University Press.

———. 2006. 'Trying to Understand French Secularism', in Hent de Vries and Lawrence E. Sullivan (eds), *Political Theologies: Public Religions in a Post-secular World*, pp. 494–526. Fordham: Fordham University Press.

Baird, D. Robert (ed.). 2005. 'Religion and Law in India: Adjusting to the Sacred as Secular', in *Religion and Law in Independent India*, pp. 7–34. New Delhi: Manohar Publishers.

Balagangadhara, S. N., and Jakob De Roover. 2007. 'The Secular State and Religious Conflict: Liberal Neutrality and the Indian Case of Pluralism', *The Journal of Political Philosophy*, 15 (1): 67–92.

Bhargava, Rajeev. 2007. 'The Distinctiveness of Indian Secularism', in T. N. Srinivasan (ed.), *The Future of Secularism*, pp. 20–53. New Delhi: Oxford University Press.

Bilgrami, Akeel (ed.). 2006. *The Crisis of Secularism in India*. Durham: Duke University Press.

Bruckner, Heidrun, Anne Feldhaus and Aditya Malik. 2004. *Gunther-Dietz Sontheimer: Essays on Religion, Literature and Law*. New Delhi: Manohar Publishers.

Connolly, William E. 1999. *Why I Am Not a Secularist*. Minneapolis: University of Minnesota Press.

Dhavan, Rajeev. 1987. 'Religious Freedom in India', *The American Journal of Comparative Law*, 35 (1): 209–54.

Frei, W. Hans. 1974. *The Eclipse of Biblical Narrative: A Study in Eighteenth and Nineteenth Century Hermeneutics*. London: Yale University Press.

Fyzee, Asaf A. A. 1963. 'Muhammadan Law in India', *Comparative Studies in Society and History*, 5 (4): 410–15.

———. 2008 [1949]. *Outlines of Muhammadan Law*. New Delhi: Oxford University Press.

Galanter, Marc. 1971. 'Hinduism, Secularism and the Judiciary', *Philosophy East and West*, 21 (4): 467–87.

Hansen, Thomas Blom. 1999. *The Saffron Wave: Democracy and Hindu Nationalism in Modern India*. Princeton: Princeton University Press.

Kant, Immanuel. 1960. *Religion within the Limits of Reason Alone*. New York: Harper & Row Publications.

Kasturi, Malavika. 2010. 'All Gifting is Sacred: The Sanatana Dharma Sabha Movement, the Reform of Dana and Civil Society in Late Colonial India', *Indian Economic and Social History Review*, 47 (1): 47–107.

Kaviraj, Sudipta. 2007. *Politics In India*. New Delhi: Oxford University Press.

Keane, Webb. 2007. *Christian Moderns: Freedom and Fetish in the Mission Encounter*. California: University of California Press.

Kozlowski, Gregory C. 1985. *Muslim Endowments and Society in British India*. Cambridge: Cambridge University Press.

Kugle, Scott Alan. 2001. 'Frames, Blamed and Renamed: The Recasting of Islamic Jurisprudence in Colonial South Asia', *Modern Asian Studies*, 35 (2): 257–313.

Madan, T. N. 1998. 'Secularism in its Place', in Rajeev Bhargava and Partha Chatterjee (eds), *Secularism and Its Critics*, pp. 297–320. New Delhi: Oxford University Press.

Mahmood, Saba. 2006. 'Secularism, Hermeneutics, and Empire: The Politics of Islamic Reformation', *Public Culture*, 18 (2): 323–47.

———. 2016. *Religious Difference in a Secular Age: A Minority Report*. Oxford: Princeton University Press.

Mudaliar, C. 1976. *State and Religious Endowments in Madras*. Madras: University of Madras.

Mukherjea, Bijan K., and Asoke C. Sen. 2010. *The Hindu Law of Religious and Charitable Trusts: Tagore Law Lectures*. Kolkata: Eastern Law House Private Ltd.

Rao, Madhava. 1934. *The Mysore Muzrai Manual.* Bangalore: Bangalore Press.

Rigopoulos, Antonio. 1998. *Dattatreya: The Immortal Guru Yogin and Avatara.* New York: State University of New York.

Sen, R. 2009. 'The Indian Supreme Court and the Quest for a "Rational" Hinduism', *South Asian History and Culture,* 1 (1): 86–104.

Sitharaman, Sudha. 2010. 'Conflict over Worship: A Study of the Sri Guru Dattatreya Swami Bababudhan Dargah in South India', in Gita Dharampal-Frick, Robert Langer and Nils Holger Petersen (eds), *Ritual Dynamics and the Science of Ritual, Volume 5: Transfer and Spaces,* pp. 205–33. Wiesbaden: Harrassowitz.

Srikantan, Geetanjali. 2012. 'The Difficulties of Religious Pluralism in India: Analysing the Place of Worship as a Legal Category in the Ayodhya and Bababudangiri Disputes', Asia Research Institute, National University of Singapore, Working Paper Series No. 187.

van der Veer, Peter. 2001. *Imperial Encounters: Religion and Modernity in India and Britain.* Princeton: Princeton University Press.

Varadachari, V. K. 2006. *Law of Hindu Religious and Charitable Endowments.* Lucknow: Eastern Book Company.

Wittgenstein, Ludwig. 1965. *The Blue and Brown Books.* London: Harper Perennial.

4

Islamic Traditions in Malabar

Boundaries, Appropriations and Dialogues

T. Hashim

It has been frequently argued that the process of modernisation is characterised by the differentiation of the secular sphere from that of the religious, which would culminate in the progressive irrelevance of religion in social life and its eventual retreat to the private sphere. The diminished role of religion in modernity would relegate it to the internal states of the social actors, where religion survives only as a right to individual belief, and if it manifests itself in public life, it is attributed to the incomplete or failed project of modernisation. The contemporary salience of political–religious movements across the world seems to represent a challenge, sometimes even constituting a threat, to the project of modernity. Of course, scholars recognise that history has proved otherwise and religion has shown no sign of leaving the public arena. In fact, it has 're-emerged', in the recent years, to become central again to contemporary political processes around the globe. Consequently, a good deal of contemporary scholarship has focused on how the so-called retreat of religion has challenged the privatisation thesis while addressing the role of religion in the public arenas. Casanova (1994) made a critical revision to the secularisation theory by distinguishing its constituent parts—religious decline, privatisation and differentiation—as independent sub-processes, but eventually saw functional differentiation as an inevitable requirement. The 'key hypothesis' of the secularisation theory came under critical scrutiny. Showing how religion and the secular inter-penetrate, Asad (2003) notes that the accompanying boundary-demarcation processes between the religious and the secular needed conceptual rethinking. As a result of these interventions, the type of questions that are being asked has shifted significantly towards examining the emergence and articulations of the religious–secular duality. As the discussion turned towards the idea of the public/private distinction, Habermas, who drew attention to the central importance of the public sphere in his genealogical work *The Structural Transformation of the Public Sphere: An Inquiry Into a Category of Bourgeois Society* (1991 [1989]), emerged as one of the most important interlocutors. According to Habermas, the public sphere, which began to emerge in the eighteenth century, developed as a social space—distinct from the state, the economy and the family—in which individuals could engage as private citizens deliberating on the common good (ibid.). Perhaps the most crucial aspect of this new social structure was its status as a space for reasoning, a realm in which reasons were forwarded and debated, accepted or rejected. Nominally, the public sphere was an indefinite open space in which all reasons could be expressed and heard but only those arguments and reasons would be accepted that could meet the assent of the participants.

Considered essential to the public sphere is the political doctrine of secularism. In modern society, there is typically a multiplicity of religious beliefs and identities, and it is argued that they can be held together only by a formal separation between religious belonging and political status, and the relegation of religious beliefs to the private sphere. To be wholly part of participatory democracy, citizens holding different religious beliefs (or none) must share something that enables them to have a common political life, a public space in which information affecting the entire political community can be exchanged and ideas debated. However, reasoned discourse in that space can take place only if religion does not dominate it. According to this conception, the public sphere is ideally a secular space central to the modern secular state, and as critics point out, Habermas paid insufficient attention to religion in his early work. Indeed, in his introduction to an influential volume *Habermas and the Public Sphere* (1992: 35–36), Craig Calhoun has noted not only Habermas's relative 'neglect of religion' but also, and more forcefully, his 'anti-religious assumptions'.[1]

A central problem for scholars of the Islamic public sphere (Eickelman and Anderson 2003; Salvatore 2007; Salvatore and Le Vine 2005) has been to problematise Habermasian conceptions of the rational, secularly oriented public sphere, which is taken to be the normative terrain on which public life thrives. Thus, the new imaginary of Islamic public sphere brought back religion into the debate wherein its proponents seek to expand the definition of the public sphere, bringing in notions such as istislah that is at the heart of the Muslim understanding of the public sphere. Istislah is a method in Islamic philosophy that is geared towards finding good in each situation by mediating between contending positions and moderating the larger process in an attempt to achieve balanced solutions for the common good of the involved parties (ibid.: 2).

Further, the bourgeois public sphere has been imagined as a site of free deliberation, signifying the core value of modernity outside the constraints of the official sphere, identified primarily with the state. Accordingly, true deliberation must be grounded in the autonomy and independence of individuals from the kind of structures of discipline and authority within which virtues are learned. However, scholars emphasising the disciplinary functions of deliberation and argumentation, on the other hand, have stressed the ideological over the dialogic aspects of the phenomenon (see Roy 1996), thus enabling an extension of an authoritative religious discourse. The resultant public is less a sphere of discussion and deliberation than one of subjection to authority, and is part of a project aimed at promoting and securing a uniform model of moral behaviour. In short, the public arena constituted by deliberation and argumentation tends to be identified as either a deliberative space of argument and contestation between individuals or as a normative space for education in community-oriented virtues. An important question to address here is, if the adherents of a religion enter the public sphere, can their entry leave the pre-existing discursive structure intact? Scholars working on the bourgeois as well as the Islamic public spheres have inadequately addressed the question of how the public sphere is a space that is necessarily articulated by power.

As pointed out, the public sphere is not just a place for carrying out debates. It is constituted by the sensibilities—memories and aspirations, fears and hopes—of the speakers and listeners as also the manner in which they exist (or are made to exist) for each other, and by the propensity to act and react in distinctive ways (Asad 2003: 185). More clearly, people who deliberate may threaten the authority of existing assumptions. Hirschkind (2006), through the idea of 'counterpublics', explores how cassette sermons circulated to discipline the power of ethical speech took public deliberation as one of its modalities. Hirschkind shows how the discursive arena explores the conceptual edifice in which deliberation and discipline, or language and power, are regarded as thoroughly inter-dependent in contrast to a space where the formation of political opinion is through inter-subjective reason. Within this context, public speech is aimed to result in pious dispositions—the embodied sensibilities and modes of expression are understood as facilitating the development and practise of Islamic virtues and Islamic ethical comportment. Hirschkind (2006: 106–07) argues that reason and religious sensibilities or deliberation and (religious) discipline are not necessarily opposed, thus opening a field of analytical inquiry that moves beyond the limits of the dichotomies of the secular–liberal discourse.

Drawing on Hirschkind, I examine the public debates among Mappila Muslim groups in Kerala—Sunni, Mujahid and Jamaat-e-Islami—on the practice of Islam, which aim at deducing a set of practical rules of conduct to guide their members in resolving the mundane issues of daily life. These groups not only follow different Islamic practices but also engage in debates with each other. The deliberation and argumentation is geared towards formulating 'correct'

Islamic practices and to arrive at an understanding of common good that aspire to constitute 'true Islam'. I focus on the practices and debates that surround the celebration of festivals, such as Milad-un-Nabi (the Prophet's birthday), Onam and Christmas, among the different groups of Mappila Muslims of Malabar in Kerala. The dialogic engagement among Mappila Muslims and the articulation of Islamic ethical norms and their embodiment as practical aptitudes are critically dependent upon the communicative practices and discursive conventions of this public arena. Within this arena, deliberation and argumentation are deployed in order to construct moral selves, to reshape character, attitude and will in accordance with contemporary standards of pious behaviour. Accordingly, the Muslim public sphere in Kerala presupposes a direct involvement of the religious leaders of Islam, of believers in discourse, activity, individual self-creation and ummah (Muslim community). By endeavouring to focus on the debates rather than the ideologies of these groups (Santhosh 2009), an attempt is made to go beyond the binary understanding of Muslim groups as revivalist versus reformist, traditional versus modern and orthodox versus heterodox.

Sociological scholarly writings have worked with the idea that the 'Muslim community' is not just a singular or homogeneous entity despite the fact that Islam is based on the monolithic idea of one God and one religious text, as the practices of approaching God and the interpretation of this singular text differ widely and are contested regularly. This is quite evident even within a supposedly singular community—the Mappilas. The idea that Muslims see themselves as oppositional binaries between 'orthodoxy' and 'reform' is not only a political claim but is also grounded in actual practices. The way one perceives the idea of 'orthodoxy' is also very important. For, how can one talk of orthodoxy when it does not constitute a body of opinion or articulate a relationship of power. 'Orthodoxy', as Asad (1986: 15) points out, 'is a distinctive relationship—a relationship of power. Wherever Muslims have the power to regulate, uphold, require or adjust *correct* practices, and to condemn, exclude, undermine or replace *incorrect* ones, there is the domain of orthodoxy' (emphasis original). Accordingly, I suggest that the term 'orthodoxy' is a function of power.

The idea of orthodoxy claims to alter the corrupt practices in religion and, while doing so, appeals to the various aspects of Islamic 'tradition', that is, it claims the authority of the scripture even as that tradition is constantly undergoing a process of modification and change. It is also important here to clarify as to what is meant by 'correct' or 'incorrect' practices. As an anthropologist concerned with how societies deal with normative ideologies, Asad argues that there is not and cannot be any fixed, essentialised orthodoxy. Being historically constituted, Islamic traditions are always subject to contestation and redefinition. That is to say, argument and conflict over the substance of Islamic traditions are intrinsic to, and constitutive of, those traditions. Hence, I assert that the practices of Islam in general and Malabar in particular should be seen as a set of complex practices that differ between groups and change within each group over time.

Mappila Muslim Groups in Malabar

Muslims of Kerala constitute 26 per cent of the population, of which more than 60 per cent is in the Malabar region. The Sunnis, the predominant Muslim community in Kerala, are registered under the Societies Registration Act 1934, and they belong to the Shafi school of jurisprudence. However, since the rise of new movements such as Mujahid and the Jamaat-e-Islami, the term 'Sunni' today has come to be understood as 'traditionalist' Muslims (Osella and Osella 2008), and these new movements among the Mappila Muslims do not give priority to the religious schools of jurisprudence. As we shall see, being a 'true' Muslim includes understanding and practising Islam 'correctly', sacrificing one's time, money and life to help others, and supporting the poor and needy among the Muslims. Underlying all these values lies a strong belief in the necessity of both spiritual and material progress, of a continued effort towards a change from what existed before. In 1989, the Sunnis were divided into two factions—one led by E. K. Aboobakar Musliyar known as the EK Sunni group, and the other by Kanthapuram A. P. Aboobakar Musliyar, known as the AP Sunni group (Kurup and Ismail 2008: 284). The AP Sunni Muslims extended their political support to the Communist Party of India (Marxist) [CPI(M)]. Their alliance with the political party, the CPI(M), has raised many debates among the Muslims of Kerala. However, the other group, EK Sunni Muslims, has been supporting the Muslim League Party. Most of the members of the EK Sunni group have been active leaders of the Muslim League. The active involvement of these different Sunni groups has attracted criticism from the Mujahid and Jamaat-e-Islami, which believe that Islam as practised by the Sunnis in Kerala deviates from 'true' Islam.

The Mujahid, another significant group among the Mappila Muslims of Kerala, is influenced by the reformist effort of Ibn Abdul Wahab of Saudi Arabia. The organisation encountered a spilt in 2002 after years of infighting. While Hussain Madavoor was the leader of one faction of the Mujahid (known as the Mujahid Madavoor group), the AP faction, popularly known AP Mujahids, named after the cleric A. P. Abdul Khader Moulavi, was the other. Another group, the Jamaat-e-Islami, is an integral part of the pan-Islamic movement in Kerala, the followers of which are generally known as political Islamists. It is believed that the Jamaat-e-Islami wanted to embrace political Islamism[2] before the events of the national Emergency (1975–77) and considered secularism and democracy to be religiously forbidden (haram). The Jamaat is branded as a fundamentalist group in Kerala as well as in India. However, the pragmatic language of Islamic activism, which combines both Islamic and social values, has provided the Jamaat-e-Islami and their youth wing, Solidarity Youth Movement (SYM), a space in the community. Metcalf (2014: 30) says:

> In 2011, core members founded a political party, the Welfare Party of India, its name signaling its secularity, inclusiveness, and stated goal of concern with the welfare of the socially disadvantaged. It adheres to the communitarian model, invoking the Constitution and law codes in the interests of preserving what they see as Muslim cultural and, increasingly, economic interests.

They engage in a variety of Islamic activism and use the media to spread their new yet flexible, pragmatic model in Kerala. Recently, the SYM has undergone a makeover to become a political party, a telling example of the secularisation process in this context. Yet another group called the Quran Sunnath Society was launched by Abul Hasan Moulavi in the second half of the 1960s. This movement became an adversary to the existing Muslim groups, since it argued for a free and liberal thinking which meant not following the *fiqh* (the four schools) and their textual interpretations.

The politically engaged religious Muslim groups, with the support of the community, compete for a share in the public sphere as the true representatives of Islam. The Indian Union Muslim League (IUML), a popular political party among the Mappila Muslims, witnessed a split in the party after the Babri mosque demolition in 1992. Consequently, many Muslim religious groups, especially the Jamaat-e-Islami and the AP Sunni group aligned with the Left Democratic Front (LDF) led by the CPI(M) and opposed the IUML, which is the prominent party supporting the United Democratic Front (UDF).[3] Moreover, these groups invoke Islamic theology to justify their political affiliations and leanings, and I hope to show how these political affiliations, mostly based on immediate pragmatic considerations, are increasingly becoming an essential part of the identity articulation of these groups along their respective theological and ideological positions.

In order to be a true follower of Islam, a Muslim is bound to follow certain Islamic tenets and moral conduct in their everyday life. The Mappila Muslims of Malabar can choose to affiliate themselves with either one of the ulema-led *maslaks*[4] (Sunni AP, Sunni EK, Mujahid AP, Mujahid, Quran Sunnath Society and Ahmadiya) or with any of the two most prominent Islamist groups who have their own political parties: the pan-Islamist inspired Jamaat-e-Islami and the National Development Front (NDF). Thus, the debates and public contestations about Islamic practices among the diverse Muslim groups form the most defining features of the contemporary Muslim communities in India and, in particular, Kerala. I would argue that these debates among the Mappila[5] Muslims of Malabar[6] presuppose an orthodox Islam, although they disagree on what constitutes orthodoxy. Undergirding the understanding of orthodoxy is the questions of what constitutes 'true Islam', in particular, among the Muslim communities in Kerala. In Malabar, Muslims live in a competitive religious public space and the debates among the Muslim groups are not only limited to intra-community issues but also extend to interactions with Hindus and Christians. Thereby, non-Muslims sometimes become the reference points in these debates.

Studies on Muslims in India: A Brief Account

Research on Islamic practices in India suggests a significant difference between the religious practices and belief systems in south India from those in the northern part of the country. This is reflected in a number of studies now available on Islam in India (Ahmad 2009; Alam 2011; Haniffa 2013; Robinson 1984). However, most of the aforementioned scholarship largely addresses the Islamic practices among north Indian Muslims and their evolution, with the exception of a few that look at the practices of Islam in south India. As Tschacher (2014: 65) says, 'This is not to say that no research has been done regarding these communities, but this research has hardly had any impact on the way Muslim societies in South Asia have been described as a whole.' The Mappila Muslims of Malabar have been the subject of a select scholarship and research focusing on four aspects, namely, the status and origin of Mappilas in Kerala, the Mappila revolt and the Khilafat movement, economic and socio-political development of Malabar, and reformist/traditionalist movements among the Mappila Muslims (Dale 1980, 1982; Dhanagare 1977; Ismail 2008; Kurup and Prabash 2000; Lakshmi 2012; Miller 1976; Mines 1975; Osella and Osella 2008; Wright 1977). This scholarship on Muslims in Kerala has largely focused on the professed theological underpinnings of the religious groups. While the theological dimensions are important components to understand the articulations of the groups, what is noteworthy is the changing nature of these articulations, which involves looking at the proliferation of Muslim groups, intra-community relations, their organisational debates and the diversity in their claims over what constitutes 'true Islam'. The focus of the rest of the essay will be on the intra-community debates to understand how the deliberations on inter-community matters frame the discourse on what constitutes the correct practices of Islam.

Before moving further into the debates, I would like to draw attention to the perspectives explaining the diversity of Islam in India. This literature can be divided into four conceptual frameworks: theory of Islamisation (Eaton 1984), co-existence (Ahmad 1973, 1976, 1981), syncreticism (ibid.) and hierarchy (Madan 2007). Das (1984: 294) comments that these perspectives have prevented scholars from seeing the diversity and wide-ranging aspects of Islam(s) and thus failed to interpret the diverse strands in the 'scripturalist' or 'textual' Islam. One way of overcoming this binary was attempted by T. N. Madan in his essay 'One among Many: Explorations in the Anthropology of Islam' (2007). Drawing on Dumont's hierarchical model of the caste system, Madan analyses the complementarities between the folk and the scriptural. Urging us to go beyond the binaries, he states that the syncretistic model of South Asian Islam does not address the crucial issue of the relative weight of the constituent elements of the syncretistic tradition (ibid.: 19). However, Madan fails to historicise the Muslim communities in South Asia, and thus 'what is encompassing' and 'what is encompassed' remain ambiguous and unclear. Finding limitations in the formulations of Madan, and borrowing from Asad (1986), I argue that Islam is best regarded as a discursive tradition, clearly indebted to Foucault's formulation of 'discursive formations' (Dreyfus and Rabinow 1982). Asad in his essay 'The Idea of Anthropology of Islam' (ibid.: 21) states:

> For the anthropologist of Islam, the proper theoretical beginning is therefore an instituted practice (set in a particular context, and having particular history) into which Muslims are inducted as Muslims. A practice is Islamic because it is authorised by the discursive traditions of Islam, and is taught by Muslims—whether by an *alim*, a *khatib*, a *Sufi shaykh*, or an untutored parent.

Asad insists that the meaning of symbols must be understood in relation to both the practical contexts within which those symbols function and the forms of social discipline by which certain readings are authorised and accomplished. The idea of discursive tradition suggests that it would be erroneous to study Islam as monolithic and essentialist, as there may be as many forms of Islam as there are Muslim communities. Moreover, it is crucial that we accept the self-identification of Muslims. If someone calls themselves a Muslim and identifies certain practices as Islamic, we must, as scholars of religious studies, begin by accepting that statement as true and then examine how these practices differ from those of other Muslims. Therefore, the question to be explored is why there are differences between the religious groups who identify themselves as Muslims. And it is here that the notion of Islam as a discursive tradition becomes pertinent, as it is constantly being reshaped to fit into an ever-changing world.

Drawing on the work of Asad (1986), I argue that tradition is a discursive formation routed in a sense of time, within which a particular understanding of selfhood is formed. This approach in studying Islam accounts for its fluidity, continual historical interpretation, and the authorisation of its religious practices and discourses. It also allows us to challenge the assumed dichotomy of Islam and modernity. Here, the understanding of tradition centres on debates around *taqlid* (adherents to the tradition) and *ijtihad* (to carry out independent interpretation) in Islamic discourses. While the Sunni Muslims advocate adherence to tradition (taqlid) in the place of individual interpretations (ijtihad) of the Quran and other Islamic sources such as the Hadith[7] and Sunnah, which is alluded to by Jamaat-e-Islami and Mujahid, the 'revivalists'/'reformists' in Islam. The reformists argue against taqlid, viewing it primarily as a set of rituals and practices that Muslims have followed unthinkingly for centuries. In Malabar, the Mujahids and Jamaat-e-Islami advocate for a greater reliance on ijtihad to liberate Islam from the outdated rituals as well as from working within the defined schools of practices.[8]

Drawing on my fieldwork, I focus on how the modern public sphere reflects and masks, often simultaneously, discourses on order, contests for hegemony and techniques of power in the Muslim community. The involvement of the Mappila Muslim religious groups in the public sphere has allowed them to transform community and religious matters into public issues, and intra-community debates into public encounters.

One of the important ideas that Eickelman and Piscatori (1996) have used to capture the nature of the debates in the context of

Muslims laying claim to the multiple truths about Islam has been the concept of 'objectification'. Objectification, according to the authors, involves three processes: first, 'discourse about Muslim tradition involves people on a mass scale'; second, there is a tendency to see religious belief and practice 'as a system to be distinguished from non-religious ones'; third, a reconfiguration of the 'symbolic production of Muslim politics' (ibid.: 39–43) that occurs as a result of the first two processes. These explicit, widely shared and objective questions are modern queries that increasingly shape the discourse and practice of Muslims of all social classes, even as some legitimise their actions and beliefs by asserting that they advocate a return to purportedly authentic traditions. Objectification is, thus, trans-class and -religion, a self-contained system that its believers can describe, characterise and distinguish from other belief systems (ibid.: 38). The different facets of objectification of Muslim religious groups can be seen in the following discussions on the debates over the celebration of Milad-un-Nabi, Onam and Christmas. My argument is that the idea of objectification is relevant to study the diversity and dialogue among the Muslim religious groups of Malabar, Kerala.

Deliberation and Argumentation: The Celebration of Milad-un-Nabi

I have followed a range of public debates among the Mappila Muslims around the issue of 'correct' Islamic practices. It could be said that the key element in gaining religious understanding and knowledge is communication. Discourses on religious practices and meanings are crucial in this process. Here I note how the idea of 'true Islam' is articulated through communication and community discourses. These debates take place in the public domain and the members of the community are aware of the multiple truth claims and arguments on the correctness of different practices. For example, the Sunni Muslims believe that Prophet Muhammad is a holy man with supernatural and divine powers and, therefore, deserves special status among Muslims. On the other hand, movements such as the Mujahid and Jamaat consider the Prophet as an ordinary man who performed extraordinary feats only because of divine intervention.

The contestation over this issue has led to the debate on the appropriate way of showing respect to the Prophet. The Sunni Muslims conduct a special early-morning prayer called moulid (an act of blessing the birth of Prophet Muhammad) glorifying the Prophet on the day of Milad-un-Nabi, soon after the ritual prayer. Apart from this special prayer, different activities such as competitions, cultural events by students, processions, feasts and decoration of the mosque premises are organised.

Unlike the Sunni groups, the Jamaat-e-Islami does not organise any processions or conduct ritual activities as part of commemorating the Prophet's birthday. It celebrates the day by inviting non-Muslims for the commemoration, conducting literary-cultural programmes to create awareness among the people, particularly among non-Muslims, about the contemporary significance of the Prophet and Islam. Contrary to the practices of the Jamaat-e-Islami, the Sunni groups have clear standpoints on the issue concerning the birthday celebration of the Prophet and they bring forth several hadiths to validate their arguments, thereby invoking tradition.

The Mujahids in Kerala have a different notion, both from that of the Sunnis and the Jamaat-e-Islami, about the celebration of Milad-un-Nabi. They do not associate any significance to the Prophet's birthday. Instead, they ascribe to the view that the Prophet's ideas and deeds are important and that they should be followed by any practising Muslim. Citing bida (innovation), Mujahids disagree with any kind of celebration,[9] calling it an unworthy innovation in Islam. This is reflected in their understanding of the Prophet's birthday. The Mujahids hold on to the notion that any celebration other than the two Eid celebrations (Eid al-fitr and Eid al-azha) is a bida and thus leads to shirk.[10] While comparing the arguments of each of these groups, it is important to note that the practices associated with Islam are not only different for each group but also their inflections have varied over time. These changes perhaps could be the result of each group's engagement in constantly defining and redefining their practices as also other kinds of influences. For example, a pamphlet of the Mujahids published in 1946 asserts the importance of the celebration of Milad-un-Nabi and moulid recitation, which we see as altered after the 1940s.

These evolving and discrepant understandings give us an idea of the manifold interpretations of the 'text' and the multiple arguments among Muslim religious groups. These doctrinal standpoints that the followers of different Muslim religious groups maintain may differ from or even contradict each other. They agree on a religious tradition and disagree on its practice.

The Celebration of Onam

The emergence of debates in the public sphere on Islam is shaped by distinct political conditions and social circumstances in different parts of the Islamic world. The participation in the public sphere is circumscribed more by interpretations, context and circumstances than by any intrinsic incompatibility or mutual exclusion. The postulated identities of religious groups or their ideological manifestos are censured in the debates. The postulated identities of the different groups or their ideological moorings come under attack when each of the groups see the other as following religious practices that are deemed un-Islamic.

The different Muslim religious groups in Malabar, in their attempt to project themselves as the ideal representatives of 'true' Islam, define and redefine what Islam is and what it is not. Therefore, the question arises as to how to differentiate certain practices as Islamic/un-Islamic. What is the yardstick to define what constitutes the un-Islamic? For instance, the Milad-un-Nabi celebration is the un-Islamic for the Mujahids and Jamaats, whereas Sunni Muslims consider it as Islamic. While the Sunni groups object to Onam celebrations (normally celebrated by Hindus in Kerala, though declared a state festival), the Jamaat is supportive of it.

The Jamaat-e-Islami, which once considered casting vote in the elections as *taghoot*,[11] as a sin and against Islamic belief, post-Emergency, began to recognise the significance of participating in the democratic political processes of the country. The radical transformation of the Jamaat, espousing a visibly secular posture and entering into a unique form of Islamic activism[12] through the formation of a secular political party, the Welfare Party of India, is an illustration of the increasing secularisation of a strand of religious groups in Kerala, a process which has made the Jamaat more aware of its identity articulations in the public sphere. As mentioned earlier, critics opine that the Jamaat, due to its recent decision to be a part of democratic politics, supports un-Islamic practices and project itself as an open group. The Jamaat-e-Islami fights 'evil practices' within the Islamic fold and thereby maintains its identity as a reformist movement. At the same time, it expresses its cultural solidarity by supporting Onam celebrations.

There is a series of questions that arises in the deliberations on Onam celebrations among the different groups. These are: Does Onam have a cultural or a religious dimension? If cultural, should Onam be considered as a symbol of social acceptance and of cultural plurality? Is Onam a Hindu or a state festival? If it is a state festival, then is Onam a cultural festival only because it is a state festival? If Onam is a religious festival, and if Muslims take part in it, should it be seen as halal (permissible) or haram (religiously forbidden)? I would like to argue that in this context, the distinction between the religious and the non-religious among the Muslim groups signifies the processes of objectification, something that had to deliberated upon.

The idea of objectification in Islam implies the changes that have taken place in relation to knowing and learning Islam. Previously, the individual learnt it from the religious elite of the community but it was now possible to learn from multiple sources ranging from pamphlets, leaflets, books, radio, television and the Internet, besides the religious elite of the community. And this objectified way of understanding Islam develops in a public space where people acknowledge that Islam plays a role in their public life (Eickelman and Piscatori 1996: 44). Processes of conscious community engagement with religious questions and concepts have no doubt been affected and altered by communication technologies and educational opportunities, but they are not entirely new processes. The processes of modernisation, being highly influenced by the mass media, have impacted upon the quotidian activities of Muslims of Malabar as elsewhere. Here, each group uses the media to project that their ideas of Islam are true and not those of the others. For instance, a newspaper *Madhyamam Daily*, supported by the Jamaat-e-Islami, carried an editorial on Onam celebrations, which reads:

> The government has announced that Onam is a state festival, and therefore, it is a people's festival. As a secular nation, it is our responsibility to partake in Onam celebrations. If there are aspects in the celebration that tantamount to being shirk (polytheism), it may be avoided. As it is a cultural (not-religious) festival we find nothing wrong in people partaking. (*Madhyamam Daily*, 27 August 2012)[13]

One may note here that the discourse around Muslim tradition involves an awareness of Muslim and non-Muslim traditions among religious followers. For instance, the Jamaat-e-Islami directs its followers to differentiate the essential and non-essential aspects of Onam celebrations. Even though it is in favour of participating in Onam, it advises its members to abstain from un-Islamic practices associated with the festival. However, the initiative of the Jamaat-e-Islami to celebrate Onam has received wider attention, criticism as well as support from different quarters and sections of politico-religious groups in Kerala. It would be incorrect to describe the Islamic practices in religious terms alone as there are other socio-political elements implicated within religion that need to be taken into consideration. For example, during the time of the Sabarimala[14] pilgrimage, Hindu devotees bring the sacred *aravana payasam*[15] from the temple and offer it to their Muslim friends. There is a contention among the different Muslim religious groups as to whether it is permissible in Islam to have aravana payasam. The Jamaat activists believe that one can drink the payasam if it is halal (permissible), but the Mujahids have a different take on it. They contend that before the payasam distribution at Sabarimala, the Hindu priests consecrate the offerings to the deity, which they believe is haram. The Mujahids and Sunni Muslims are of the opinion that the Jamaat-e-Islami's liberal approach towards the consumption of aravana payasam and the celebration of Onam festival tantamounts to being pseudo-secular. However, the splinter group of Mujahid has a different view on the issue.

The arguments of the Mujahid Madavoor group are revealed in the words of the Hadith scholar, A. Abdussalam Sullami:

> Taking part in the Onam celebrations is not at all against Islamic beliefs and practices. Onam is a commemoration of unity and diversity. There is no problem in being part of other religious festivals. At the same time, we think eating food on the occasion of the Prophet's birthday is haram as also in the case of Muharram. (*Mathrubhumi Daily*, 12 August 2006)

As a counter-response, the AP Mujahid group declared that Onam is a religious and not a cultural festival. *Sneha Samvadham*, a magazine published by the AP Mujahid group, has severely criticised the decision of the Jamaat-e-Islami and the Madavoor Mujahid group to participate in the Onam celebrations. The magazine states that Onam is purely a religious and not a cultural celebration and vehemently criticises the policy of the secular government of using Hindu symbols as cultural–national symbols. It states:

> It was in the 1960s that the Pattom Thanu Pillai Ministry decided to declare Onam as a state festival. Until the 1960s, the celebration was purely religious and there was no dispute over Onam celebrations. While the Hindus celebrated Onam, the Muslims and Christians celebrated Eid and Christmas respectively. It is purely religious and has nothing to do with the secular fold. From the very outset, when the government decided to include Onam as a state festival, the intellectuals opposed the decision because of the religious element in the celebration. (Primrose 2012: 11–18)

The group, in its magazine, criticised the government's attempts at the Hinduisation of a secular state and predicted that there would be disputes over the celebrations in the future. They questioned the authority of a secular state to adopt religious symbols and the religious status given to this festival as also the plan of the government to impose Onam as a state festival. The group insisted that its followers should not take part in any of the Onam celebrations.

The articulations around questions of religious identity and execution of the same at the individual level are being problematised by the Mappila Muslim religious groups. As a result, followers transform religious beliefs into a reflexive system, thereby broadening the scope of religious authority and redrawing the boundaries of their groups. The implication of this process of objectification of Islam is that religious beliefs and practices are increasingly seen as systems (*minhaj*) to be distinguished from non-religious ones (Eickelman and Piscatori 1996: 42). The most crucial point to keep in mind is the fragmentation of authority among the contemporary Muslim religious groups in Kerala.

In this context, it is interesting to see the take on Onam by the Muslim groups. They accept the Onam festival, for it is claimed to be a state festival with secular character. This leads us to think about the idea of secularism as a state project and as a social process (see Iqtidar 2011). Here, secularisation can be discussed at two levels: one, at the level of the process of a split between the public and private spheres. The other one is seen as a social process which involves both the process of accepting religious practices in public and also involving rationalisation of these beliefs, which Eickleman and Piscatori (1996) termed 'objectification'.

The Celebration of Christmas: Halal or Haram?

The discussions on the celebration of the Prophet's birthday and Onam celebrations point to the fact that there is no single or unanimous opinion among the Muslim groups. In this last section, I would like to draw attention to the debate over the celebration of Christmas, which has been a source of critical engagement among the Muslim religious groups in Kerala. All the religious groups, that is, Sunni, Mujahid and Jamaat-e-Islami, except for the Quran Sunnath Society, are unanimous over the belief that celebrating Christmas is shirk and is against the basic doctrines of Islam. According to Christian belief, Prophet Jesus is the son of God and Christmas is celebrated as his birthday. In contradiction, Islam believes that Jesus was sent as a prophet of God just as God sent Prophet Muhammad to deliver the word to the people of his time, and therefore, to associate God with Jesus and to worship him as an 'idol image' is tantamount to shirk. Islam also believes that God has no form, is singular and has no children, wife, father or mother. On the other hand, the Quran

Sunnath Society, which swears by the Quran and the Hadith believes that over the years, Christmas has lost its religious connotations and has become more of a celebration and a family occasion where people gather to share gifts with each other. Tanalur (2013: 36), a Quran Sunnath Society leader says: 'Regarding the celebration of Christmas, we do not find any commandment in the Quran directly. We do not believe that hadith will give us the right directions.'

Although the Islamic dictates do not restrain people from participating in other religious celebrations, they impress upon the idea that the other religious celebrations should not be actively celebrated by the Muslims, as they are considered haram and will not go well with the idea of a monotheistic approach of Islam. Even then, there exists an everyday explanation to participate in these celebrations under the logic that the prophets of all the religions, be they Mohammed, Eisa or Moses, are the same, and that one has to respect their teachings.

While the hadiths constitute commentaries on the Quran by the companions and disciples of Prophet Muhammad, the Quran still forms the ultimate source for authenticating practices, and hadiths are acceptable to the extent that at least two disciples/saints validate an interpretation. This being the case, they argue that the Hadith can only be taken as a supplementary explanation of ideas and injunctions of the Quran thereby placing a highly restricted role for individual interpretations of the Quran. I have, by adopting an ethnographic approach, attempted to illustrate how the varied religious practices open up a certain awareness about the different paths available to lead a pious Islamic life. The competing claims of these Muslim groups and the attempts made by their ideologues and leaders to convince people that the practices they suggest are *sahih* (correct), while others are not, force a critical engagement with the notion of Islam as a cohesive religion, deepening the realisation that there is not one Islam within the Muslim milieu of Malabar in Kerala.

Conclusion

An inquiry into the arguments put forward regarding the claims of 'true Islam' and duties of Muslims among different groups offers significant material for the debates over secularisation which have been concerned with the (ir)relevance of religion in the public sphere.

My study of the debates among the Mappila Muslim groups in their agreements and disagreements over different issues adds to the debate on secularisation. It also adds to our understanding of the public sphere which, in this case, is inhabited by multiple Muslim groups and their articulations. As it questions the perception of the category of Islam as monolithic, this study adds to the literature on Islam in India which is most often derived from work done in north India.

I have shown in the essay the dynamics of the public sphere in Malabar and its constant engagement between and among groups over what are perceived as issues to deliberate on the concept of a 'true Islam'. The engagement entails contesting each others' claims to authenticity, while justifying one's claims as true. This has meant a constant designing and redesigning of the dictates of Islam for others and also for oneself, through shuttling between the understandings derived from texts and context. Thus, it could be argued that the public sphere in Malabar is a receptacle of multiple groups engaged in claiming 'true Islam', which is not only influenced by their understandings of their text and everyday religious practices, but is also dictated by the socio-political conditions that these groups negotiate within Indian democracy.

As they access, engage and interpret texts, agreements and disagreements among them periodically emerge. They may converge at times and depart at others, but the followers of each group maintain their interpretation to be the right one. For us, what is of concern is the question: Under what circumstances is a particular kind of theological explanation adopted and why? An important aspect of 'objectification of religion' is that religion is not emptied out of its transcendental value, but is transformed into a more historically situated, critically analysed set of beliefs and practices. The Muslim religious groups in Malabar, Kerala, are constantly involved in debates and contestations over their beliefs and practices. They are, at the same time, open to making changes in their interpretations of the text as a result of these dialogues and discussions that they are engaged with in the public sphere. This involves not only accepting interpretations, but also affirming differences. It is important to note that these debates and dialogues, and the resultant changes that have been made to their conceptions, have meant that there exists a space for plural views. Further, we see how practices are debated/articulated in the context of the micro-politics of the region as well as the larger dictates of Islam. To explore the importance of the public space in Malabar, it is necessary to not only understand how consensus on issues is reached and collective will is seemingly forged, but also how debates across incommensurable frameworks persistently break down, negotiations and persuasions fail, and how the different languages of debate remain mutually comprehensible to participants as they draw references and seek validation for their arguments from the same religious doctrines.

Notes

1. Yet, in the last several years, Habermas has turned increasingly to questions of religion. See, for instance, Habermas (2002).
2. Syed Abul Ala Maududi, the founder of Jamaat-e-Islami, reiterated that the objective of the Jamaat-e-Islami is the establishment of Islam or political Islamism as revealed by God and *hukmat-e-ilahi*, meaning 'rule of God'. He also held that there is no essential difference between state, society and government and all are part of the larger Islamic order anchored in sharia. His political concept is totally centred around an ideology of nothing above Islam, beyond Islam and against Islam. For details, see Kurup and Ismail (2008).
3. Kerala politics is characterised by two opposing political coalitions: CPI(M)-led LDF and the Indian National Congress–led UDF. These two coalitions have been alternatively assuming power in the Kerala assembly elections since the 1980s.
4. Maslak refers to the schools of jurisprudence being followed, for example, Hanafi, Shafi, Maliki or Hanbali. However, in colloquial Mappila usage, 'maslak' is also often employed to distinguish between the different kinds of more recent groupings within Sunnis, for example, Mujahids, Jamaat-e-Islami and Quran Sunnath Society.
5. Mappila is also spelled as Mappilla, Maplah, Moplah and Moplamar. Etymologically, it has been glossed as a contraction of *Maha-pilla* (literally, big child, a title of honour conferred on immigrants). The term 'Mappila' is used to refer to Christians in the southern part of Kerala.
6. The northern part of Kerala, which consists of the present-day Kasargod, Kannur, Wayanad, Kozhikode, Malappuram and Palakkad districts, together called Malabar, was part of the Madras Province before the formation of Kerala state.
7. The Hadith is collection of reports purporting to quote what Prophet Muhammad said verbatim on any matter. The term comes from Arabic, meaning 'report', 'account' or 'narrative'
8. The four major schools of jurisprudence for Sunni Islam are Hanafi, Maliki, Shafi and Hanbali. Apart from the Quran and Sunnah, the Sunni organisations

completely depend upon the four schools of jurisprudence. See Kurup and Ismail (2008: 253).

9. Bida is a kind of un-Islamic innovation. Bida is distinct from *ilhad* (heresy). Heresy is considered to be an act of conscious rebellion and bida, the result of confusion, especially as it refers to disagreement with the authority of pertinent Prophetic tradition.
10. Shirk is the sin of practising idolatry or polytheism, that is, the deification or worship of anyone or anything other than the singular God, that is, Allah. Literally, it means ascribing or the establishment of partners placed beside God. It is a far more serious sin than bida.
11. Taghoot means 'to cross the limits', 'to overstep boundaries' or 'to rebel'. In Islamic theology, the word refers to idolatry or to worship of anything other than Allah.
12. In the case of Islamism, Ahmad (2009) argues that Islamism itself is changing, from being opposed to secularism to actually supporting it in the Indian context.
13. All the quotes from Malayalam dailies and magazines that appear in this essay are English translations of the original Malayalam text.
14. Sabarimala Sree Dharma Sastha Temple, dedicated to Lord Ayyappa, is the most prominent among the Sastha temples in Kerala.
15. The prasadam (transvalued religious offering by Hindu worshippers) at the Sabarimala temple is aravana payasam.

References

Ahmad, Imtiaz (ed.). 1973. *Caste and Social Stratification among Muslims in India.* New Delhi: Manohar Publications.

——— (ed.). 1976. *Family, Kinship, and Marriage among Muslims in India.* New Delhi: Manohar Publications.

——— (ed.). 1981. *Ritual and Religion among Muslims in India.* New Delhi: Manohar Publications.

Ahmad, Irfan. 2009. *Islamism and Democracy in India: The Transformation of Jamaat-e-Islami.* New Jersey: Princeton University Press.

Alam, Arshad. 2011. *Inside a Madrasa: Knowledge, Power and Islamic Identity in India.* New Delhi: Routledge.

Asad, Talal. 1986. 'The Idea of Anthropology of Islam', Centre for Contemporary Arab Studies, Washington, DC.

———. 2003. *Formations of the Secular: Christianity, Islam, Modernity.* Stanford: Stanford University Press.

Calhoun, Craig (ed.). 1992. 'Introduction', in *Habermas and the Public Sphere*, pp. 35–36, Cambridge: MIT Press.

Casanova, José. 1994. *Public Religions in the Modern World.* Chicago: The University of Chicago Press.

Dale, F. Stephen. 1980. *Islamic Society on the South Asian Frontier: The Mappilas of Malabar 1498–1922.* Oxford: Clarendon Press.

———. 1982. 'Islamic Society on the South Asian Frontier: The Mappilas of Malabar', *The American Historical Review*, 87 (2): 521–22.

Das, Veena. 1984. 'For a Folk Theology and Theological Anthropology of Islam', *Contributions of Indian Sociology*, 18 (2): 293–300.

Dhanagare, D. N. 1977. 'Agrarian Conflict, Religion and Politics: The Moplah Rebellions in Malabar in the Nineteenth and Early Twentieth Centuries, *Past & Present*, 74 (3): 112–41.

Dreyfus, Hubert and Paul Rabinow. 1982. *Michel Foucault: Beyond Structuralism and Hermeneutics*. Chicago: University of Chicago Press.

Eaton, Richard M. 1984. *The Rise of Islam and the Bengal Frontier, 1204–1760*. Berkeley: University of California Press.

Eickelman, Dale F., and James Piscatori. 1996. *Muslim Politics*. Princeton: Princeton University Press.

Eickelman, Dale F., and John W. Anderson. 2003. *New Media in the Muslim World: The Emerging Public Sphere*. Indiana: Indiana University Press.

Habermas, Jürgen. 1991 [1989]. *The Structural Transformation of the Public Sphere: An Inquiry into a Bourgeois Society*. Cambridge, Massachusetts: MIT Press.

———. 2002. *Religion and Rationality: Essays on Reason, God, and Modernity*. Cambridge: Polity.

Haniffa, Farzana. 2013. 'Piety as Politics amongst Muslim Women in Contemporary Sri Lanka', in Filippo Osella and Caroline Osella (eds), *Islamic Reform in South Asia*, pp. 171–20. London: Cambridge University Press.

Hirschkind, Charles. 2006. *The Ethical Soundscape: Cassette Sermons and Islamic Counterpublics*. New York: Columbia University Press.

Iqtidar, Humeira. 2011. *Secularising Islamists? Jamaat-e-Islami and Jamaat-ud-Dawa in Urban Pakistan*. London: University of Chicago Press.

Kabeer, V. S. M. 2012. 'Mujahid Prasthanathil Sambavikkunnath, Prajaranavum Vasthuthakalum', *Varthamanam Weekly*, 1 (2): 2.

Kurup, K. K. N., and E. Ismail. 2008. *Emergence of Islam in Kerala in 20th Century*. New Delhi: Standard Publishers.

Lakshmi, L. R. S. 2012. *The Malabar Muslims: A Different Perspective*. New Delhi: Cambridge University Press.

Madan, T. N. 2007. 'One among Many: Explorations in the Anthropology of Islam', *The Eastern Anthropologist*, 60 (1): 1–25.

Metcalf, Barbara D. 2014. 'Being Muslim in South Asia', in Robin Jeffrey and Ronojoy Sen (eds), *Being Muslim in South Asia: Diversity and Daily Life*, pp. 18–41. New Delhi: Oxford University Press.

Miller, Roland E. 1976. *Mappila Muslims of Kerala: A Study in Islamic Trends*. New Delhi: Orient Longman.

Mines, Mattison. 1975. 'Islamisation and Muslim Ethnicity in South India', *Royal Anthropological Institute of Great Britain and Ireland*, 10 (3): 404–18.

Osella, Filippo and Caroline Osella. 2008. 'Islamism and Social Reform in Kerala, South India', *Modern Asian Studies*, 2 (3): 317–46.

Prabash, J. 2000. 'CPI (M)'s Muslim League Dilemma', *Economic and Political Weekly*, 35 (34): 3009–11.

Primrose, P. V. A. 2012. 'Onam Agoshathinte Mathavum Dhesheeyathayum' (Malayalam), *Sneha Samvadham*, 2 (1): 11–18.

Robinson, Francis. 1984. 'Islamic Society on the South Asian Frontier: The Mappilas of Malabar 1498–1922', *Modern Asian Studies*, 18 (1): 157–61.

Roy, Olivier. 1996. *The Failure of Political Islam*. Cambridge, MA: Harward University Press.

Salvatore, Armando. 2007. *The Public Sphere: Liberal Modernity, Catholicism, Islam*. McGill: Palgrave Macmillan.

Salvatore, Armando and Mark Le Vine. 2005. *Religion, Social Practice, and Contested Hegemonies: Reconstructing the Public Sphere in Muslim Majority Societies*. New York: Palgrave Macmillan.

Santhosh, R. 2009. 'The Process of Religious Identity Formation: A Sociological Study of Religious Organisations in Kerala, South India', unpublished Ph.D. thesis, Centre for the Study of Social Change and Development, Institute for Social and Economic Change, Bengaluru.

Tanalur, Basheer. 2013. 'Oradharsha Prasthanathinte Dhayaneeya Anthyam', *Vedadharshanam Magazine*, 6 (2): 36.

Tschacher, Torsten. 2014. 'The Challenges of Diversity: "Casting" Muslim Communities in South India', in Robin Jeffrey and Ronojoy Sen (eds), *Being Muslim in South Asia: Diversity and Daily life*, pp. 64–86. New Delhi: Oxford University Publications.

Wright, Theodore P., Jr. 1977. 'Muslims and the 1977 Indian Elections: A Watershed?', *Asian Survey*, 17 (12): 1207–220.

Newspaper and Web Sources

Basith, Abdul. 2012. 'Hate Campaign against IUML Minister in Kerala', June 2012. Available at http://twocircles.net/2012jun07/hate_campaign_against_iuml_minister_kerala.html (accessed 16 November 2017).

Kesari Daily (Malayalam), 24 June 2012.

Madhyamam Daily (Malayalam), 8 June 2012 and 27 August 2012.

Mathrubumi Daily (Malayalam), 12 December 2006 and 23 June 2012.

Siraj Daily (Malayalam), 19 February 2014.

Thelicham Reporter (Malayalam), 7 June 2012.

5

Piety and the Civic

The Solidarity Youth Movement and Islamism in Kerala, South India

Shahul Ameen K. T.

This essay explores how the Jamaat-e-Islami Hind's Kerala chapter—the state wing of the Indian Jamaat-e-Islami, a transnational 'Islamist' organisation formed under the leadership of Syed Abul Ala Maududi in 1941 in Lahore—has contributed to shifts in the concept of Islamic 'reformism'. The essay revolves around the ideology and activism of the Solidarity Youth Movement (SYM), the youth wing of the Jamaat-e-Islami Hind's Kerala chapter (Kerala Jamaat, hereafter).[1] Formed in 2003, the SYM has forged different religious and civil society engagements, which had been so far absent in the discourse of Islamic reform headed by the Jamaat. Unlike the parent organisation, the SYM directly participates in ongoing people's movements that address issues pertaining to development and its discontents. It organises civil society initiatives, namely, *samaravum sevanavum* (struggle and service), around issues such as ecological degradation, protection of human rights, rehabilitation processes and the Adivasi and Dalit land rights programme in Kerala. Addressing these issues, the organisation creates platforms for civil society initiatives across ideological and religious divides. Such solidarities arguably interrogate the state's programmes from the perspectives of subaltern groups and invite religious and non-religious groups to raise questions around victimhood caused by the state and capitalism. The organisation also responds to everyday political developments in which the state and non-state actors are involved. Interestingly, these practices are articulated both in terms of *ibada* (divine worship) and *paura dharmam* (citizens' responsibility) among the practitioners of the SYM. I argue that such discursive meaning-making processes lead to a reimagination of the civil–religious binary on the one hand, and transformation of the Jamaat-e-Islami on the other. This essay thus brings to fore how the discourse of Islamism itself changes as the SYM engages with questions of civil society, development and marginalisation in the context of Kerala.[2]

What accounts for the changing engagement of the Kerala Jamaat from Islamic and Muslim community–centric reformism to participation in contemporary civil society issues pertaining to human rights and ecological concerns through the SYM? Scholars of Islam have identified similar shifts within Islamism in varied cultural contexts across the world. Broadly speaking, the analytical terms 'Islam *mondain*' (Otayek and Soares 2007: 17–19), 'discursive tradition' (Asad 1986: 14–15) and 'civil Islam' (Hefner 2000) explore the manners in which Muslims design their religion in a secularising world situation. The descriptive term 'post-Islamism', however, has gained currency in the academia, which denotes the civil–democratic transformation of Islamism (Roy 2004; Bayat 2007). It also indicates Islamists' endeavours towards combining religiosity with 'liberal' ideals such as human rights, freedom, liberty and plurality. Elaborating this term, Bayat (2007: 11) writes: 'It is an attempt to turn the underlying principles of Islamism on its head by emphasising rights instead of duties, plurality in place of singular authoritative voice, historicity rather than fixed scripture, and the future instead of the past.' In his view, Islamic groups' internal contradictions and societal pressure accelerate a qualitative shift from Islamism to post-Islamism. Such a move, according to him, also imbibes strategies and modalities to tackle with transforming social, political and economic spheres (ibid.: 11–12).

Can the notion of post-Islamism address the Kerala Jamaat's strategic shift? At the outset, this model, grounded primarily in the Middle East and North African socio-political experiences, provides little scope to address the nature of Islamism in South Asia. Here, Islamist groups variously participate in postcolonial electoral democratic politics and culture. For instance, the Jamaat-e-Islami of Pakistan, contrary to the understanding of post-Islamism as a contemporary trend, had long-lasting affiliations with trade unions and progressive political movements of the country (Iqtidar 2011). Shehabuddin (2008) explores the Bangladesh Jamaat-e-Islami's involvement in women's self-help groups, an initiative of local self-governmence. When the Students Islamic Movement of India (SIMI), an offshoot of the Jamaat-e-Islami Hind (India), got radicalised and separated from the parent organisation in the early 1980s, the Indian Jamaat made alliances with human rights organisations and invoked the rhetoric of minority rights enshrined in the Indian Constitution (Ahmad 2010). Different shapings of the Indian Jamaat—for instance, the moderation of the Jamaat-e-Islami Hind and the radicalisation of SIMI—also demonstrate distinct processes of Islamisation, but these are not reducible to the framework of post-Islamism. In particular, the distinct geographic and historic specificities of Kerala's religious reformism cannot be analysed with a linear notion such as post-Islamism.

Adding another impasse on scholarly understanding, Indian sociological studies define Islamic movements, particularly Islamism, as a 'great tradition' derived from Islamic scripts, thereby alien to the South Asian tradition of 'lived Islam' or Sufi Islam (Ahmad 1981; Troll 1989).[3] 'Secularism' studies, on the other hand, have revolved around the issues of identity politics, community radicalisation, Muslim personal law and communal violence—these studies maintained a distance from studying post-Independence Islamic movements (Bhargava 1998). Meanwhile, a range of studies in the postcolonial context has illustrated the centrality of religious movements, including Islamist ones, in the modern public sphere. These studies demonstrate the state's role in shaping modern religion and religious movements.[4] Highlighting this view, Iqtidar (2011: 41) writes of 'the emergence of modern state and its attempt at managing religious practice and thought within a colonial context in North India as a key development that made Islamism possible'. Similarly, the new ethnographic studies on Islamism posit the analytical focus at the creative intersection between democratic practices and religion.[5] Challenging an essentialist understanding of Islam, these studies demonstrate the trajectories of the globally informed historical specificities of Islamic movements. Likewise, scholars have also situated Islamic movements in a larger network of social institutions and relations (Navaro-Yashin 2002). Needless to say, these explorations delineate how Islamic movements adopted religious scriptures and other discursive traditions in shaping a variety of religious/social articulations and modalities of programme coordination.

It is with reference to these new ethnographic studies that I delineate the case of the SYM. The essay accounts for the SYM's ideology and praxis in relation to the religious, civil and political actors of Kerala. Engaging with the SYM, I shall explore how the movement created a novel signification to scriptural traditions as well as customary usages of the Mappila Muslims of Malabar.[6] Engaging with the SYM's articulation of certain cardinal concepts—ibada (service to God), *muamalat* (social dealings), *khilafat* (divine deputy) and *haqq* (obligation, right)—the essay brings to fore how the youth wing of the Kerala Jamaat brought important shifts in the concerns of religious movement/organisation, and thereby the relation between civil society, electoral democracy and Islamism. Postulating the SYM's agency as a reflexivity of Islamism,[7] I demonstrate the emerging civil–religious concerns of Kerala. Indeed, this inquiry is implicated to think through the contemporary making of religion and politics, with special reference to Islamic movements.

The Ideological Routes of the SYM

The SYM, according to a practitioner, draws insights from 'the world liberation movements'.[8] A leader validates its 'struggle and service' with supporting quotes from the Quran and the Hadith.[9] SYM practitioners also draw on the legacies of the Mappila Rebellion in its 'protests' and participation in people's movements. In my interview with Kuttil Muhammadali, the first president of the SYM (2003–05), he underscored *sanatana moolyaghal* (eternal universal values) as the basis of the ideology of the SYM.[10] These values comprise compassion, tolerance, care and fraternity to humanity and nature. In an interview with Arifali, the *amir* (president) of the Kerala Jamaat, it was pointed out that 'Gandhi's notion of Ramarajya' might be equivalent to the principle of both the organisations—the Jamaat and the SYM.[11] In his view, this Gandhian notion denotes a desire for a justice-oriented nation, which characterises the respectful inclusion of religion. On the occasion of the Social Auditing Programme of the SYM, he further explained that Maududi's thoughts were the SYM's best reference. C. Davood, the media person of the Kerala Jamaat, located the lineage of the SYM in the philosophy and practice of the Students Islamic Organisation (SIO) the student wing of the Jamaat.[12] A good number of the leaders define its activities as ibada, service to God or Allah, and this approach has a mass appeal among the practitioners.

The SYM frames its ideological roots from certain events, movements and personalities. For instance, the organisation conducted a programme called Samakalika Keralam Thuhfathul-Mujahidin Vayikunnu (Contemporary Kerala Reads Thuhfathul-Mujahidin) in Malappuram in February 2010. On this occasion, the *Thuhfathul-Mujahidin*—an Arabic text written by a Sufi saint that 'calls' Muslim believers for a battle against the Portuguese colonial power in the context of sixteenth-century Malabar—was interpreted to stress the core of *mathasamoohikatha* (religious sociality). This notion denotes the activities of the religious leaders to create a better society and fight for economic and political liberation. Similarly, the 'heroic' symbolism of the Mappila Rebellion (1921) is frequently employed in the SYM's protests against 'new imperialism'.[13] Though the organisation does not share the concerns of the socio-religious reform movements of late nineteenth-century Kerala such as women's education, it claims inspirations from those upheavals: 'Definitely, we travel through the same route opened by the Sri Narayana Movement and other religious movements.'[14] Addressing Malabar's backwardness in education and employment, the SYM launched a programme called the Malabar Nivarthana Prakshobam (the Malabar Renovation Protest) in November 2011. The title and mode of this protest was an adaptation of a larger movement that took place in the Travancore region in 1893. The Travancore movement demanded that the government should fulfill the educational and employment needs of the people. Thus, in different ways, the SYM strategically appropriates the *modus operandi* of some of the popular and historic protests of Kerala. When questioned about other appropriations, the general secretary of the SYM replied:

> Being an Islamic expression, the Solidarity retains its roots in the soil of the *desham* [country] and expands globally. It maintains debate-oriented relationships with the left and other social movements in Kerala, and follows an Islamic tradition that absorbs *nanma* [virtues] from different corners. It continuously incorporates goodness from international, national and regional traditions but maintains a Kerala identity. The SYM echoes the ideas of the people of Kerala.[15]

Resembling the disposition of contemporary Islamic movements, the SYM also maintains public visibility and strategic ambiguity in its ideology (Huq 2008; Schielke 2009). Drawing on various interpretative cultural resources and practices—by presenting translated verses of the Quran, by narrating incidents from the Mappila Rebellion, by reciting Dalit poetry, by exhibiting snapshots from the Arab Spring or by quoting the Fundamental Rights of the Indian Constitution—the SYM articulates its ideology. It invokes the rhetoric of diverse movements such as human rights movements, new social movements, neo-leftism, post-Islamism, youth movements, and Dalit and Backward Class movements. Suffice to say, these plural articulations have been performative in the public concerns/issues of Kerala. Corresponding to the SYM's activism, the Kerala Jamaat finds a way to participate in the dominant 'secular' and 'left' public sphere of Kerala, into which its entry was denied on the charge of Islamic fundamentalism. The SYM's engagements reshape the concerns of the Kerala Jamaat as it addresses questions pertaining to human rights and environment. The following section thus discusses how the SYM practitioners interpret Islamic scriptural and other traditions, including common usages, and engage in the civil society concerns of Kerala.

Divinity and Civil Initiatives

According to SYM practitioners, God, humankind and *paristhiti* (environment/nature) are closely inter-related.[16] Allah is the *rabbul-alameen* (nurturer/lord of the 'worlds'). In this notion of 'worlds', humankind and paristhiti are included, and all creatures are mandated to serve God. Among them, human beings hold a special privilege, namely, khilafat, the power to implement sharia (the divine jurisprudence). Apart from serving God, human beings are obligated to implement divine jurisprudence. They are also delegated for *dawa* (invitation to the path of Allah), to invite other human beings towards *din* (belief/religion). How can humankind serve God? What of sharia should a human as a *khalifa* (representative of Allah) implement and invite humanity to join? How do 'environment/human rights' come into the domain of ibada, khilafat and sharia? Addressing these questions, the SYM draws the theology of struggle and service:

> Definitely each grain of sand, blade of grass, planets, day and night, and seasons have their respective *dharmam* [duty] to perform. The rhythm of their performance is the existence of universe, nature, earth and even humankind. Nothing was created for a futile purpose. Each one's duty and its fulfillment remain important. Since they perform their [divinely assigned] duties, [we] have to maintain them in a divine way. Being God's representatives, nature's preservation has always been the supreme responsibility of humans ... "He brought you forth from the earth and hath made you husband it" [Surah Hud: 61]. "Then we appointed you viceroys on the earth after them that we might see how you behave" [Sura Yunus: 14]. (Shameem 2007: 102)[17]

Drawing on the notion of dharmam, T. K. Abdulla, an SYM advisor and a senior member of the Jamaat, presented the religious character of 'nature' and 'earth'. Because of Allah's will, earth's components such as sand and seasons follow a mutual co-existence. Presenting verses from the Quran, he affirms that the maintenance of nature has been a divinely assigned duty of humankind. Similarly, he highlights the divine law of human dharmam in which importance is given to the protection and promotion of nature and human culture.

> A human is Allah's representative on this earth. Being a representative, he has two complimentary dharmams. According to the first, humankind should rule the world by following justice and the law of Allah, namely, sharia, which is devoted to the practice of *adil*-based *hukum* [justice-based divine rule] in this world. When the Quran said that Davood Nabi [Prophet David] was appointed as the khalifa, Allah meant the same. *Imarathulard* is the second meaning of human khilafat. This notion addresses issues such as building, maintaining and expanding the earth [/nature]. (Abdulla 2007: 18)

Resembling this view, an SYM practitioner also pointed out that human beings must preserve and maintain the 'earth, plateaus, rivers, trees, continents, and mountains'.[18] Furthering the list, conservation and upholding of human and non-human life—'the essential components of nature'—also become a human khalifa's responsibility. The practitioner sketched out how a human ought to perform his/her divinely given dharmam towards the earth and human life:

> As per Allah's plan, human relations with nature must be friendly and cooperative, and the former cannot exploit the latter. The Prophet's words, "Allah has compelled [you] to be righteous in everything", definitely clarify what the human being's relation should be with all living and non-living things. [Once] the prophet looked at Uhad Mountain and said "Oh, mountain, I love you and you love me"; this throws light on Islam's perspective on nature. While a human uses natural resources, he has to preserve them for the lives of future generations. Islam puts forward this idea. In the Koran's statement "everything on the earth is created for you", the word "you" refers to all humans who will live in this world till its end. [Being the khalifa] we are responsible not only to maintain the goodness of the earth but also to ensure its fruitfulness ... The holy text defines a holy struggle and it is nothing but one's work for feeding the poor. The Koran teaches: "One should help another one for gaining Allah's mercy". [Moreover], the holy text questions all kinds of social injustice and domination, especially on the poor. It insists that the believer works for the liberation of humanity by ensuring good food, air and shelter.[19]

Through Islam's interpretative resources such as the verses of the Quran and Hadith, the SYM articulates the promotion of environment and the protection of humankind as one's responsibility. In the SYM practitioners' view, the organisation was formed to address these 'divine' duties. As a divine mission, the SYM develops its civil initiatives against the violators of nature and human rights that, according to the practitioners, include multinational corporates, development-induced state, dominant social forces and their nexus. The SYM draws its visions from the Quran, an interpretative resource, which simultaneously reflects upon the ongoing civil programmes and shows a departure from the notions of ibada that are present in the traditional religio-cultural context. In an interview, an SYM practitioner elaborates the notion of ibada of the SYM in the following way:

> Allah created mankind to worship Him. Through ibada, mankind expresses obedience and submission to the will of its creator, Allah. In popular view, ibada consists of *shahada* [testifying to one's faith], *salat* [prayer], *zakat* [giving alms], *saum* [fasting during the month of Ramzan] and haj [pilgrimage to Mecca] only. However, ibada is not limited to these five pillars. It contains more matters, which are instructed in the Quran and Hadith. Further, the terrain of ibada is not limited in the matters pertaining to God and human relations only. It inheres muamalat, the conduct of humankind towards each other. It also contains the prescribed mode of conduct with flora and fauna, earth and sky and the universe. The Muslim, the one who submitted his will to God's will, has the duty to perform these ibada and dawa ['call' to observe ibada]. Since each Muslim is a khalifa, representative of God, both the duties are assigned to him.[20]

The SYM practitioners bring the logic of Islamic praxis to civil concerns, without violating the expectations of public conscience. Participating in such a plural public conscience on the environment and human life, the SYM articulates the 'Islamic' logic of these movements of civil practices. Its position thus creates a dual argument in the public sphere about the SYM's character, either as the transformation of Islamism or as the tactic of Islamism. The SYM provides religious interpretation for its ecological as well as human rights concerns, and seeks collective acceptance in Kerala's public sphere. Thereby, the SYM leaders and practitioners conceptualise their concern with living and non-living things within the terrain of worship. Accordingly, they perceive endeavours for human welfare and environmental protection as an 'intrinsic' attribute of their service to God. In the following section, I will show how this articulation of worship faces contestations as the SYM seeks acceptance from other Muslim groups.

Contested Ibada in the Muslim Public Sphere

The SYM repeatedly criticises the traditional Sunni organisations' notions of ibada.[21] It assigns *anustanikata* (ritualism) to the Sunni ideas of ibada. The Sunnis, in the SYM viewpoint, are concerned about performing certain ibada—the five pillars, for instance—and selected muamalat only. Through *waaz* (long speech at mosques), especially during the nights of the holy month of Ramzan and at the shrines of saints and martyrs, they recurrently highlight the importance of namaz and *zaum* (fasting during Ramzan). Different groups of Sunnis emphasise more on rituals such as dikr (a ritual of remembrance of God), *dua* (collective prayer), moulid (a ritual in which poetry about Muhammad's life is recited) and namaz (compulsory prayer). These rituals contain social performative aspects, and they are habitually designed for the Sunni followers. The Sunnis strictly set their rituals in locations such as mosques, madrasahs and shrines or at houses, and discourage the SYM-type 'street-centric' ritual performances. Regarding ritual presentation, one could arguably say that the Sunnis prefer a 'veil' from the public gaze while they perform their collective rituals. Interpreting bazaars as centres of *iblis* (devil) and *fitina* (distress), the majority of the Sunni ulema repeatedly discourage the Muslim youth's presence in streets, instead encouraging its presence in mosques and the compulsory five-time namaz in unison: 'Nobody from the street comes to your *qabar* [grave] and finds out your *paraloka* [otherworldly] success; you have to work for it by doing compulsory *amalukal* [rites and rituals].'[22] This consideration of a Sunni leader reflects the Sunni disposition of public issue–centric articulations of religiosity.

According to the SYM, the Sunnis dismiss Islam's *adhatyatmaka* (devotional) facets in its dealings with public issues. Though the

Mujahid movement led by the Kerala Naduvathul Mujahideen (KNM) has a putative history of Muslim socio-religious reformism, its minimal participation in civic issues is pointed out by the SYM. The Indian Union Muslim League (IUML), however, is presented as a 'community'-based political party.[23]

> The Sunnis limit the scope of ibada in *anustanikata* [ritualism]. They pray and do other ritual services like dua [prayer]. Listen to their talks and observe their deeds that emphasise the husband's duty towards his wife, son's towards father and so on. These are incomplete understandings of ibada. Why don't they deal with the duty towards the environment and fellow non-Muslim citizens? They disregard these dimensions of Islam. Though the Mujahid movement presented Islam's *ijtihad* tradition and reformist ideals, it failed to express its outlook on civic issues. [Moreover,] by presenting Islam for Muslims only, the Mujahid dismisses Allah's central identity presented in the holy Quran, that is, *rabbulalamin*, cherisher of worlds. [...] IUML is a political group of the Muslim community only, and thereby it failed to think on larger politics of environmentalism and human rights in which Muslim's issues also are included.[24]

The SYM's notion of ibada establishes religious grounds for its practice. It consciously places such a constituted notion of ibada amongst the Muslim groups who likewise hold variegated and interconnected notions of ibada, as the essence of their organisation. Presenting ecological and human rights–centric meanings of ibada, the SYM attempts to draw its own and the Jamaat's Islamic character, which has been questioned in the history of the Islamic movements of Kerala. Further, it refashions the agenda of Islamic religious groups towards pro-ecological and human rights–oriented civic initiatives, along with the existing practices, including philanthropy. Such a reconstitution of ideology and practice, nevertheless, involves tremendous socially informed theological contestations and negotiations between the different Muslim groups. Moreover, those processes take place in the terrain of the public sphere in which plurality and everyday state intervention prevails.

The IUML, a Muslim political party, has utilised public platforms to present the SYM as a 'non-secular' 'Maududian' mask of religious fundamentalism. 'It is a fake pro-Adivasi, Dalit, environmentalist face of Maududism', argued an IUML leader.[25] Further, the SYM has been criticised in the IUML circles for not addressing Muslim 'community' issues. 'Solidarity is a good name for a cement company', said a youth leader of the IUML commenting on SYM's 'non-Islamic' and 'non-Muslim' title.[26] These statements reassert the IUML's self-perception as the political representative of the Muslim community. At the same time, being a partner in the parliamentary political system and in coalition governments, the IUML leaders do accept and work for ensuring the 'common good' of plural communities, in which Muslim 'issues' are also involved. Thus, the IUML—as a Muslim minority community–based political party in Indian democracy—has the complementary role of being the custodian of Muslim interests and a party in plural electoral democracy. Addressing these dimensions of the IUML's practice, P. K. Kunhalikutti, the former IUML minister of industries and information technology in the government of Kerala, pointed out: 'Politics is a religious activity for me. Involvement in public issues is the greatest ibada. Ibada means good deeds. Our *niyyat* (intention), that is, intention of the mind, has to be clear. Help the poor. That definitely is religion.'[27]

Representing the Mappila Muslim–dominated constituencies of Malabar, the IUML invokes notions such as 'Muslim interest' and community development. It contests elections and participates in coalition governments. Aligned with the expectations of the coalition front, including the idea of 'collective responsibility', it usually produces discourses on public good and development. These discourses change the notion of Muslim interest to an extent and generate an understanding that argues that general good leads to Muslim good as well. 'A good deed indeed is a service to God', the IUML members claim. 'Do *amal* (good practice) by pleading Allah's *rahmat* (mercy)', the IUML members often repeat these words. 'Be merciful upon the creature to gain the Creator's mercy', an IUML leader translated for me from the Hadith.

The Sunni Student Federation (SSF), the student wing of the AP Sunni group, finds considerable 'non-Islamic' externalities in the ideology and practice of the SYM. 'Left-front vocabularies, modes of struggle, bargaining techniques and intellectuals guide the organisation', an SSF supporter pointed out.[28] In his view, instead of growing inward towards Islam, the SYM shows an outward turn, which highlights non-Islamic traditions. He believed that the SYM espoused the ideas of the communist movements and failed to uphold Islam in its pure form. Instead of presenting communist ideas in the post-communist era, the SSF demands the SYM to present the exclusive religio-cultural properties of Islam. Therefore, the SSF wants to replace the scope of *Native Bapa*, a hip-hop album on human rights violation, with 'Burda' and 'Moideen Mala', centuries-old Mappila ritual performance. Moreover, the SSF finds 'struggle and service' potentials in religio-cultural rites and rituals of the Mappila Muslims, which are placed against the 'communist' character of the SYM. The SSF argues that the correct performance of rites and rituals itself meets social and spiritual responsibilities of Muslims.

As service to God, Sunnis perform *salat* (prayer) in unison, conduct *iftar* (the evening meal that breaks the daily fast during Ramzan) parties, celebrate saint days and conduct dikr conferences. As part of these ritual performances, they mobilise food, money and clothes for orphanages and destitute homes, schools and madrasahs, and provide financial help for the marriage of poor Muslim women, girls' education and health. Similar to the activities of the Jamaat and the Mujahid, they give *zakat* (alms) to the needy and engage in philanthropy, ranging from hospital service to educational scholarship programmes for Muslims. Interestingly, extending their social services beyond the community, the Sunnis, at present, do recognise the importance of public issues like afforestation programmes. For example, *Risala*, a weekly of the AP Sunni group, started publishing essays on waste, global warming, environmental decay and so on. Yet, it is the SYM that takes the credit for the Muslim groups' new emergence with civic concern:

> Regarding the Solidarity, Islamic religious organisations shared different kinds of doubts. "It is not Islam; not *tawheed*", they accused us ... [However,] at present almost all religious organisations, especially their student and youth organisations, imitate us [the SYM] and carry out public and civil issues with reference to Islam.

> The SYM never went for theological debates [the common practice of the Mappila Muslim religious groups] to transform them. And, it influences their agenda as contemporary Kerala witnesses.[29]

Though the Sunnis have shown an inclination towards the SYM-type public issue–oriented civil initiatives in recent years, they utilise their energy, money and social capital to conduct, for instance, a salat gathering instead of building a house for an Adivasi family. The Sunnis make sure that their zakat is individually given to a *vishvasi* (true believer) of Islam than collectively for a common cause. Indeed, the Sunni leaders tell the SYM to prioritise ibada such as namaz and the five pillars. Unlike the Sunni get-togethers, the SYM engages with a wider, plural public. At the sites of civic engagements, the SYM practitioners perform namaz. In the midst of a conference on human rights violation held at Koduvally in March 2013, the SYM leaders stopped for namaz. Those who do not perform namaz, including Muslims, found it a useful interval. Moreover, there was no compulsion that invited 'Muslims' to perform namaz. Here, the namaz marked a moment for thanks-giving. Through this ritual performance, the practitioners asked for mercy of God for the ongoing programme.

Similarly, during its large-scale tenth anniversary closing conference held at the Kozhikode beach, the *azan maghrib* (call for compulsory prayer just after sunset) echoed from the nearest mosques. As a pre-planned move, the SYM volunteers set the same venue for the salat, and it was performed under the *imamate* (leadership) of a senior Jamaat leader. As part of many ritual acts in the prayer, the imam (the leader of the prayer) recited verses from the Quran to complete the ritual circle. While performing the second *rakat* (ritual cycle just after the second *sujud* [prostration]), the imam recited 'Surah An-Nasr' (The [divine] Help) of the Quran: '[1] When there comes Allah's help and the victory, [2] and you see people entering Allah's religion in multitudes, [3] then pronounce the purity and praise of your Lord, and seek forgiveness from Him; surely He is Ever-Relenting.'[30]

These events highlight the performative aspect of religious and civic components of the SYM's engagements, and how they resonate with the region's enduring public discourse of civic initiatives. The

Indian National Congress (INC) has three members of the legislative assembly (MLAs) who pledged to devote their public life for the cause of the environment and for protecting the greenery of the earth. In Kerala's micro-level gatherings—at schools, clubs, madrasahs, self-help groups and churches—the questions of ecological protection are promoted as important agenda. At present, *sramadanam*—an individual/collective act of helping others without expecting any monetary returns and for fulfilling social and/or divine commitment—includes ecological concerns as well. Thus, we need to understand and situate the SYM in the globally informed state-wide political praxis and cultural concerns. In the next section, I elaborate on how the SYM interprets a customary usage of the region in articulating its religio-civil practice.

Haqq and Its Civil Society Interpretation

The Malabar region has a long association with the Middle East through trade as well as the Islamic teachings of Hadrami Islamic ulema. The recent Gulf migration has contributed to this relation through an economic and cultural exchange of labour, goods and remittance. This relation has been unbroken, longstanding and direct. It has been argued that the social and cultural life of the Malabar region shows the well-rooted influence of Yemeni and Egyptian culture rather than that of Indo-Persian culture (Miller 1992). In this context, I map the social performance of an Arabic customary usage, that is, haqq in the region. This examination aims to situate the SYM's interpretative transformation of the conceptual trope of haqq in the context of the movement.

The term 'haqq' has multiple usages in Malabar. Mappila Muslims use the term as one of the qualities of Allah. 'The truth' has been the meaning in this context. Sometimes, it is recognised as the opposite of the word *batil* (false or unacceptable). Following the Sufi tradition, *anal haqq* (I am the truth) gets enacted in interesting ways in the everyday life of the Muslims in Malabar. Haqq is also defined as the 'right' (or belongings) of a person and/or a community, which is protected and promoted by other fellow beings. For instance, people say, '*arante haqq edukarut*' (do not take others' belongings), which implies one's responsibility upon the 'right' of other fellow beings. This particular interpretation of haqq has a number of social implications in Malabar.

The community leaders rehabilitated the Mappila Muslim children who were affected by the Mappila Rebellion of 1921. Orphanages were seen as the religious responsibility of the community leaders and, simultaneously, the *avakasham* (right) of the orphans. The orphanages were constructed across the Malabar region. These orphanages were conceptualised both in terms of ibada, (service to God) and muamalat (deeds for human welfare). Mostly Muslim children were enrolled in these orphanages. Meanwhile, responding to secular democracy, educational institutions of the Mujahid and the Jamaat—education being another responsibility of the ulema and community leaders as well as the right of the Mappila Muslims—enrolled 'non-Muslims' as well. However, many of these institutions were known as Mappila institutions. When the community experienced massive Gulf migration as well as religious revivalism from the early 1980s onwards, Islamic organisations of Malabar started articulating their 'Islamic' duties and responsibilities more vigorously. In recorded long speeches of the Sunni ulema, for instance, sex, *mahr* (dower), food and clothes were identified as rights of the wife guaranteed by her husband. Similarly, qabar (grave) and *kafan* (shroud) were defined as the rights of the dead body and the responsibility of the ummah (the Muslim community), among others. Overall, the Islamic groups developed and widely articulated a discourse of religious duties-cum-responsibilities across the Malabar region.

Participating in this public discourse on haqq, the Mujahid movement went a step further. It conceptualised the significance of zakat in a much broader manner. It professed that the poor should 'fight' and get their right/share from the distributable wealth of fellow Muslims. In effect, the movement discouraged the common practice where 'needy' Muslims visit and collect the share of zakat from wealthy Muslims. Instead, the Mujahids instructed the donor of the zakat to calculate the zakat amount as per the religious norms and distribute it 'secretly' among the poor, *miskeen* (destitute) and other deserving people. As an alternative, its practitioners collected the share of their individual zakat, purchased durable items such as auto-rickshaws, small shops and tailoring machines for that amount and distributed these items among the 'needy'. Apart from zakat, they collectively distributed *zakat-ul-fitr*, a charity given to the poor at the end of the fasting in the month of Ramzan.

The Sunnis criticised this collective zakat distribution practice. As against this, they instructed Mappilas to dispense zakat personally to 'deserving' individuals. At the same time, the Mujahids' concept of charity faced an internal dilemma. While distributing the collected money and other things as a religious act, some of the non-Muslim households requested for a share. There were cases in which the Mujahid members distributed some of these items, especially sacrificial meat, among non-Muslim neighbours. A group of Mujahid ulema interpreted this act as unacceptable because it did not meet the niyyat of the believer. However, a group of young Mujahid leaders interpreted Muslim's responsibilities towards non-Muslim people's livelihood. Drawing from various Hadith traditions, this group stressed the human responsibility towards 'non-Muslims' and extended the scope and reach of haqq.

In a similar vein, the SYM practitioners invoked haqq to generate a plural collectivity in civil society among the protesters and supporters of human rights and ecological issues. It was used to build issue-based alliances with different groups. In fact, this customary usage enabled the movement a range of mediation right from its involvement in the people's movement for ecological rights to questioning the state's pro-capitalist industrial policies in association with other protesting civil society groups. Moreover, the trope of haqq as a religio-civil act legitimised the participation of other religious movements. At the same time, it opened the space for those the practitioners describe as the 'beaten-up', including Adivasi and Dalit groups. These groups were considered to be legitimate candidates in the domain of haqq—groups whose rights should be protected and promoted by the civil society in which religious movements were legitimate members. Thus, the SYM urges its practitioners to dedicate their energy to ensure the means of livelihood of these 'marginalised' groups.

> Tomorrow's world should be for the beaten-up. We cannot rest until their liberation. We have to mobilise our consciousness for

> their new era. The era will emerge when our night prayers and day struggles converse ... We give priority to others like the Adivasi ... Indeed, it comes from our faith.[31]

In his speech, the founding president of the SYM frames the question of social justice as haqq and the rhetoric demands that the practitioners work for the subjugated in society.

Placing their concern with this-worldly praxis, the SYM, participated in the movement against Hindustan Coca-Cola Beverages Private Limited in Plachimada. It supported the Adivasi protest movement that demanded that the cola company shut down its plant that contaminated ground water and released toxic waste into agricultural land. Expressing solidarity with the Adivasis, the SYM and other protesters declared that access to pure drinking water was a right of the people. The protest collectives further raised demands for a 'responsible' government that should ban the production and distribution of Coca-Cola in the state. Extending these demands, environmental activists, plant-affected Adivasis and the SYM practitioners marched to the Palakkad Collectorate and thereby drew the attention of the district collector towards the issue. To unite Adivasis around the question of water rights, it also conducted an international Adivasi *sammelanam* (conference) in Palakkad. Its 'Stop Check Post, No Entry for Coca-Cola' programme physically blocked the trucks of the company at the state border. The 'Oru Kudam Vellam Oru Pidi Ari' (One Pot Water, Handful of Rice) campaign also addressed the livelihood and drinking water issues of the Adivasis. In connection with these protests and involvements, the SYM conducted its first state-level conference in Palakkad, the drought-prone and cola-affected region of Kerala. Forty thousand people assembled for the conference and demanded the state to ban the production and distribution of Coca-Cola in Kerala. Here, cola became a symbol of exploitation by multinational corporates in nexus with the state. In such a context, the SYM's varied engagements highlight the rights of Adivasis and create the platform for protesters and supporters of human rights and ecological movements in the realm of civil society. The organisation builds relationships with different groups on the one hand, and organises against political power's nexus with corporate interests on the other. Here, the movement articulated people's movement as a locus of varieties of mediation, in which the Islamic movements' role was also deeply imbricated.

Conclusion

Providing platforms for the subjugated groups to present ecological and human right concerns, the SYM recurrently upholds their issues in Kerala's public sphere. Refraining from debates on ritual practices, SYM compels the practitioners to undertake 'struggle and service' for the cause of marginalised communities such as Dalits and Adivasis. Building 'issue'-based alliances across civil society groups, the SYM formulates a notion of religio-civil 'solidarity' as it engages with the politics of the marginalised. These solidarities necessitate the organisation to incorporate varied ideas and concerns into the working ideology of the SYM. Situated in the plural public sphere, the SYM incorporates these ideas in a rather creative manner. On one level, they articulate an agenda drawn from Islam's interpretative resources as well as customary usages. Its notion of khilafat defines human beings as God's this-worldly representatives with divine duty, the maintenance of earth/nature and the preservation of His creatures, mainly the weaker ones. Here, unlike the public pietism thesis (Hirschkind 2006; Mahmood 2005) in which 'prayer [ibada] becomes an embedded desire and need in itself' (Cannell 2010: 92), the SYM's notion of ibada overtly leads to a reconfiguration of the civil–religious binary as well as the concerns of Islamism.

In particular, the SYM brings forth the notion of ibada and haqq into the domain of the plural public sphere and civil society movements of Kerala. It has carried interpretative resources of Islam as it engages in the civic concerns of the region. The practitioners present their praxis as a complementary relation of piety and civic action, and they call upon humankind towards such actions. The SYM thus strives for creating solidarity among people's movements and issue-based collaborations across social divides against their common enemies. Without creating a counter-Muslim public (Hirschkind 2006), its rhetoric for solidarities not only replaces 'exclusive' Muslim issues into the realm of public sphere discussions on human rights, but also stimulates 'Muslims' to participate in new civil initiatives. Through civil politics, it judges, denounces and evaluates the actions of the government. One could evoke Rosanvallon's (2008) notion of counter-democracy in this context. Moreover, the SYM's public engagements enhance the Jamaat's participation in the dominant 'secular' and 'left' public sphere of Kerala.

Notes

1. All quotes from fieldwork narratives and vernacular sources in this essay have been transalated by the author from the original Malayalam.
2. Robinson (2008: 206) defines Islamism as folows: 'In the second half of the twentieth century, the process of renewal mutated to develop a new strand, which claimed that [religious/Islamic] revelation had the right to control all human experiences and that *state power* must be sought to achieve this end. This is known to many as Islamic fundamentalism, but is usually better understood as Islamism' (emphasis added). This term, however, has a discursively—rather than rhetorically—produced 'usage' in different contexts.
3. Scholars have identified the pivotal role of Islamic movements for a larger process called 'Islamisation' (Aggarwal 1969; Ahmad 1969). These understandings, however, do not look into the sociological aspects involved in the making of Islamic movements in India. Meanwhile, a group of historians and political scientists have explored the dynamism of Islamic movements in British India (Metcalf 1982; Minault 1982; Robinson 2001; Sanyal 1999; Sikand 2002). Positing Islamic movements at the intersection of politics and economy, these writings foreground the blurring of 'reformism' with 'traditionalism'. These studies also account for the importance of human endeavours, especially that of charismatic leaders, and the role of social forces in the making of Islamic movements in the medieval and colonial periods (Alam 2004; Zaman 2002). Though this literature empirically delineates the complex texture of Islamic movements, it does not provide an approach that is helpful to study the distinctiveness of religious movements in the context of the post-Independence political scenario.
4. For a review of these studies, see van der Veer (2002).
5. See, for example, essays in the special issues of *Modern Asian Studies*, 42 (2008), and *Journal of Royal Anthropological Institute*, 15 (2009: S1–S240).
6. Kerala witnessed unprecedented social movements of Dalit and Adivasi groups in early years of the current century (Bijoy 2008). Public visibility and social pressure of these social movements arguably shaped the praxis of the SYM.
7. See, for example, Uberoi's (2003: 122–23) understanding of civil society as the locus of 'God-realisation' or 'self-realisation'.
8. Apart from the freedom movements of Asia and Africa, the political upheavals of Latin America and Vietnam receive recurrent appearance in the discourses of the Kerala state as 'the anti-imperial liberation movements'. Interview with a Kerala Jamaat leader, Kozhikode, January 2012.

9. Interview, Kozhikode, January 2011.
10. Interview held at Chennamangaloor, March 2011.
11. See interview in *Mathrubhumi Weekly*, 13–19 June 2010, p. 13.
12. Interview held at Hira Centre, Head Office, Kerala Jamaat, February 2011.
13. See, for example, *Native Bapa* (2013), a hip-hop album directed by Muhsin Paleri, which frequently gets highlighted in the SYM discourses.
14. Interview, Kozhikode, October 2012.
15. Views of T. Muhammad Velom, General Secretary, SYM. Interviewed at Kozhikode, May 2013.
16. Along with paristhiti, the SYM practitioners interchangeably use words such as *mannu* (soil), *bhoomi* (earth) and *prakriti* (nature).
17. The words of Muhammed Shameem, state committee member, SYM.
18. Interview with Shameem and other members at Hira Centre, Kozhikode, February 2012.
19. The summary of a workshop talk of T. K. Abdulla, held at Hira Centre, Kozhikode, on the theme of development; summary prepared by K. T. Hussain.
20. Interview with an SYM practitioner, Februry 2012.
21. The term 'Sunni' denotes 'traditionalist' or 'Orthodox' Muslims who stand opposed to the organised reformists—the Jamaat and the Muhahid movements. E. K. Aboobaker Musaliar and Kanthapuram A. P. Aboobaker Musaliar lead the two factions of Sunnis, who constitute the largest portion of the Mappila Muslims of Malabar.
22. Interview with Abdurrahiman, imam of a Sunni mosque, Malappuram, February 2011.
23. The IUML was founded on 10 March 1948 in Madras. Unlike the All-India Muslim League's (AIML) demand for a separate Muslim nation, the IUML accepted the Indian version of a plural secular democracy, the Constitution, rule of law and a parliamentary federal system.
24. Interview with P. I. Naushad, President, SYM, February 2012.
25. From a recorded speech delivered by M. A. Shaji, an IUML leader
26. Ibid.
27. Interview published in *Mathrubhumi Weekly*, 13–19 June 2010, p. 25.
28. Interaction with Nuaiman K. A., January 2012.
29. Interview with Muhammad Velam, February 2012.
30. 'Surah An-Nasr' of the Quran.
31. The presidential address of Kuttil Muhammadali at the venue of the first state-level conference, 24 April 2005.

References

Abdulla, T. K. 2007. 'Vikasanam, Islam Oramukam', in A. A. Haleem (ed.), *Vikasanam, Paristhiti Aagola Muthalalitham* (Malayalam), pp. 17–24. Calicut: Solidarity Youth Movement.

Ahmad, Aziz. 1969. *An Intellectual History of Islam in India*. Edinburgh: Edinburgh University Press.

Ahmad, Imtiaz. 1981. *Ritual and Religion among Muslims in India*. Delhi: Manohar.

Ahmad, Irfan. 2010. *Islamism and Democracy in India: The Transformation of Jamaat-e-Islami*. New Delhi: Permanent Black.

Aggarwal, P. 1969. 'Islamic Revival in Modern India: The Case of Meos', *Economic and Political Weekly*, 4 (42): 1679–81.

Alam, Muzaffar. 2004. *The Languages of Political Islam in India*. New Delhi: Permanent Black.

Asad, Talal. 1986. 'The Idea of an Anthropology of Islam', Occasional Papers Series, Georgetown University, pp. 1–22.

Bayat, Asef. 2007. *Making Islam Democratic: Social Movements and the Post-Islamist Turn*. Stanford: Stanford University Press.

Bhargava, Rajeev (ed.). 1998. *Secularism and Its Critics*. New Delhi: Oxford University Press.

Bijoy, C. R. 2008. 'The Plachimada Struggle', *Economic and Political Weekly*, 41 (41): 4332–39.

Cannell, Fenella. 2010. 'The Anthropology of Secularism', *Annual Review of Anthropology*, 39: 85–100.

Hefner, Robert. 2000. *Civil Islam Muslims and Democratization in Indonesia*. New Jersey: Princeton University Press.

Hirschkind, Charles. 2006. *The Ethical Soundscape: Cassette Sermons and Islamic Counterpublics*. New York: Columbia University Press.

Huq, Maimuna. 2008. 'Reading the Qur'an in Bangladesh: The Politics of "Belief" among Islamist Women', *Modern Asian Studies*, 42 (2–3): 457–88.

Iqtidar, Humeira. 2011. *Secularizing Islamists: Jama'at-e-Islami and Jama'at-ud-da'wa in Urban Pakistan*. New Delhi: Permanent Black.

Mahmood, Saba. 2005. *Politics of Piety: The Islamic Revival and the Feminist Subject*. Princeton, NJ: Princeton University Press.

Metcalf, Barbara D. 1982. *Islamic Revival in British India: Deoband, 1860–1900*. Princeton, NJ: Princeton University Press.

Miller, Roland E. 1992. *Mappila Muslims of Kerala: A Study in Islamic Trends*. Madras: Oriental Longman.

Minault, Gail. 1982. *The Khilafat Movement: Religious Symbolism and Political Mobilization in India*. New York: Columbia University Press.

Navaro-Yashin, Yael. 2002. *Faces of the State: Secularism and Public Life in Turkey*. Princeton: Princeton University Press.

Otayek, R., and S. Soares (eds). 2007. *Islam and Muslim Politics in Africa*. New York: Palgrave Macmillan.

Robinson, Francis. 2001. *The Ulama of Farangi Mahal and Islamic Culture in South Asia*. Delhi: Permanent Black.

———. 2008. 'Islamic Reform and Modernities in South Asia', *Modern Asian Studies*, 42: 259–81.

Rosanvallon, Pierre. 2008. *Counter-democracy Politics in an Age of Distrust.* Massachusetts: Harvard University Press.

Roy, O. 2004. *Globalised Islam: The Search for a New Ummah.* London: Hurst.

Sanyal, Usha. 1999. *Devotional Islam and Politics in British India: Ahmed Riza Khan Barelwi and His Movement, 1870–1920.* New Delhi: Oxford University Press.

Schielk, Samuli. 2009. 'Being Good in Ramadan: Ambivalence, Fragmentation, and the Moral Self in the Lives of Young Egyptians', *Journal of the Royal Anthropological Institute,* 15: S24–S40.

Shameem, Muhammed. 2007. 'Vikasanam, Paristhiti, Islam', in A. A. Haleem (ed.), *Vikasanam, Paristhiti Aagola Muthalalitham* (Malayalam), pp. 101–23. Calicut: Solidarity Youth Movement.

Shehabuddin, Elora. 2008. *Reshaping the Holy: Democracy, Development, and Muslim Women in Bangladesh.* New York: Coliumbia University Press.

Sikand, Y. 2002. *The Origins and Development of the Tablighi-Jama'at (1920–2000).* New Delhi: Orient Longman.

Troll, C. W. (ed.). 1989. *Muslim Shrines in India.* Delhi: Oxford University Press.

van der Veer, Peter. 2002. 'Religion in South Asia', *Annual Review of Anthropology* 31: 173–87.

Uberoi, J. P. S. 2003. 'Civil Society', in Veena Das (ed.), *The Oxford India Companion to Sociology and Social Anthropology,* pp. 122–23. Oxford University Press: New Delhi.

Zaman, M. Q. 2002. *The Ulama in Contemporary Islam: Custodians of Change.* Princeton, NJ: Princeton University Press.

6

Adjudication of Personal Law and the Question of Secularity

An Analysis of Judicial Practice in the Sharia Adalats of Uttar Pradesh

Suchandra Ghosh and **Anindita Chakrabarti**

Through an ethnography of *dar-ul-qaza* or sharia *adalats*,[1] this essay attempts to unpack the process of adjudication of Muslim personal law in India where the state, religious as well as local-level bodies assess different rights and duties to resolve family/civil disputes. The emergent plural adjudication system raises important questions for the concept of secularity as multiple forums arbitrate on the question of family/civil law based on religious affiliation. The Muslim personal law in India has had a long history of reform. In the post-Independence period, the key issue has revolved around reconciling majoritarian governance and citizenship rights with the civil freedom of the religious minority groups. Balancing between the claims for national unity on the one hand, and upholding plurality and difference on the other has always resulted in the mutually exclusive choice between personal law and demands for a uniform civil code (UCC). In this essay, we argue that it is only by drawing our attention to how the adjudication of personal law actually takes place in contemporary India that we can begin to think beyond this sharp binary. The ethnography of dispute resolution at a dar-ul-qaza suggests how a close collocation between civil and religious forums guides the adjudication of personal law and thereby decentres some of the assumptions regarding personal law in India.

We begin by drawing attention to the fact that the concept of justice in the context of personal law is not a straightforward one. It dwells on the fault lines of rights and trust/affect. The predicament is captured in Béteille's (2012: 109) argument that while the subject of right is encoded in the rules and one can resort to a court of justice in case of a breach, trust is implicit, and once it is breached, one does not know to whom one should turn. Adjudication of personal law best exemplifies this situation. The breach of trust and its redressal are never a straightforward movement to the courts of justice. Personal law covers marriage, divorce, inheritance and custody, and here rights remain entwined in the language of duties and affect. We argue that before we bring further changes in Muslim personal law, we need to understand the functioning of the law, the litigants' perception of the disputes and how they resolve them.

We found that as petitioners brought their disputes to local bodies, sharia courts as well as at civil and family courts, their legal praxis created a space of inter-legality. Petitioners approached very different forums of adjudication in order to address and resolve different types of 'personal' disputes/troubles. At times, a particular forum evoked the authority of another to resolve a case. Yet, as Redding (2014) has observed, an over appreciation of the 'rule of law' principle in legal scholarship has led to a disparagement of non-state law. As a result, the actual mechanism and the procedures of law in the venues outside secular courts have remained unattended (ibid.: 962). However, in recent years, a body of research has focused on how legal practice is localised and decentralised by multiple legal actors including a number of non-state actors (Lemons 2010; Solanki 2011; Vatuk 2017). These non-judicial actors range from political parties and trade unions to local *mahila mandals* and *seva ashrams*,[2] to list a few (Suneetha and Nagaraj 2006: 4357–58). We take this research as our starting point and illustrate how litigants, especially women, access a range of non-state institutions, in our case dar-ul-qaza, as and when they deem appropriate.

How do we understand the concept of agency in this context? How do the litigants exercise their agency in dealing with their personal problems and negotiating strained personal relations? Vatuk (2001: 228) has shown how the societal ethos of paternalism pervades the judicial reasoning at family courts where the judges are more eager to save the institution of marriage than the woman. Vatuk (2017: 32) has argued that the problems that the women face in their personal lives are not essentially due to law—however imperfect and inaccurately implemented they may be—but they lie in the 'cultural configurations of gender and law and their relationship to state'. The 'Muslim woman' of the legal texts is embedded in her local, social context of *biradari*,[3] class and sectarian differentiations. In this essay, we show how a litigant perceives the legal or moral nature of a dispute and chooses a tribunal for redressal/guidance. Her legal choice is also informed by the economic and social milieu she inhabits just as they influence the decision-making at the different forums of dispute resolution.

Analysing some of the cases brought to dar-ul-qazas over a two-year period, and drawing on interviews with lawyers and judges at the civil and family courts of Kanpur, the essay shows how and why petitioners decide to approach a particular court and how cases get resolved, many a time, in collocation between the secular and religious forums. We found that a decisive majority of the cases at the dar-ul-qaza were appeals by women petitioners for divorce, maintenance and complaints against their affines. Many cases were also brought to address the validity or licitness of marriage as well as divorce. The findings give us an insight into how the 'personal law' of religious minorities works within the judicial structure of a secular nation state. The process of adjudication of personal disputes, we argue, has important lessons for understanding the concept of secularity in a democratic state, marked by plurality and difference. Concomitantly, the linkage and the collocation between the 'courts of justice' as they adjudicate on kinship, affect and household economics raise new questions on religious rights, citizenship and secularity.

The fieldwork for this study was conducted primarily at the Deoband-affiliated dar-ul-qaza of Kanpur. At the same time, a few cases were followed at the Farangi Mahal and Nadwatu'l-'Ulama (Nadwah) of Lucknow, and at the family and the civil courts of Kanpur.[4] The disputes, whether they involved marriage, divorce, inheritance or vicious quarrels between a woman and her husband's sister, followed an interesting pattern.[5] Analysing the cases, we attempt to understand how in a secular democracy, the process of dispute resolution is shared by religious adjudication forums and the state. This essay emphasises the need to understand legal praxis and its multi-vocality in order to address the issue of judicial reform of Muslim personal law. The *suo motu* public interest litigation (PIL) brought by the Supreme Court on the issue of gender discrimination suffered by Muslim women due to practices such as triple talaq and polygamy, and the subsequent judgement in August 2017 that invalidated triple talaq, form the backdrop of the fieldwork.

The essay is divided into the three sections. The first section maps the religious and secular adjudication structure in the city of Kanpur. Here, we pay attention to the emerging informal units within the secular legal landscape and the procedural aspects of the sharia courts. The second section attempts to understand how certain disputes are brought to the dar-ul-qazas as the litigants perceive them as problems that can be resolved only at this forum. Yet, many cases get curiously tangled with other judicial forums. The third section looks into this crossover and dialogue between the religious forum and the secular forum of the family/civil courts—the functioning of dar-ul-qazas and their linkages with the judicial units. At times, the collocation is intended, either by the court or the litigants, but in other cases, the crossover to different forums is unintended and contingent. In the concluding section, we raise the question of secularity as it unfolds in the context of personal law and the plural legal landscape in India.

The Structure of Adjudication Sites: Sharia Adalats and Civil Courts

The judicial system in India has a well-defined hierarchical structure. It has the Supreme Court at its apex, followed by the high courts and the district courts. The district courts have their criminal, civil and family courts, and each of these juridical units is further constituted of the parent and additional courts. A dispute, when brought to a family/civil court, is registered at a parent court where it is heard for the first time. Depending on a case and the burden of cases on a parent court, the judge refers the case to one of the additional courts. In the Kanpur District Court, there are five parent courts. The family court settles marriage, divorce, maintenance and custody disputes. Here we would like to mention that by the Family Court Act 1984, a *vakil* (advocate representing a party before the judge) is not required. Yet, as a practising advocate of the Kanpur Family Court remarked, suitors are generally unaware of the legalities of the court proceedings and, therefore, prefer to hire lawyers.[6] In recent times, in the matters of family dispute, there has been an emphasis towards mediation rather than litigation in family courts. Along with the courts, a mediation unit, a *lok adalat*[7] and a *mahila thana* (all-women police station) function to resolve family disputes. Civil suits that are considered to be solved through mediation are also referred to the mediation unit.

Mediation in matrimonial cases follows a definite trajectory. After a case is registered at the family court, if a judge feels that it can be solved through counselling, it is referred to a mediation centre. Resolution through mediation is a preferred form of judicial settlement, where relief is drawn up by mutual consent of the suitors. A mediator negotiates a *samjhauta* (agreement) between the parties, on which the court gives a decree. But, at times, mediation yields no result, and the case is then dismissed and reverted to the court for hearings. Mediators are practising lawyers of the district court. No remuneration/salary is paid for this work. There is a sense of recognition, and the mediators anticipate that in the near future, some remuneration will be allocated for this work.[8]

The lok adalat is constituted under Section 22 of the Legal Services Act 1987, and is functional once in a month, usually on the last Sunday.[9] It decrees in those disputes that have already been solved by out-of-court settlements. It looks into matrimonial and property cases, but delivers judgements after hearing a case only once. The mediation unit of the Kanpur District Court, also known as the *mahila paramarsh kendra*, functions to expedite the judicial process. Headed by a district judge, the Kanpur unit operates two hours daily, from three to five in the afternoon, and it is functional on all the weekdays.

The mahila thana is a unit affiliated to the state police department that looks into the cases of family disputes brought by women, including those of domestic violence.[10] The regular employees of the police department, social workers and non-governmental organisation (NGO) personnel serve as mediators. Cases that are perceived to be resolved through counselling are considered here for settlement. If the mahila thana fails to mediate between the parties, cases are referred to the mediation unit of the local family court. Drawing attention to the less bureaucratic and informal adjudication structures and their functioning, we note the inter-play of formality and informality in the current judicial system. The dar-ul-qazas, on the other hand, despite having no legal recognition, follow a structured litigation procedure. While the rigour of court procedure is comparable with the state courts, they work with a different judicial and moral logic as they adjudicate disputes in family matters.

At the dar-ul-qaza, the qazi's[11] service is considered as a part-time, voluntary work. We were told that the dar-ul-qaza operates on the principle of *iman* (faith), and thereby in performing his task, a qazi offers *khuda ka khidmat* (religious service), and that his aim is not to earn a living (*saadat ka rah doosra hai*). Before a qazi is appointed, it is verified that an incumbent has a decent income so that he does not fall prey to financial corruption. The dar-ul-qaza accepts only a fixed nominal fee from the petitioners. The Deoband dar-ul-qaza in Kanpur is located on Rizvi Road of Parade Chauraha, half a mile away from the district court and the mahila thana in the city.[12] Both the qazi and his assistant officiating at the dar-ul-qaza were trained at Dar al-Ulum Deoband, an Islamic seminary of higher learning in Deoband, Uttar Pradesh. We were told that after acquiring his degree as alim (an expert in Islamic law and theology), the qazi also underwent a year-long training at Imarat-e-Shariah, Patna, Bihar. Established in 2002, the dar-ul-qaza operates under the name Mahkama-E-Shareeya and is located in a large Muslim ghetto in downtown Kanpur.

Unlike the state judiciary, there is no clear appellate structure in sharia adalats. But a litigant who is dissatisfied with a dar-ul-qaza judgement can either appeal for a review of the verdict at *sadar* (national headquarters of the same legal school) or take his/her case to a popular legal school (for instance, Farangi Mahal or Nadwah) for re-examination. In Lucknow, we followed cases at Farangi Mahal.[13] The dar-ul-qaza is functional twice a week and its popular *dar-ul-ifta*[14] not only responds to those who physically approach them for fatwa, but also to those who reach them via email.[15] Over a period of time, we found that a network of local imams, *muftis*[16] and the heads of the neighbourhood (mohalla) panchayats work in close alliance with the dar-ul-qaza. In the course of *tahqiqat* (investigation) of a case registered at his court, the qazi often gets in touch with an imam from the neighbourhood where the petitioner belongs. This is based on the assumption that the imam of a mosque in a neighbourhood is usually aware (*'kaun kitna pani me hai'*) of those residing in its vicinity. Local information is gathered in order to find out about the petitioners and their disputes. An imam is sometimes part of the mohalla panchayat that settles disputes through *salisi* (arbitration). Besides, other local notables and influential persons, whom petitioners may also deem fit to mediate, are inducted at the mohalla level. However, compliance to such settlement depends on the discretion of the petitioners. When issues are complex and the council perceives that problem-solving is unlikely, it may refuse to intervene and refer the case to a sharia adalat or a state court.

The sharia adalat in Kanpur functions on all days of the week, except *juma* (Friday). On the weekdays, petitioners visit the sharia adalat for *zubani maslah* (enquiry) on their cases, register new complaints or submit documents, while on Sundays, the cases are heard. On an average, the sharia adalat hears five to six cases on a particular day.[17] The preferred written language of these sharia adalats is Urdu, though they accept claims and petitions in Hindi. There are no stenographers at the sharia adalats, but recently it has installed a computer to type out the final verdicts of the cases.

What is the judicial procedure at these dar-ul-qazas? It approximately takes two to three hearings to solve a case. But, sometimes, a case can get settled in a single hearing. It was said that the solutions are sought according to the guiding principles laid out in the Quran and Hadith. At first, a written petition is submitted. The contact details of the defendant are noted down to intimate him/her about the complaint. Subsequently, a summons is sent to the defendant to appear before the dar-ul-qaza.[18] However, if a *fariq* (party) to a lawsuit intends to delay the judicial process, he/she might evade accepting the summon order. Then the dar-ul-qaza sends a messenger to inform that the party is required to be present at the dar-ul-qaza. The respondents are urged to report within a maximum of 15 days from the date of receiving the summon order. In a divorce case, if the defendant refuses to receive the summons, the dar-ul-qaza can issue an *ex parte* order to settle the case. But the dar-ul-qaza adopts such a measure only after following the due procedure, which includes notification in the local Urdu dailies.[19]

At the court, both the plaintiff and the defendant are called to testify their respective accounts of a case submitted to the dar-ul-qaza, and they come with their witnesses. The dar-ul-qazas have defined a set of qualifications for its witnesses. A witness in a case can never be an immediate kin of the litigants. Yet, he/she should be well informed about a dispute and the petitioners. The witness must also belong to the same neighbourhood/village as that of the suitor. The judicial procedure at the dar-ul-qaza privileges oral testimony over written documents. When written documents are presented, they have to be validated by witnesses. This makes it imperative to affirm the probity and reliability of the witness. Further, there is a standard process of verification. At the start of an interrogation, a witness is cautioned not to lie to the dar-ul-qaza, as lying at this premise is like making false admissions at a mosque. Next, the witness's relationship to the suitor is enquired into. At a dar-ul-qaza, a vakil (person representing a case before the qazi on behalf of the litigant) can be present, but unlike in civil courts, the vakil is not a lawyer.[20] Here, the parties present their respective accounts and verification is done with help of the witnesses. Litigants sometimes seek judicial review in cases that have already been tried and decided by a dar-ul-qaza. We were told that appeals for a review of judgements could be made at the Deoband dar-ul-qaza of Zakir Nagar, Delhi.[21]

To understand the process of adjudication, we need to understand that in both the state courts and the dar-ul-qazas, the question of winning or losing treads the delicate terrain of affect and kinship. In both the forums, as the structure of the civil judiciary suggests, litigants are encouraged to explore the possibility of solving their case through discussion and negotiation. In civil/family courts, when a judge sees the prospect of resolution through negotiation rather than by *bahs karna* (arguments), the case is forwarded to a mediation unit. Figure 6.1 captures the structure of the courts with its multiple forums for redressing family disputes, and also shows that these multiple forums operate alongside other informal dispute-resolution systems such as the dar-ul-qazas. The following section explores how litigants decide on the appropriateness of a forum for dispute resolution.

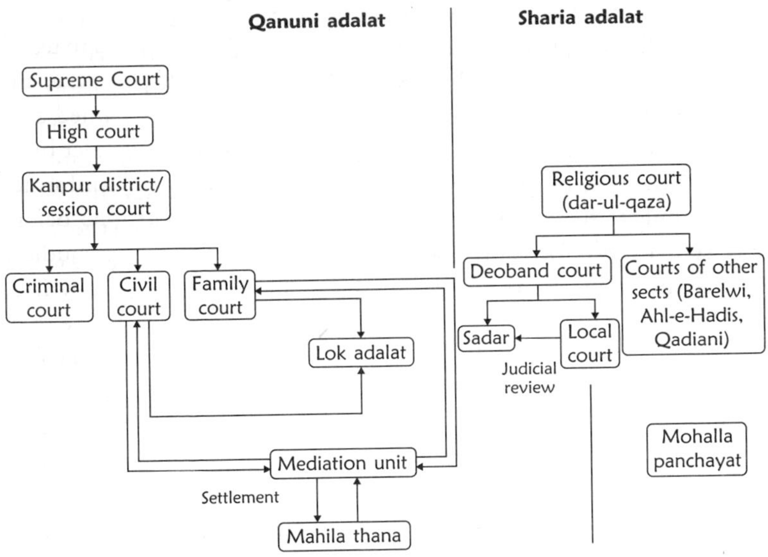

Source: Compiled by the authors.

Figure 6.1 *Structure of the Courts*

It addresses the question: When and why do litigants decide to approach a dar-ul-qaza? Here, we focus on the cases and the disputes that are brought before the dar-ul-qaza, and the petitioners' expectations from the judicial forum.

Appropriate Adjudication Sites: Why Come to a Dar-ul-qaza?

During the first few visits to the family court in Kanpur, the lawyers we interviewed informed that there were very few 'Muslim cases' at the civil/family courts. During her next visit, Ghosh met a young Muslim woman, Nazma Biwi, who was withdrawing her case from the family court.[22] She wanted her maintenance claim to be adjudicated with the mediation of the local imam of the mosque where she had her *nikah* (marriage). She believed that she would get a favourable settlement at this tribunal, as the people who would be adjudicating knew her well. She said that her case was subjudice at the family court for seven years.[23] The decision to revert to the mosque committee of her neighbourhood was informed by her familiarity with the judicial setting. She felt that it was a forum where she could participate and negotiate. We frequently noticed manoeuvring between the tribunals, especially in matrimonial disputes and sometimes also in cases of property disputes. But there were also cases where the petitioners deemed the sharia adalat to be the appropriate forum and resolved their problems at this site. In this section, we discuss cases that were brought only to the dar-ul-qazas and the modalities by which the cases were settled. We focus on the rationale adduced by the petitioners for the choice of the tribunal and the manner in which the qazis resolved the disputes.

Women often approach dar-ul-qazas to obtain marriage dissolution. By *khula,* a wife appeals (*mutalva*) for divorce to her husband and in lieu has to let go her mahr and *nafaka* due to her in *iddat.*[24] While it is not mandatory to come to a dar-ul-qaza to plead for khula, she is often compelled to seek mediation of a qazi due to her husband's reluctance to respond to her divorce appeals. When the qazi is convinced that the husband is withholding khula to harass his wife and is not committed to the relationship, or does not have the capacity/intention to fulfill the duties to his wife, he takes the initiative and dissolves the marriage by *faskh*.[25] We found several cases where women petitioners approached the dar-ul-qaza for marriage dissolution by faskh. In a case, a woman plaintiff deposed that two years ago, her husband had abandoned her along with her children, and that he had not come back since. Her marriage, she described, had been fraught with financial difficulties. Whenever she tried to compel her husband to work harder or earn more, the latter retaliated by threatening to abandon her. One day, he left her with the children at her natal home. Allegedly, he had repudiated the marriage before leaving and had forcibly taken away her jewellery and kept them in his sister's custody. The dar-ul-qaza accepted her plea and initiated the proceeding to investigate the case. Although the plaintiff was unaware of her husband's whereabouts, the court sent a summon order to the man's sister's place. His parents were dead and his elder sister was called by the qazi. The sister declared that her brother was missing for the past few years and that she did not have any information or knowledge of him. The court in order to be absolutely certain and then take a call on the marriage, asked the plaintiff to produce two witnesses who could support her claim. She brought her brother and his wife as witnesses, while her parents corroborated their account.[26] The court then directed the plaintiff and her family to publish a search notice for the husband in a local Urdu daily. The qazi advised her to circulate the newspaper advertisement among the husband's relatives, friends and acquaintances. The procedure was carried out and her husband was still untraceable. The plaintiff was a young woman with small children, and her parents expressed their inability to support her for long. Her brother had supported her for some time, but the qazi perceived that the existing financial arrangement was not sufficient to sustain her. He revoked the marriage. While this was a case where the woman wanted a divorce, in other cases women approached the qazi to resolve dilemmas emerging from a threat (or pronouncement) of divorce.

We found a few cases emerging from the issue of the 'triple talaq' pronouncement. A woman deposed at Farangi Mahal, Lucknow, seeking a fatwa. She said, following a quarrel with her husband, she began to fret and refused to eat. It infuriated her husband who threatened that if she would stop eating after every fight, he would divorce her. Since he repeated the threat several times, she was apprehensive whether it had revoked their marriage. The fatwa that was issued stated that talaq did not take place. The mufti explained that the husband had only threatened and not issued talaq: The husband had no of intention of divorcing his wife; he used threat to discipline her. But if it was a threat, why did they bother to come to Farangi Mahal to clarify? The wife responded to Ghosh by explaining that marriage was not just a relationship between two individuals but here Allah was the witness. Ibada (worship) does not merely imply keeping fasts, offering namaz and paying zakat (annual donation as per Islamic law). It encompasses the everyday life of an individual. In an event of talaq pronouncement, it is the responsibility of the couple to accept the pronouncement and separate. By accepting the annulment, the couple fulfills a farz (duty) to God.

In another case, the wife had left her marital home with her children after a fight with her husband. She moved in with her parents. During their separation, the husband, in a fit of rage, fuelled by alcohol, pronounced talaq over the phone. But as he calmed down, he realised his mistake and wanted her back. Even his wife wanted to reunite. But the man's father-in-law had overheard him pronouncing talaq and compelled him to consult a cleric for a verdict on the status of their marriage. The couple came to Farangi Mahal for a fatwa. The couple looked nervous as they sat in a corner of the dar-ul-qaza with their two children. The question for the fatwa was sent inside, and when the mufti appeared to declare the fatwa, the husband looked repentant and remorseful.[27] He admitted having pronounced talaq in a state of inebriation. He was not in his consciousness as he pronounced talaq and did not even remember how many times he said it. The mufti cognised the husband's lack of intent behind the pronouncement, and with a sharp rebuke for indulging in alcohol, he dismissed the case with a fatwa. The couple was encouraged to renew their marriage as the dar-ul-ifta judged the pronouncement as 'a babble under influence of alcohol'.

Understanding divorce in Islam is contingent on comprehending nikah as a religious contract that is embedded in a network of rights and duties with God as the ultimate embodiment of the relationship (Bowen 2012). From this standpoint, partners entering a nuptial tie oblige the divine by following the terms of the contract, and in conforming to these principles, they live their faith (ibid.: 145). We were told that it is a man's responsibility to provide *khan-pan* (food), *ghar-makan* (shelter) and *gosalbzi ki farz/haq pe zauziyat* (sex). Impotency is a legitimate *vajah* (ground) on which women appeal for divorce at the dar-ul-qaza. A case was brought to the Kanpur dar-ul-qaza where despite repeated denials by the husband (defendant), the qazi believed the plaintiff's complaint of impotency against her husband. In this case, medical reports were sought by the qazi for *tahqiq talav* (investigation). The dar-ul-qaza made it clear that it would judge the case based on the medical reports. When the reports were presented, the qazi consulted them and granted divorce. Though medical reports were considered as the most important evidence in this case, other cases followed a very different trajectory where they were not even asked for. The settlement was in favour of the wife as the dar-ul-qaza ruled for divorce. A few other cases on similar grounds were reported to the dar-ul-qaza, but it did not always consider medical reports as adequate evidence for adjudication.

In another case (in which the couple were parallel cousins before their marriage), the wife stated that they never had a physical relationship, and her husband sat in silence.[28] The qazi interpreted the man's silence as evidence of the charge. He did not oppose the divorce either. In this case, the qazi did not ask for any medical reports, although the woman had persuaded her husband to undergo tests after experiencing sexual inaction in their marriage. Though remedial measures were suggested by the doctor, the man did not seek any medical help. At this point, the wife returned to her parents and decided to file for divorce. Judging the complaints and the case circumstance, the qazi ruled a divorce. The man's father expressed apprehension over the mention of impotency in the *talaqnama* (divorce agreement in written form). He requested the qazi to mention some other complaint (*ittafaqi ki vajah*) as the basis of divorce. The qazi scolded the defendant for marrying even after knowing his physical infirmity and cited a verse from the Quran to educate him on how it is a duty, in case of incapacity, to control one's urges than marry and ruin another life. While pronouncing the verdict, the qazi asked the defendant to pay the mahr and nafaka that were due to the woman.

Citing his inadequate income, the husband's family members requested him to bring down the amount. A lengthy negotiation between the parties ensued.

Petitioners come to the dar-ul-qaza with the expectation of mediation in family quarrels. A middle-aged woman came to the dar-ul-qaza in Kanpur with her brother over a conflict with her sister-in-law (brother's wife). She complained that her sister-in-law did not fulfill her duties to her in-laws. We understood what constituted the 'duties' as she elaborated on the flaws on her sister-in-law—how her sister-in-law would not do the household chores and was not respectful towards her in-laws. While mentioning this, the plaintiff showed a scar on her hand, alleging that her sister-in-law had hit her. Further, she complained that her sister-in-law would often leave home (*bhagti hai*) on frivolous grounds and move in with her parents. The real ground of contention, however, was that the sister-in-law wanted to live separately with her husband and their child. From the qazi's inquiry, it emerged that while the brother earned for the family, the finances were managed and controlled by his sister. The dar-ul-qaza wanted to hear the sister-in-law's version of the case, and the sister-in-law responded to the dar-ul-qaza's summon.

On the day of hearing, the parties came to dar-ul-qaza with their respective parents. The sister, the plaintiff in this case, argued that her family was concerned for her brother's child. She raised the concern that her sister-in-law often ate from her nephew's share of food. This annoyed the qazi. He scolded her saying that a mother is always concerned about her child's well-being and so was her sister-in-law. He advised the plaintiff to focus on the well-being of her sister-in-law and her child. When she tried drawing attention to her sister-in-law's behaviour, the wife argued that the plaintiff and her mother were excessively intrusive in her marital relationship.[29] They imposed many restrictions on her, even on her eating habits and physical movements. The court inferred that the plaintiff and her mother were interfering in the relationship between the couple. Apprehensive that their constant interference might further harm the couple's relationship, the qazi advised the husband to find an accommodation on rent and set up a separate household with his wife and child. To the defendant, he advised that she should stay at her in-law's place for a week and see if she could adjust. If not, she should call up and report, and then accordingly, the qazi would decide on the marriage. It became clear that the qazi did not place much importance on the plaintiff's charge. During the course of the hearing it emerged that two of the plaintiff's brothers had moved out and were living with their wives and children. She was apprehensive that this brother might do the same. He was the only earning member in the household and the family depended on him. The *ray* (judgement) did not satisfy the sister, who wanted the qazi to chastise her sister-in-law and also make suggestions to discipline her. The qazi's suggestion that the couple should shift to a separate household created a stir in the room where the hearing was taking place.

Later, the assistant qazi explained to us that according to Islam, a daughter-in-law has no obligation to take care of her in-laws. It is by virtue of her *ikhlaq* (conduct) that she looks after his parents. Rather it is a husband's obligation to provide for the wife (food, sex and shelter) and look after her well-being. Nevertheless, it is a son's responsibility to look after his parents and also his sister in the absence of their father. It so turned out that the qazi's verdict disciplined the sister, not the sister-in-law.[30] The case was a matrimonial conflict but the real contestants were the sister and the wife. The husband was a silent spectator, seeking restoration of the marriage.[31] We found a pattern where conflicts routinely arose over the control and the management of family *kharcha* (finances). In her claims for maintenance, the wife often identified the sister-in-law as an adversary rather than the husband.

The dar-ul-qaza deliberates and adjudicates on maintenance in marriage.[32] Yet it is argued that it lacks the authority to enforce financial settlements (Lemons 2010: 31). Nevertheless, we found petitioners approaching the dar-ul-qaza for maintenance settlements after decrees had been issued at a state tribunal. A petitioner came to Farangi Mahal for non-payment of the maintenance that was settled by the local mahila thana. She alleged that her husband had promised to comply with the maintenance ruling, but very soon, the maintenance was discontinued. At the dar-ul-qaza, she identified her sister-in-law as the adversary, complaining that her husband was under the influence of his sister and that following his sister's advice, he had stopped all communications with her and their daughters. Her husband was settled in Saudi Arabia. The petitioner pleaded before the qazi to allot a higher emolument as monthly maintenance and issue an order to effectuate a regular payment of the amount. In this case, we saw that as the mahila thana failed to enforce a regular payment of her maintenance, the petitioner appealed at the dar-ul-qaza.

Women also come to the dar-ul-qaza to claim their share in property as well as to seek clarity on the question of their quranic share. They sometimes also seek the qazi's intervention in property distribution. An elderly woman came to the dar-ul-qaza with her daughter. She told the qazi that her two elder sons had unfairly acquired a major share of their father's property. They took over their father's transport business and ousted the younger brother from it. They had also got the ancestral house registered in their names. She lamented that neither her daughters-in-law nor her sons took care of her. She had five daughters, and except the youngest one, all were married. She was worried for her youngest daughter and, therefore, had decided to come to the dar-ul-qaza to ask for the daughter's share in the family inheritance. She wanted a redistribution of her husband's property. She said that she was unwell and did not want to go to the civil court. The daughter interjected to point out that if they took recourse to the civil court, by the time the judgement came, their mother might be dead without having the resources for treatment and care. The mother informed that she had consulted her sons before approaching the dar-ul-qaza and they had agreed to her proposal of redistributing the property in consultation with the qazi. The assistant qazi calculated the property share of the different members in the family. A one-eighth share was assigned to the plaintiff. The rest of the property was also divided: two-thirds of the property was for the sons, and the daughters were given a one-third share each.

We found that the sharia adalat was also a legal site where women petitioners came to appeal for what they perceived a breach of haqq (right).[33] They appealed to the moral authority of the qazi, drawing attention to the (mis)conduct of family member(s). A case was brought to the sharia adalat in Kanpur after a verdict had been passed by the civil court in the city. The dispute was over an old house. The civil suit was originally filed by the plaintiff's sister's son who was also her step-son. The plaintiff had married her sister's husband when she died. Her sister had a son and a daughter and she had four children. Legally, the house belonged to her sister as her husband had gifted it to her before she died. Following the rules of inheritance, the civil ruling had favoured her sister's children. The plaintiff was upset with the verdict as she felt deprived of the share in her husband's property. She approached the qazi with the argument that she had raised her sister's children as her own. She appealed for a property settlement that would guarantee an equitable share of the property to the children from both the marriages and also mentioned that she was looking after her ailing husband and hardly had any source of income. The qazi observed that the civil ruling in this case was in consonance with Islamic law. He decided to refer her case to the neighbourhood mosque so that, taking cognisance of her situation, the local imam could intervene and influence the parties to come to an agreement through compromise.[34] The trajectory of the case, from the *qanuni adalat* (civil court) to the dar-ul-qaza and finally to the mohalla mosque committee, shows how plaintiffs approach different forums to address and resolve personal disputes and claim their rights—legal as well as moral. This inter-linkage we map in greater detail in the following section.

Dar-ul-qaza and Civil Court: Inter-linkages and Collocation

In this section, we examine how cases are often subjected to legal scrutiny at both dar-ul-qazas and courts. This legal pluralism could either be initiated by the litigant or emerge as a requirement of the judicial procedure. At times, procedural requirements make it necessary for a sharia adalat to seek help from a secular legal institution. On other occasions, the court is approached for its enforceable authority. In this section, we discuss how a complex pattern of inter-legality is set in motion, as litigants seek resolution and redressal on matters ranging from family quarrels to bitter property disputes between brothers.

In a *virasat* (inheritance) case brought to the sharia adalat of Kanpur, a property obtained through inheritance had to be divided between the legal heirs of the deceased (four daughters, two sons and the wife).[35] The qazi examined the competing claims in 'the light of sharia' and delivered a decree. Devolution of property followed. But one of the sisters was dissatisfied with the verdict and she approached the Kanpur Civil Court. However, the civil court judge (as narrated by the qazi) became aware of the dar-ul-qaza's adjudication on the case. He summoned the judgement and enforced it.[36] This case shows the importance given to sharia judgement at a civil court in inheritance cases. On the other hand, there are cases that follow a reverse trajectory, from the civil court to the dar-ul-qaza, as the latter was considered to be a more appropriate forum by the civil court judge.

We followed a case that was initially registered at the Kanpur Civil Court, but subsequently got resolved at the dar-ul-qaza. The dispute was over property. A man claimed that he had bought a house in Kanpur city in his younger brother's name and this he did to escape tax liability. Since his brother was not employed at that time, he got the property registered in his name. A few years later, the brothers decided to prepare a wasiyatnama (will) for the property transfer, to avoid the expense of re-registration.[37] Later, when the property value escalated, the younger brother, unable to resist the possession of the property, denied the wasiyatnama. This prompted the elder brother to file a case at the Kanpur Civil Court. During the court proceedings, he stated that if his younger brother could swear in the name of Allah that the property belonged to him, he would relinquish his claim over it. At this point, the judge said that if the siblings were to settle the case through *qasm* (oath taking), they should take their case to a sharia court and bring the verdict to the civil court.[38] In this case, the court's perception of what could be a reasonable and satisfying judicial procedure from the litigants' point of view determined the appositeness of the legal forum.

We reconstructed the case from the elder brother's submission on the dispute at the dar-ul-qaza. The elder brother registered a fresh suit at the Kanpur dar-ul-qaza. Next, a summon order was sent to the younger brother to report at the dar-ul-qaza. Although the younger brother initially refused to appear, later he responded to the order. The qazi decided on the dispute, and both the plaintiff and the defendant accepted its verdict. The elder brother had claimed earlier that his brother had not invested in the property at all, but when they came together at the dar-ul-qaza, the elder brother was silent as the younger brother refuted his claim. The qazi perceived his *khamoshi* (silence) as evidence of the younger brother's shared ownership of the property. After long discussions, which involved bargaining and negotiation between the brothers, the qazi pronounced the decision. While a 60 per cent share of the property was allotted to the elder brother, the remaining 40 per cent was given to the younger brother. At the beginning of the arbitration, the qazi made the parties sign an agreement that they would accept and comply with its judgement. The dispute was settled, and the petitioners submitted a copy of this settlement to withdraw the civil suit.

We found that in certain cases, the appeal for marriage dissolution at the dar-ul-qaza involves the court's intervention. This intervention is used to exert pressure on a recalcitrant party to appear before the dar-ul-qaza. In this context, the court acts as a disciplining agent. This happened in a khula case registered with the dar-ul-qaza of Kanpur. The case dragged at the dar-ul-qaza for two years due to non-cooperation from the husband, until the qazi advised the wife to take the case to a family court. The qazi justified his advice by stating that as the husband was ignoring the summons from the dar-ul-qaza, the order from the civil court would compel him to respond. But at this point, the deliberations took an unexpected turn. The qazi asked the wife to write down the gifts that she wanted to recover from her in-laws, but she refused to draw this list. She told the qazi:

> I am already fighting a civil suit on the same dispute and these proceedings (as you know) are full of fake claims (*qanunan me jhooth hota hai*). The legal notice has my statement that I left my jewellery at my in-law's place. But, here, if I am asked to submit a list of the items that are with my in-laws, I can only make a true claim, which then will contradict my legal notice. I am apprehensive that if the dar-ul-qaza document reaches my adversaries, my civil case will be jeopardised.

At this point, it was revealed that the plaintiff had already lodged a dowry harassment complaint under Section 498A of the criminal procedure code (CrPC).[39] The husband did not appear at the dar-ul-qaza. Finally, after waiting for six months and publishing a notification in the local Urdu daily, the qazi dissolved the marriage by invoking faskh.

Another case where the wife had complained of domestic violence and registered Section 498A of the CrPC against the husband was brought to the dar-ul-qaza. The charge of domestic violence was against the husband. But during the hearing, the wife began to sob. At this point, the qazi took her to a quiet corner of the room where she was asked to narrate her problems. She said that the real culprit was not her husband but her father-in-law. She alledged that he had made attempts to sexually harass her. She gave the example of him peeping into the bathroom while she was taking a bath. Her husband was unwilling to take action against his father. While weeping in the corner of the room, she told the qazi that she was relieved that she could finally express the 'real' problem in her marriage. Because of family honour and social prestige, she could not articulate her real marital trouble. The qazi advised her that the couple should set up their own residence. As with this case, women often felt that they could freely express their problems without apprehending moral threat or worrying about the legal merit of their argument.

Sometimes, adjudication can become unduly complex because of a procedural lapse. A wife had appealed for divorce at a dar-ul-qaza of Nadwah. As the qazi found the husband unnecessarily delaying the case, he invoked faskh and released the wife from her conjugal tie. After she observed iddat, her husband, who so far had not responded to the qazi's summons, appeared at the dar-ul-qaza and contested the divorce. He submitted a petition stating that he was unaware of the marriage dissolution appeals and, therefore, would not accept it. At this point, it emerged that prior to filing her divorce appeal at the sharia court, the wife had registered charges of domestic violence and dowry harassment against her husband at the Allahabad Family Court. Since the summons were not received by the husband, the dar-ul-qaza needed to put up a notice in the Urdu newspapers before invoking faskh. The qazi, therefore, reopened the case for a fresh hearing from his side. The husband agreed to the divorce, but on the condition that she withdraw all the charges from the Allahabad Family Court. She readily agreed. The qazi was disappointed to hear that the plaintiff had also approached the family court with her dispute and had not disclosed it. The case shows the judicial procedure of the dar-ul-qaza and how a lapse in this procedure led to the reopening of the case.

Apart from the property dispute case between the brothers, in a few other cases too we saw how the civil/family courts value the judgements of the dar-ul-qaza in their decision-making. When a Lucknow Family Court judge heard that a parallel adjudication was taking place at Nadwah, he decided to wait for the latter's verdict. Yet, despite a ruling by the civil court (after a settlement was made) that no more petitions should be filed on the same dispute at any other court, sometimes cases were filed at the dar-ul-qaza. In all likelihood, such 'legal forum shopping' is not informed to the judicial authorities. But conversely, when a case is filed at a dar-ul-qaza, the qazi tries to find out either directly from the suitors or indirectly through its own networks if any suit is already filed on the same dispute at any other court. Solanki (2011: 280) has noted how petitioners approaching the dar-ul-qaza are required to sign a consent form stating that they have approached the judicial unit on their own and they agree to abide by its decisions. Dar-ul-qazas also expect petitioners not to approach a state court for a fresh plea in a case that has already been settled at a sharia adalat. But, in our field, we have found that at times the dar-ul-qaza advises its petitioners to seek assistance of the state court when the authority and the force of law are required to resolve a case. On the other hand, the state court seeks support from the sharia adalat by referring to its verdicts in making judicial decisions. The cases discussed in this section throw light on the judicial procedure in the adjudication of personal law and indicate how the dar-ul-qazas and the state courts function in collocation.

The ethnography of the dar-ul-qaza helps us understand the context of judicial reasoning. As Stiles (2003, 2009) has argued, every instance of judicial reasoning can only be comprehensively understood if, other than court documents, the cultural context in which legal reasoning takes place is also cognised. The academic discussion on the personal law issue in India, we argue, would benefit by taking cognisance of the field view of legal praxis. In the concluding section of the essay, we argue how the ethnography of an emergent judicial landscape and the adjudication of personal law in India have something to offer to the discussion on secularity as well as the personal law debate in India.

Conclusion

The perceived incompatibility between secular state law and non-state religious laws and norms has been challenged by scholars whose work illustrates an emerging landscape of inter-legality (Tschalaer 2012).[40] Theoretically, adjudication forums such as the dar-ul-qaza do not have any legal standing, yet in practice, they are interconnected with and complementary to the judiciary from the perspective of the petitioner and her 'case' (Vatuk 2003: 144). Solanki's (2011) work on Mumbai has offered a fine-grained analysis of this interaction between the state and the societal adjudicating units as a shared adjudication system in addressing the issues of marriage and divorce. How do state courts, and civic as well as religious bodies interact in the adjudication of marriage and divorce in legally plural societies? Solanki traces the complexity of this process and the gaps between the law and its practice (ibid.). In this essay, we have shown how litigants consider different adjudication forums as appropriate for resolving their personal disputes and how judicial practice creates a field of inter-legality.

The judiciary functions through formal, institutionalised procedures, but the dar-ul-qazas functioning outside the realm of the state also exercise rigour in their procedure (Redding 2014: 979). The state courts operate through a judicial hierarchy that connects local courts to the apex tribunal. By contrast, dar-ul-qazas have no enforceable authority. Dar-ul-qazas are aware of the 'duality' of their position in the legal/social landscape—their jural/moral authority, on the one hand, and the unenforceability of their orders, on the other. Moreover, we found that, as did Kozlowiski (1995: 896–97) in his work on Hyderabad, when a defendant was non-cooperative and unresponsive to the sharia adalat's summons, the qazi sometimes counselled the petitioners to seek assistance from a civil authority.

Marriage, divorce, custody and maintenance are the subjects dealt with under personal law. But we tend to miss the point that for those seeking a resolution to their family disputes and failed marriages, it is more a question of a personal trouble/misery than law. For women, the dar-ul-qaza serves as an efficient site for quick and inexpensive divorce, as compared to family courts. At the same time, it is only at this forum that certain religio-legal problems could be brought (as discussed in the second section of the essay). We argue that from the litigants' point of view, the dar-ul-qaza is often not an alternative unit of dispute resolution but rather an appropriate site for adjudication.[41] Our ethnography also suggests that women exercise their agency in deciding where they should take their cases and in negotiating the transactions. We have shown how dar-ul-qazas adjudicate as women approach them for problems ranging from trouble with the father-in-law to khula on grounds of the husband's impotency. These *personal* problems, from the litigant's point of view, are not so much a matter of *law* but rather of finding the appropriate forum for resolving them. Depending on the nature of the problem, litigants decide which legal forum to approach and at times evoke the authority of another forum to settle cases.

We argue that only by shifting our focus from legislation to legal practice, with greater attention paid to the institutional aspects of law and the litigants' point of view, can we move beyond the sharp binary between gender justice and the rights of religious minorities. An institutional ethnography of religious, community-level *jamaat*s (local councils) and family/civil judicial units would help us to think through the personal law debate.[42] The case of dar-ul-qazas and the space they share in the secular judicial landscape throw light on how the religious and the secular institutional spheres negotiate their boundaries. Basu (2003) has discerned an 'interpellation' of religion in the secular court's adjudication of personal law. Illustrating how innovation and plurality through which a complicated system of personal law functions, she argues that as religion interpellates in law, the judiciary 'modify, expand and contradict' the legislative provisions (ibid.: 132–40). It is through this process that secularism in the Indian context gets articulated and reinforced. To this argument, the ethnography of the dar-ul-qaza and the dispute-resolution process described in this essay adds a new dimension. It shows how personal disputes over inheritance and maintenance get addressed and resolved through, what we call, the 'collocation' between the religious and civil judicial sites. Thereby, the essay foregrounds the sociological insight that the questions of tangled personal disputes are as much questions of affect and *akhrat* (afterlife) as they are of law.

Notes

1. While the people call these forums dar-ul-qaza, in academic literature they are usually referred to as sharia courts. These two terms are used interchangeably in this essay.
2. Mahila mandals are women's committees organised by the women from a neighbourhood/locality. Seva ashrams are councils organised by local committees as an endeavour towards social service.
3. Biradaris are caste groups; in this case, among Muslims whose members follow a particular occupation.
4. In Kanpur city, there are a few dar-ul-qazas, each with a separate sectarian affiliation. These sects differ in their interpretation of sharia. But in practice, there is only one dar-ul-qaza affiliated to the Jamiat Ulema-e-Hind of the Deoband school that functions regularly in the city. So, sometimes people with the other sectarian affiliations also approach the court for dispute resolution.
5. Uttar Pradesh has a Muslim population of 19.26 per cent. The figure is calculated from the population data provided in the 2011 Census.
6. Vatuk's (2001) ethnography of the Chennai Family Court also shows that although litigants are allowed to argue their case before a judge, they are generally whisked away by lawyers, immediately as they step inside the courts. But the litigants' court presence is crucial, and in the cases where petitioners fail to appear on three consecutive dates of hearing, their cases get dismissed (ibid.: 229–30).
7. Informal judicial unit within the family/civil court that pronounces verdicts in the cases that have already been settled out of court through compromise.
8. Interview with a family court lawyer of Kanpur District Court.
9. The mediation unit of the Kanpur District Court functions under the Jila Vidhik Seva Pradhikaran and was set up in 2008. The unit was created at the directive of Allahabad High Court to deal with family and civil cases.
10. Mahila thanas [all-women police stations (AWPS)] were first started in Uttar Pradesh in the 1990s, with the objective of realising a 'speedy and quality disposal of cases' relating to women. The initiative was first started in Lucknow, but gradually over the next two decades, these police stations came to be set up in 71 more districts. By 2010, AWPS were established in all the districts of Uttar Pradesh (*Times of India*, 6 April 2010).
11. The qazi is the one who adjudicates and arbitrates, functioning like a judge.
12. In its vicinity lies the Barelwi-affiliated sharia adalat of Khuli Bazaar. Though we were first introduced to this sharia adalat, we soon found that it was not functioning as a dispute-resolution centre but was chiefly committed to distributing amulets, a protection against evil eye and divine disputes, so to speak.

13. Farangi Mahal is an illustrious family, which traces its descent to the eleventh century mystic, 'Abd Allah Ansari of Herat. Its ancestors migrated to India from Medina during the early years of the Delhi Sultanate. In 1559, Emperor Akbar made a revenue-free grant to Mulla Hafiz. More than a century later, in 1692, the Mulla's great-grandson Qutb al-Din was murdered in a land dispute in which he had no role. To compensate for this loss, Emperor Aurangzeb granted to his family the possession of the sequestered property of a European merchant in Lucknow. The family occupied the castle in 1695, and thereafter, they gradually populated its neighbourhood. The family later came to be known after the name of the palace that was bestowed on it, and it still retains its lofty stature (Robinson 2005: 1–2). One of its family members, Maulana Khalid Rasheed Farangi Mahali, is recognised as a local leader. He runs madrasahs including a separate madrasah for girls. He is politically active and his opinion on any issue of public interest carries weight among a certain section of the Muslim population.
14. Dar-al-ifta is an institution of Islamic legal jurisprudence where fatwa seekers approach a qazi/mufti for queries in their religious and ethical matters. It also functions as a space for dispute resolution in matters related to the sharia.
15. Fatwa is a juristic opinion issued by a Muslim cleric for an ethical breach. The problems that are amenable for treatment by a fatwa should be specifically associated with the violation of *din* (religious obligation). The problem should be presented in writing, in Urdu before a mufti, who, on evaluating it in light of the Quran and the Hadith, gives a response. Generally, one party presents the problem before the mufti and the fatwa is handed over to him. Although a fatwa is not morally binding on an individual, it is valid so far as the parties to it comply with the declaration. *Faisla*, on the other hand, is a judicial decision made by means of an elaborate adjudication procedure in decision-making where the presence of both parties is mandatory. And in case, either of the parties is absent, the relief is granted in favour of the petitioner present, as a benefit of doubt.
16. An Islamic scholar who responds to those seeking solutions to ethical dilemmas by issuing fatwas.
17. Farangi Mahal accepts *likhit javab* (petitions for fatwa) on all the weekdays, except Friday. The dar-ul-qaza conducts its procedure twice in a week, between two and four in the afternoon on Wednesday and Thursday.
18. If either of the parties has a genuine reason to defer a case, the request is granted.
19. Shahar (2008) has suggested a re-evaluation of the state's role in policy formulation in Islamic law and an increased attention to its procedural aspects, particularly as qazis and muftis have more autonomy in the realm of procedure than in interpretation. The changes or adaptations in Islamic law, he argues, are most often achieved by reforms in judicial procedure (ibid.: 140–41).
20. Zubaida (2003) has argued about the institution of vakils and the redundancy of their role in dispute settlement during the Mamluke period. It was observed

that in an Islamic court, a vakil was not an individual educated or literate in law, but an influential person known for his connections, who would be chosen for the role based on his skills in pleading and persuasion. Yet the jurists would not always approve their presence at court, due to the belief that *vakala* (plural of vakil) are open to enriching themselves by deceit and corruption (ibid.: 45–46).

21. In a different context, Powers (1992) has argued that the appellate system in Islamic law functions under specified and limited conditions. Primarily, a judgement is considered for review only after it is ascertained that the decreeing judge is incompetent to issue the said verdict. Otherwise, a judicial review may be ordered, if there is a complaint that the adjudication process has not complied with law. If a judgement is in dissonance with prescriptions of the Quran, Sunnah or even the *qiyas* (principle of analogy used in interpreting Islamic law), then a judicial review may be ordered (ibid.: 324).
22. We use pseudonyms in the essay to protect the identity of the interlocutors and litigants.
23. Rudolph and Rudolph (1999: 258) have drawn on their findings from a village tribunal in newly independent India. They pointed out that resolution in the cases that came for scrutiny before the panchayat was obtained through compromise between parties. There was no absolute triumph or defeat in the cases. Yet, both the parties would go home satisfied that they understood the arguments and the developments in their cases.
24. Khula refers to a mode of divorce in which a wife appeals her husband for marriage dissolution. Mahr is an entitlement that is accrued to a woman on her marriage. She has an absolute right over it and the amount is decided keeping in view the potential husband's *hasiyat* (ability) to fulfill it (*ada karna*). It is required that a husband should hand over the mahr before he consummates the marriage. Iddat is the obligatory waiting period that a wife has to observe following her divorce. It is only after this period that she can remarry. The period extends over three lunar months, primarily to determine whether the woman is pregnant from her previous marriage. If that is the case, the former husband is liable to bear the expenses of delivery and maintenance of the child. Nafaka is the maintenance due to a divorced woman from her husband during the period of iddat.
25. Faskh refers to a divorce invoked by qazi where the husband's consent is not required. *Talaq-i-tafwid* is a mode of marriage dissolution at the initiative of a wife such that if a stipulation for divorce that was incorporated at the time of marriage (in consultation with a prospective wife and her parents) is breached, the marriage will be deemed annulled with immediate effect. Sometimes, at the event of a contravention of stipulation, the wife will be entitled to live apart from the husband and still be maintained by him (Carroll 1982: 279–80). In our field, we did not find such cases of divorce.
26. A witness can never be an immediate kin member of a petitioner, whose account he/she is supposed to testify, that is, a parent or child, while those in a parallel

relationship, such as a brother, a sister or an uncle may serve as witness. Yet there are instances where the court observes exception in counting those as witness who may not otherwise qualify for the task, for want of evidence. But primarily he/she should be well informed about the dispute in question as well as the petitioner, and must also belong to the same mohalla or the village as that of the suitor. (Interview with qazi, Farangi Mahal Lucknow, September 2016.)

27. Stiles (2003) followed contested divorce cases in the Islamic courts of Zanzibar. She found that in adjudication, a qazi would not merely look at the actions leading to divorce. He would rather cognise the intentions of the actors who were party to divorce. A qazi would often assess an act in terms of its interpretative meaning, drawing on the local cultural context (ibid.: 273–76).
28. Drawing on an ethnography of sharia courts in Zanzibar in the adjudication of family cases, Stiles (2009) observed that the charge of impotency adduced by a wife in a matrimonial case can be an effective means of persuading a husband to enact 'an immediate divorce'. The potential shame and the embarrassment expressed in a relatively public forum of the court would often prompt a husband to end marriage in a haste (ibid.: 59–60).
29. We notice a similarity with the patterns of argument drawn up by research on litigants' orientation in court proceedings—the manner in which they framed their arguments. Based on their observations of 1,000 litigants, Conley and O' Barr (1990: 59) differentiated between relational and rule-oriented litigants. The sister's mode of arguing approximately follows the former model.
30. Drawing on an ethnography of Islamic courts in the Gaza city of Palestine, Shehada (2009) argued that a judge does not merely implement the law based on the details documented in the case, he is also a member of the community, and uses his local, contextual knowledge to give judgements. The judges thus influence not just the individual who is seeking a legal remedy but also the life in the community (ibid.: 257).
31. Lemons (2010) observed that in her field she would often hear that among Indian families, disputes that appear as disagreement between couples would actually be grappling with the conflict between their parents (ibid.: 36).
32. Tucker (1994) explored marriage practices and the associated entitlements for women in Syria and Palestine in the seventeenth to eighteenth centuries. She found that a marriage, once consummated, would make the husband liable for certain responsibilities. The husband thus provided for his wife and children and the obligation was binding on him, irrespective of his wife's ownership and control over resources. The social norm required a husband to provide at a level that is appropriate to her background (ibid.: 269).
33. The concept of haqq bears similarity with the Western notion of 'right'. Yet, in the Islamic legal discourse, it is better understood as the rights of individuals that have connection with the divine who framed it. But drawing on the usage of haqq in Moroccan society, Geertz (1983) found haqq being used more as 'correct behaviour' than 'correct understanding'.

34. The qazi's assistant explained that the sharia adalat usually does not accept property disputes, as petitioners often dismiss settlements on property if they do not find them favourable. But they do entertain requests to give their expert opinion on property distribution.
35. Virasat is the Islamic provision of transferring one's material assets to the legal heirs.
36. Interview with qazi, Barelwi dar-ul-qaza, October 2015, Kanpur.
37. A legal document that sanctions the transfer of property to individuals who are not the legal heirs. Sharia permits passing on at the most a one-third share of one's property. The remaining portion of the property should compulsorily be distributed among the legal heirs.
38. We would like to draw attention to Uberoi's (1968: 78–79) observations on the appropriateness of oath in the Islamic legal procedure. The Muslims of the northern highlands of Afghanistan (also known as Andarabis, after the place where they reside) highly regarded the act of swearing by the Quran. Both inside and outside the court, oath-taking was attributed great value, and the act largely determined the liability or non-liability of an offence. Nevertheless, liability in any civil or criminal offence was determined by the following five criteria, sequentially placed in their order of importance: (a) the confession by the accused or defendant; (b) the evidence presented by the eyewitnesses, in adequate number and with the required qualifications, in support of the plaintiff's claim; (c) administration of the solemn oath by the Quran, to the accused or defendant, declaring non-liability; (d) abstention from the oath by the accused or defendant; and (e) proof by the 'categorical indications', that is, by inference from the facts and circumstances documented by the assessors. The court procedure required the plaintiff to adduce legally valid proof for a complaint, and it was imperative that the defendant must swear an oath of non-liability before the qazi to establish his innocence. But if the defendant refused to take an oath, the plaintiff was asked to take an oath instead. Often, on the criterion of 'circumstantial evidence', the case got dismissed as unproven or inadmissible, or the plaintiff was declared a slanderer and calumniator (ibid.).
39. Lemons (2010) had referred to a similar case of a wife seeking divorce, but there, the woman had registered a property theft case against her in-laws. The court sent an order to the qazi (who had earlier investigated the case) to certify divorce to the couple. The court further reminded the wife to return all the gifts given to her by her husband or in-laws. Thus, we see a civil court judge relying on the qazi's service and also influencing the decision-making at religious court.
40. Lemons (2010: 169–71) notes how a 'non-legal' normative order co-exists along with the state and is shaped by it, creating a field of inter-legality or legal pluralism.
41. Vatuk (2017) noted that for a woman facing a problem in her personal life, the dar-ul-qaza is often an alternative site of dispute settlement. Her argument is that a family court is the last resort for a woman who has a plurality of

institutions—affiliated to state as well as others in the community—to redress her problem (ibid.: 42).

42. We would like to mention Stephens' (2018) nuanced study of the sutured negotiations between secular law and Islamic law in the colonial context that throws new light on this old debate.

References

Basu, Srimati. 2003. 'Shading the Secular: Law at Work in the Indian Higher Courts', *Cultural Dynamics*, 15 (2): 131–52.

Béteille, André. 2012. *Democracy and Its Institutions*. New Delhi: Oxford University Press.

Bowen, John. 2012. *A New Anthropology of Islam*. Cambridge: Cambridge University Press.

Carroll, Lucy. 1982. 'Talaq-i-Tafwid and Stipulations in a Muslim Marriage Contract: Important Means of Protecting the Position of the South Asian Muslim Wife', *Modern Asian Studies*, 16 (2): 277–309.

Conley John M., and William M. O'Barr. 1990. *Rules versus Relationships: The Ethnography of Legal Discourse*. Chicago and London: University of Chicago Press.

Geertz, Clifford. 1983. *Local Knowledge: Further Essays in Interpretive Anthropology*. USA: Basic Books.

Kozlowski, Gregory C. 1995. 'Loyalty, Locality and Authority in Several Opinions (Fatawa) Delivered by the Mufti of the Jamiah Nizammiyah Madrasah, Hyderabad, India', *Modern Asian Studies*, 29 (4): 893–927.

Lemons, Katherine. 2010. 'At the Margins of Law: Adjudicating Muslim Families in Contemporary Delhi', Ph.D. dissertaion, University of Berkeley.

Powers, David S. 1992. 'On Judicial Review in Islamic Law', *Law and Society Review*, 26 (2): 315–42.

Redding, Jeffrey. 2014. 'The Case of Ayesha, Muslim "Courts", and the Rule of Law: Some Ethnographic Lessons for Legal Theory', *Modern Asian Studies*, 48 (4): 940–85.

Robinson, Francis. 2005. *The 'Ulama of Farangi Mahall and Islamic Culture in South Asia*. Delhi: Permanent Black.

Rudolph, Lloyd I., and Susanne Hoebar Rudolph. 1999. *The Modernity of Tradition*. New Delhi: Orient Longman Limited.

Shahar, Ido. 2008. 'Legal Pluralism and the Study of Darul-Qazas', *Islamic Law and Society*, 15 (1): 112–41.

Shehada, Nahda. 2009. 'Negotiating Custody Rights in Islamic Family Law', in Thomas G. Kirsch and Bertram Turner (eds), *Permutations of Order Religion and Law as Contested Sovereignties*, pp. 88–105. Surrey: Ashgate.

Solanki, Gopika. 2011. *Adjudication in Religious Family Laws Cultural Accommodation, Legal Pluralism, and Gender Equality in India*. New Delhi: Cambridge University Press.

Stephens, Julia. 2018. *Governing Islam: Law, Empire, and Secularism in South Asia*. Cambridge: Cambridge University Press.

Stiles, Erin E. 2003. 'When Is a Divorce a Divorce? Determining Intention in Zanzibar's Islamic Court', *Ethnology*, 42 (4): 273–88.

———. 2009. 'The Laws of Marriage: Sexuality, Impotence, and Divorce Suits in Zanzibar's Islamic Courts', *Journal of Women Living under Muslim Laws*, Dossier 32–33, Sexualities, Culture and Society in Muslim Contexts: 59–74.

Suneetha, A., and Vasudha Nagaraj. 2006. 'A Difficult Match: Women's Actions and Legal Instituions in the Face of Domestic Violence', *Economic and Politcal Weekly*, 41 (41): 4355–362.

Times of India. 2010. 'UP First State to Have a Mahila Thana in All Districts', 6 April. Available at https://timesofindia.indiatimes.com/city/lucknow/UP-first-state-to-have-a-mahila-thana-in-all-districts/articleshow/5764919.cms (accessed 13 April 2017).

Tschalaer, Mengia Hong. 2012. 'Competing Model-Nikahnamas: Muslim Women's Spaces within the Legal Landscape in Lucknow', *Journal of Law and Social Research*, 3: 65–80.

Tucker, Judith E. 1994. 'Muftis and Matrimony: Islamic Law and Gender in Ottoman Syria and Palestine', *Islamic Law and Society*, 1 (3): 265–300.

Uberoi, J. P. S. 1968. 'District Administration in the Northern Highlands of Afghanistan', *Sociological Bulletin*, 28 (1): 65–89.

Vatuk, Sylvia. 2001. '"Where Will She go? What Will She Do?": Paternalism toward Women in the Administration of Muslim Personal Law in Contemporary India', in Gerald James Larson (ed.), *Religion and Personal Law in Secular India*, pp. 226–50. Bloomington, IN: Indiana University Press.

———. 2003. 'Muslim Women in the Indian Family Courts: A Report from Chennai', in Imtiaz Ahmed (ed.), *Divorce and Remarriage among Muslims in India*, pp. 137–60. New Delhi: Manohar Publishers

———. 2017. *Marriage and Its Discontents: Women, Islam and the Law in India*. New Delhi: Women Unlimited.

Zubaida, Sami. 2003. *Law and Power in the Islamic World*. London: I. B. Tauris.

7

Religious Activism and Secular Ethos

Muslim Organisations and Palliative Care in Kerala

R. Santhosh

Sitting in his modest house near Areekode, a small town in Malappuram district of Kerala, Muhammad Ali, popularly known as Ali Master tells me, 'It is the religious obligation of every Muslim to help people like palliative care patients and our organisation is just taking the lead. In fact, we argue that these patients, irrespective of their religious affiliation, are rightful recipients of zakat,[1] and I can prove it based on quranic verses.' He was explaining the theological as well as philosophical foundations that prompted the Kerala Nadwatul Mujahideen—an influential Muslim reformist organisation in Kerala, popularly known as the Mujahid movement of which he is a member—in taking the lead in a highly successful palliative care initiative in the Muslim-majority Malappuram district of the state. The Mujahid movement has been at the forefront of this initiative in Malappuram, mobilising volunteers as well as resources from the community for the effective dissemination of palliative care for terminally ill patients in the district. Ali Master's explanations on the theological basis of the Mujahid activism in palliative care and the deliberately adopted secular ethos in its implementation in a multi-religious society like Kerala opens up interesting ways of exploring the nature of Islamic activism and prompts us to revisit the secular–religious binary that is ubiquitous in the discussion on Islam and modernity.

What is striking in the activism of the Mujahid organisation in the field of palliative care in Kerala is a curious mix of the religious and the secular that defines the contours of such activism. While the Mujahid members of the palliative care movement vouch by their religious inspiration and present their activism as Islamic dawa,[2] they are highly conscious about the secular ethos and modalities of their execution in the public domain. This careful negotiation of the boundaries between religion and the secular has made these voluntary groups highly effective in terms of mobilisation of human as well as other resources. The model is appreciated by different religious communities whose patronage it receives as benefactors as well as the beneficiaries of such activism.

In this essay, my interest is to explore the ways through which the Islamic dawa is carried out as palliative care voluntarism by Mujahid volunteers and the ideologies and ethos that shape this form of activism. I suggest that this particular case provides us with an opportunity to revisit the debate on Islam and secularism and explore the processes through which Muslim communities in different socio-political contexts negotiate with secularism and secularisation. I contend that the term *mathetharatvam*—the Malayalam equivalent of secularism—used quite often by Mujahid leaders while explaining their palliative care activism and the numerous modalities through which they try to adhere to this principle is a process of civic activism. This process, I suggest, is typical of Muslim reformist organisations like the Mujahid, as the very emergence of Islamic reformism in the Indian subcontinent also heralded the inescapable process of secularisation in the form of rationalisation during its momentous encounter with modernity. I present this case also to further a methodological argument that calls for context-specific ethnographic research that looks into the practices and everyday experiences of Muslim communities to understand their negotiations with modernity and its concomitant institutions.

Primary data in the form of qualitative interviews and participant observation at different sites of the palliative care movement in Kerala serve as the basis of my analysis. I conducted fieldwork in several phases in 2012 as well as in 2013, primarily in the Malappuram and Kozhikode districts of the state, where the movement has been highly active and successful. I made several visits to palliative clinics in these districts to understand their system of in-patient and out-patient caregiving, community participation in terms of volunteering, resource mobilisation and overall coordination. I also conducted in-depth interviews with several key informants, both medical practitioners and senior volunteers who were instrumental in conceiving and popularising the movement in Kerala. Several leaders of Mujahid movements and active volunteers were interviewed to understand their motivation and involvement in the functioning of these clinics.

The Context: Palliative Care and Mujahid Activism in Kerala

The palliative care movement in Kerala has been hailed as one of the most successful initiatives in the field of palliative care in the developing world. The World Health Organisation (WHO) has declared it as a model worth emulating (Stjernsward 2007). The first palliative care clinic was established in Kozhikode in 1993 by the NGO Pain and Palliative Care Society (Rajagopal and Kumar 1999). Soon it was realised that the most vital component for making the palliative care initiative successful was not doctors or other medical professionals but a group of active volunteers and genuine patronage by the local community. The attempt to involve the community in the palliative care initiative received a fillip with the initiation of a project known as the Neighbourhood Network in Palliative Care (NNPC) in the Malappuram district. Under this programme, local volunteers were trained to identify terminally ill patients in their locality and provide necessary basic medical aid with the help of trained professionals. Dr Suresh Kumar, one of the key persons active in the NNPC initiative, argues that this initiative revolutionised the way in which palliative care was organised. The NNPC has been an important factor in the success of the palliative care movement in Kerala. This community-led initiative replaced the previous hierarchical doctor-led structure in palliative care with a network of community-based, volunteer-led, autonomous initiatives (Kumar 2012).

The palliative care movement in Kerala is significant both for its reach and for the overwhelming community support it enjoys. It is estimated that out of the total 310 palliative clinics in the country, 250 are in Kerala. Almost 50 per cent of the terminally ill people in the state are covered under the palliative care scheme, while the corresponding national figure is only 2 per cent (Paleri and Numpeli 2005). Kerala also designed the NNPC programme where volunteers from the neighbourhood are identified and trained in providing palliative care (Kumar and Mathew 2005).

The palliative care movement is highly successful in northern Kerala, especially in two districts—Malappuram and Kozhikode. In the Malappuram district, almost 70 per cent of the chronically ill are covered under this initiative in comparison with the state average of 50 per cent (Vijay and Mukta 2009). More than 20,000 bedridden patients in the district are getting regular care at home through the local self government–led home-care programme with community participation. Similarly in the Kozhikode district, nearly 1,000 volunteers visit almost 10,000 houses every week to attend to patients who are bedridden with cancer, stroke and spinal injuries (ibid.). While Kozhikode has the highest number of palliative clinics, numbering 39, the Malappuram district is placed second with 33 clinics, and these numbers are much higher in comparison to the number of clinics in other districts of the state. These two districts are also ahead of all others in collecting financial contribution from the community for palliative care.

Typically, a palliative care clinic focuses on the four main services: (a) provision of home-care services where a team of trained medical professionals along with volunteers make scheduled visits and provide necessary medical care to the bedridden patients; (b) out-patient clinics, where patients visit the palliative clinics and avail consultation and medicines from doctors; (c) distribution of medicines and equipment such as waterbeds, crutches, wheelchairs and oxygen cylinders to the houses of the patients; and (d) organising income-generating activities and rehabilitation programmes for bedridden patients. Though each clinic functions as an independent unit, there are umbrella organisations in all the districts of Kerala that coordinate and facilitate the functioning of these clinics. Volunteers play a pivotal role in the running of palliative care clinics, as each volunteer is entrusted with a given geographical area for monitoring, and he/she is expected to conduct a survey to identify patients who require palliative care. After this, the volunteer helps the patients register themselves at the clinic and submit a comprehensive report on the patients' economic and family situation. Subsequently, a team of doctors, nurses and volunteers visit the house of the patient and administer the necessary clinical procedures like dressing of the wounds and catheter change. Based on the economic condition of the family, each patient is categorised as very poor, poor, middle-class and rich. While all medicines and equipment are chargeable for the rich, some concession is given to those categorised as the middle-class, and these items are supplied free to the poor and very poor households. Periodic visits by the volunteers supplementing the visits of medical teams ensure social and emotional support, better compliance with medical/nursing instructions, timely reporting of symptoms to the doctor and financial support (Kumar 2012).

The overwhelming success of the palliative care movement in these two districts and in the northern Malabar region of the state has been largely attributed to Islamic activism and charity. Prominent in these developments have been Muslim organisations, particularly the Mujahids led by Dr Hussain Madavoor. The Mujahids have mobilised their organisational networks to support palliative care work, including the establishment of clinics in most parts of these districts. Jamaat-e-Islami has also ventured into palliative care but on a more modest scale, with a single clinic in Malappuram district. Though traditionalist Sunni organisations have not established their own clinics, they also encourage their members to support the initiatives of the palliative care movement.

The decision of Mujahids to venture into the field of palliative care underscores a sense of deeper reflection and engagement with the questions of 'true piety' and devotion. Dr Abdul Rahman, one of the leaders of the Mujahid student wing and a central figure in the popularisation of the palliative care movement, points out that the organisation used to have lively debates during the early 1990s regarding the nature of Islamic dawa. Many youngsters like him argued that Islamic activism could not be limited to preaching Islamic tenets, and that it needed to extend to other areas of human concerns and take up issues of public interest. He points out, 'We used to have heated debates on whether tree planting can be considered as Islamic activism, and finally we could convince other members that yes, it can be, and gradually we moved to more concrete actions like providing medical aid to patients in the Calicut Medical College.' Later, the Mujahid decided to utilise its organisational resources to spread palliative care clinics across the districts of Malappuram and Kozhikode and directed its members to actively participate in its functioning by volunteering and mobilising resources.

One of the often-heard refrain of the palliative care volunteers is that money is never a constraint for the activities of the clinic and the community is more than willing to donate as they are aware of the noble work of the clinics. These clinics function on the basis of micro-funding, and money is mobilised from the community on a continuous basis. Several innovative methods are employed to collect money from the community. Small collection boxes with an appeal to donate to palliative clinics are ubiquitous on the cash tables of most shops in the Malabar region, and they constitute one of the steady sources of regular income to the clinics. A second form of financial mobilisation is to have a list of contributors, including individuals and institutions who pay a fixed monthly donation to the clinic, and in a typical palliative clinic, individual monthly donation varies from Rs 10 to Rs 3,000. Similarly, schools, colleges, small industries, bus operators, auto-rickshaw drivers and banks too pay this monthly donation, ensuring a constant flow of income. The most significant form of financial mobilisation takes place during two occasions, one on the world State Palliative Care Day on 15 January and the other in the month of Ramzan. During the State Palliative Care Day, every palliative clinic organises extensive volunteer squads to visit households, shops and other institutions within its reach and collect money, and this turns out to be a significant sum for each clinic. The other important financial contribution comes in the month of Ramzan, through individual contributions or through the organised zakat committees. Besides, all mosques undertake special collection drives immediately after the Friday prayer during the Ramzan month, thus collecting a significant sum. For example, in Pulikkal Palliative Care Clinic, one of the active palliative clinics in Malappuram district, the total income for the year 2011–12 was Rs 20,41,182, out of which the collection during Palliative Care Day yielded Rs 2,63,097, and the Ramzan collection, Rs 8,80,515. The remaining money was collected through monthly and box collections. Medicines worth Rs 4 lakh were donated by the different local self-governing bodies of the state.

Palliative care has outgrown its initial purpose of providing care to the terminally ill and has extended itself to that of a safety net, albeit in a limited way. It identifies very poor families that are provided with foodgrains, provisions and other essential items for their subsistence, as they can buy these items from designated shops and the palliative care clinic settles the bill on a monthly basis. Likewise, at the time of festivals, food kits and dress materials are distributed among these families. Notebooks, pens, textbooks, umbrellas and so on are supplied at the beginning of the school year to children from these families.

As mentioned earlier, the lion's share of the financial contribution for the palliative clinics is collected in the month of Ramzan from individual contributors and mosques, and needless to say, the notion of zakat underlies this heightened form of charity. Palliative movements make use of myriad forms of zakat and *sadaqa*[3] to ensure sufficient funding for their functioning. Reformist organisations including the Mujahid have succeeded in setting up centralised zakat committees, and even the traditional Sunnis have begun to follow suit. The major arguments in favour of zakat committees are their transparency and fairness, and maintaining the anonymity and dignity of the receiver. Reformist organisations, while criticising the traditionalists who insist on distributing zakat individually, argue that individual zakat-giving has vestiges of a feudal value system and the donor expects permanent obeisance from the receiver. According to the reformists, on the other hand, the zakat committees ensure an impersonal and just system of distribution. Mustafa, one of the active volunteers of palliative care, points out that there is no consensus among various religious groups on whether zakat can be given for the purpose of palliative care. But the reformists assert that nowhere in the Quran is it mentioned that only Muslims are the rightful recipients of zakat. The palliative care patients, irrespective of their religious identity, can receive zakat.

Mujahid as the Islamic Reformer and Reflexive Believer

The religious life of a Mujahid is an explication of his reformist convictions as he strives to maintain a distinctive religiosity from the traditional Sunnis. Reflecting the wider tendencies of Islamic reformism, Mujahids are against the practice of shirk (attribution of partners to God), bida (innovation in worship) and taqlid (blind following) with a stress on ijtihad (reasoned interpretation). In the specific socio-cultural context of Kerala, these reformist ideas get translated into the cultivation of specific religious practices and dispositions that include abstinence and opposition to shrine worship and dargah visits, the celebration of the Prophet's birthday and singing Arabic-Malayalam songs eulogising Prophet Muhammad as part of traditional rituals; insistence on delivering the Friday *qutba* (public sermon) in Malayalam; and above all, insistence on the exclusive dependence on the Quran and Hadith in opposition to traditional Sunnis, who extensively use the 400-year-old Shafi text *Fatul-mueen* by Sheikh ZainudhinMakhdum II (Osella and Osella 2008). Mujahids have been at the forefront of Islamic theological and organisational contestations in Kerala for the past several decades, thereby creating a vibrant Islamic public sphere resonating with debates over 'true Islam' (Santhosh 2013)

Every Mujahid volunteer I came across in the palliative care units in the Malappuram and Kozhikode districts depicts himself as a deeply religious person with a larger interest in the transformation of society into a better world. The volunteers eloquently elaborate on the role played by the Mujahid movement in the reformation of the community in particular and the Kerala society in general. The typical reformist discourse of fighting 'ignorance' and 'blind beliefs' within the community marks these narratives. The volunteers remind me that but for the Mujahid movement, the community would still be steeped in ignorance and blind beliefs, struggling under the yoke of exploitative ulema. They proudly point out that the traditional Sunnis who opposed these reformist activities had no option but to follow the reformist and progressive steps initiated by the Mujahid, especially in matters such as secular education and gender questions.

Underlying these narratives is the argument that a correct, rational understanding of Islam is the driving spirit behind all these achievements. The same argument is used by Mujahid volunteers to distance themselves from and criticise the traditionalist Sunnis, who allegedly follow religion in a non-rational, blind manner, thereby failing to understand the emancipatory capacity of Islam, which according to these activists is founded on a strong humanitarian ethos. The most prominent theme in these narratives is the ability of the reformist to think and practise Islam in a rational way, thereby opening up newer vistas of Islamic engagement in the community for its betterment. Basheer, one of the senior volunteers of palliative care in Nilambur, in the Malappuram district, tells me:

> Since my childhood, I was influenced by the Mujahid ideology and activities. I felt that Islam is not something to be reduced only to rituals and followed in a blind manner. I began to read the Quran in Malayalam and contemplate its meanings, and therefore, I could go into a much deeper understanding of Islam, which was distinctly different from those offered by the local clergy. That was a transforming experience, as I could understand how forcefully the Quran urges believers to strive for the service and upliftment of others. I felt that that Islam is highly radical, and it depends on my rational faculties to make sense of its emancipatory potential and derive inspiration for personal as well as societal transformations.

The constant reflection and contemplation on the religious obligations of a 'true Muslim' and the anxiety about the ultimate evaluation of their life after death are tellingly evident in the words of Mujahid activists when they explain the religious motif of these activities. Basheer recites the Hadith by Imam Muslim (Muslim ibn al-Hajjaj), which asks the believer whether they visited the ill and fed the hungry, and argues that these questions are eternally valid. Basheer also liberally quotes instances from the life of Prophet Muhammad where he became the embodiment of service and kindness to his fellow human beings. He argues that a believer can mechanically recite these verses, be content with it and carry on with his Islamic religious life with all the accompanying rituals. But for a true believer, these verses are commandments that urge him to reflect on one's life and bring in necessary changes in the right direction. At the end, human beings will be answerable to God and the eternal life in heaven depends on the activities in this world.

The religious motif of the Mujahid volunteers is more clearly articulated by Ali Master who concedes that for many of them, the question of heavenly reward in the afterlife is a profound inspiration. But he argues that for many others, including himself, palliative activism has a larger humanitarian motif, a profound sense of obligation as a human being to the creator. As the sole being created by God with discerning and rational faculties, palliative care provides him the platform to fulfil his fundamental obligation to the creator. These faculties demand a true believer to be sensitive to the pain and sufferings of people in their immediate surroundings and do whatever is possible to ameliorate that. For him, the fundamental demand of Islam is to have a compassionate heart and an urge to strive for a better world. Whether he would be rewarded in this world or in the afterlife is not a matter of concern for him.

To illustrate this point further, Ali Master tells me that one of the contentious issues regarding the mobilisation of funds for palliative care among different Muslim organisations is the question of whether zakat can be channelised to palliative clinics. He points out that the Mujahid movement vehemently argues that palliative patients are the rightful recipients of zakat and it can be given to any patient irrespective of their religious affiliation. While the Jamaat-e-Islami concurs with this view, the traditional Sunnis oppose it. The theological reasoning of reformists in this case is particularly interesting. Ali Master shows me the quranic verse on zakat (9.60) that spells out the eligible groups for zakat donation and points at the fifth category, usually described as those in 'bondage' or in 'captivity'. While the conventional explanation for this term is to refer to Muslims captured by enemies who needed to be ransomed and also men from other tribes enslaved by Meccans and Medinans, Ali Master gives a completely different interpretation for this term. He argues that though these terms might have meant people in bondage or slavery during the time of the Prophet, as a true believer, he has the right to interpret this category as the people who are permanently bedridden, who are in bondage of illness and who are captives of terminal illness. He emphasises that these interpretations, though unconventional, reflect the spirit of Islam, as it requires the believers to make sense of the Holy Quran in different socio-political contexts. He also adds that not resorting to such rational and reflexive interpretations of these verses is a gross injustice to the spirit of Islam.

For the Mujahid activists, the rational faculty that they use to identify new vistas within Islam also enable them to develop an imagery of a better society, one that is infused with Islamic principles and ideals but capable of functioning in a multi-religious and secular context. In all their narratives, they highlight this compatibility argument and are quite candid in admitting the extra-religious influences in their thinking about social progress and development. Basheer himself was an activist of the Kerala Sastra Sahitya Parishat, an organisation that aimed at instilling a scientific temper and environmental consciousness in Kerala during the 1980s and 1990s. Basheer points out that the activities of the Parishat helped him broaden his worldview on issues such as social justice, environmental protection, women's question and public health. He argues that while the Parishat presents these issues from a secular point of view, his reading of Islam and the Quran has helped him develop similar perspectives through an Islamic point of view, and there is no contradiction.

Ali Master also acknowledges the lingering legacy and influence of the Communist Party in the Malappuram district, which provided a pro-poor thrust to political and social activism. He points out that no religious or social organisation in Kerala can claim to be unaffected by the emancipatory campaigns of the Communist Party and nor can the Mujahid organisation. He says, 'Definitely the Communist Party and its ideology have influenced us. They could gain acceptance among the masses only because they directly got involved in the everyday struggles of the ordinary people and were a committed lot to the core.' While appreciating the emancipatory project of communism and the dedication of its activists, Ali Master points out that Islam is equally revolutionary, and it is up to the believers to make use of its emancipatory message for the well-being of society. Ali Master points out that he had absolutely no issues in working along with atheists like Dr Mathews, who played a pivotal role in initiating palliative care clinics in the Kozhikode district, and he is quite appreciative of the latter's commitment and dedication to the cause of palliative care patients. For, it is not their religious belief that matters but rather their conviction and dedication in the service of the people who are in need of palliative services.

As mentioned earlier, the word 'mathetharatvam' appears quite frequently in the narratives of the Mujahid activists while explaining the motif and functioning of the palliative clinics. This term is used to indicate two inter-related ideas: one that they have no preferential treatment towards any religion and remain equidistant from all, and second, the emphasis on the constricted role of religion in the daily affairs of running these clinics. Expectedly, the equidistance tenet is put into practice not by refusing to engage with religions but, as is typical of Indian secularism, by maintaining a uniform acceptance of all as illustrated by their practice of distributing festival kits at the time of festivals such as Onam, Vishu and Bakrid.

The Mujahid leaders point out that the explicit invocation of religion needs to be severely contained in the ideological as well as practical aspects of initiatives like palliative care. The organisation acknowledges the necessity of limiting the sphere of religion within certain boundaries, and this realisation is the result of a deeper understanding of the immediate social reality as well as its socio-political connotations. During my initial interaction with the office-bearers of the Pulikkal Palliative Clinic, they were reluctant to identify the palliative care clinic with the Mujahid organisation and only gradually became open to discussing the organisational affiliation of these clinics. The leadership emphasised the point that in many places, the Mujahid volunteers might have initiated the clinic, but it was strengthened and maintained by all. Ali Master, who is often invited by other palliative clinics to provide training and guidance, told me,

> In many places, our initial meetings with Mujahid activists were held in our mosque, but then we insisted that subsequent meetings be held in secular places. Similarly, we just named these clinics simply as palliative clinics of a given place but never with any words or symbols signifying religious or other meaning.

Ali Master points out that Islamic dawa needs to be reinvented constantly so as to make it relevant in the changing socio-cultural contexts. He points out that Kerala society has witnessed rapid changes and that the traditional structures of family, public health and caregiving have undergone drastic transformations and have posed serious challenges. Factors such as the mushrooming of nuclear families with limited manpower to take care of the terminally ill, the rapidly increasing number of cancer patients due to lifestyle changes and, above all, the crippling treatment costs for terminal diseases in the bourgeoning private healthcare system warrant immediate intervention from the community. 'These changes can be of lethal consequence to a family with moderate income as well as resources, and we as religious activists see tremendous significance in intervening in such a scenario to ameliorate the difficulties of these families', he says.

The active involvement of volunteers from divergent socio-religious backgrounds and the unstinting support and patronage of the multi-religious community makes it mandatory for the Mujahid activists to explicitly downplay the religious patronage of palliative care initiatives. I would argue that notwithstanding the practical compulsions of a multi-religious context in which the palliative care initiative functions, this downplay is a reflection and acceptance of broader understandings of a secular philosophy and ethos. These Islamic activists seem comfortable with the philosophical moorings of secularism and its relevance in a multi-religious context. What is striking is the explicit invocation of the secular demarcation between public and private spheres, and the insistence on the circumscribed scope of religion in the public sphere of palliative care initiatives. As the philosopher Charles Taylor (1999: 52) argues, secularism is applicable to non-Christian societies everywhere that have become modern, and 'equidistance' and 'inclusion' represent the essence of secularism. The functioning of palliative care clinics and the articulation of the Mujahid activists explicate Taylor's argument about the omnipresence of secularism in modern complex societies. They appear fully consonant with the idea that a functioning democratic society requires some commonly recognised definition of 'the good life', and secularism in the sense of equidistance and inclusion is, therefore, inevitable (ibid.).

The Mujahid activists share a larger imagery of creating a compassionate and humane society that cares for its suffering members, and for them, palliative care provides an avenue to strive in that direction. In this endeavour, while Islam inspires them, they are ready to welcome others who are inspired by other religions and also by non-religious ideologies. There is a visible acceptance of the legitimacy of alternative ideologies and their right to co-exist in a plural society. Invocation of mathetharatvam explicitly summarises this inclusion of multiple inspirations, both religious and non-religoius, as well as the necessity of keeping religion within specific boundaries while striving for a common cause in a multi-religious society.

I also want to highlight the specific socio-political context in Kerala in particular and India in general, where the discourse of secularism becomes increasingly appealing to the Muslim organisations. Enshrined in the Indian Constitution, the promise of secularism as the non-imposition of the majoritarian religion and the freedom to practise, profess and propagate one's religion seem to be most significant reassuring factors for the religious minorities in India. The specific trajectory of Indian democracy and the ascendance of Hindutva politics have made Muslim organisations realise the significance of a secular promise by the Constitution. Ahmad's (2010) work—which illustrates the transformation of the Jamaat-e-Islami from an organisation founded on the ideals of Maududi that despised democracy, nationalism and secularism to an organisation that most vocally supports secularism in the contemporary Indian context—is a testimony to such transformations necessitated by the specificities of Indian democracy and the political context.

The composition of the public sphere in Kerala is an amalgamation of numerous groupings bonded by affiliations stemming from caste, religion and ethnicity, leaving very little space for truly non-religious, rational organisations. These religious articulations are welcomed by citizens as well as by the state as long as they are not seen as disturbing the communal harmony of society or directly challenging state authority. The Mujahid movement has successfully entered such spaces provided by the state and civil society to project a lofty goal as the site of their religious activism. Non-Mujahid members of the palliative clinics, both Muslim and others, though identifying the initiative as led by the Mujahid, are comfortable in working with them as long as the leadership functions within a non-partisan and inclusive framework. In the Pulikkal Palliative Care Clinic, I came across several volunteers, both Muslims and non-Muslims, who say that they do not have any ideological affiliation to any organisation and they are happy with the way the palliative care clinic has been functioning in Pulikkal as it is doing some meaningful work for the people. Quite often, activities like palliative care by the Mujahid are widely seen by Muslim leaders as a desirable model worthy of emulation by other organisations. Given the Indian socio-political context where Muslim organisations are constantly watched for their credentials and loyalties, the initiative of palliative care is seen as a worthy example of 'noble Islamic activism'. For the Mujahid, this discourse is important also because their activities portray a 'true picture of Islam' and not its distortions reflected through violence, hatred and fundamentalism.

In the remaining part of the essay, I want to locate the specific case of Islamic activism by the Mujahid volunteers in the larger context of Islamic reformism and secularisation. The literature on the emergence of reformist Islamic movements emphatically points out that the foundational transformations happened during its encounter with modernity.

Islamic Reformism and the Imperatives of Secularisation

It is evident that the Mujahids envision Islamic activism as a way of praxis—as an avenue where theological principles and belief systems are put into practice in everyday life with specific emancipatory objectives. While doing so, the Quran as well as hadiths constitute a discursive tradition from which they judiciously choose appropriate theological tenets to substantiate varied interpretations of dawa, which increasingly reflect preoccupation with secular issues and concerns. The case of Mujahid activism in palliative care clearly reflects this 'this-worldly' orientation and, I contend, also reflects the inescapable process of secularisation that is characteristic of Islamic reformism. The visible secular rhetoric that the Mujahid leaders adopt while explaining their role in the palliative care movement is indicative of a deeper and inescapable process of secularisation that has been taking place within Islamic communities for several decades.

In the Indian subcontinent, the reformist traditions and organisations, such as Shah Waliullah, Ahle-Quran, Ahle-Sunnath, Jamaat-e-Islami, Deobandi School and Tablighi Jamaat, brought in fundamental changes in which Muslims experienced their religion. Most of these movements, though aimed at thwarting the advent of colonial modernity epitomised through Christianity and colonial rule in India, gradually incorporated a series of underlying features of modernity. The exhortations to go back to 'the fundamentals of Islam', as espoused by all these movements, cannot be assumed to be a reactionary response to colonial modernity and an attempt to return to an old and pristine Islamic past. Several scholars have pointed out that though these movements claim that they are returning to a pristine past and *the* tradition, in reality all these movements are specifically modern (Asad 1986; Madan 1997, 2006; Nandy 1990; Reetz 2006; Robinson 2008; Sanyal 1996; Turner 2001). Turner (2001) further points out that fundamentalists and reformists are not traditionalists because a traditionalist would argue that the gate to ijtihad (interpretation) is closed. By contrast, fundamentalists are involved in reinterpretation by the very act of imposing their perspective over customary practices that have existed in the past through a compromise or rapprochement with Islamic traditions (ibid.: 40).

The contingencies of modernity with which Islam was forced to negotiate resulted in the production of a series of ingenious practices that redefined Islamic religiosity in a radical manner. The response of Islam to modernity and the ways of negotiation were neither unitary nor singular. A complex series of highly differentiated and diverse responses was produced in different socio-cultural contexts. It was neither Islamic theology nor the basic tenets of modernity that determined the nature of such responses. On the other hand, a complex set of factors and the specific socio-historical contexts played a pivotal role in deciding the nature of Islamic negotiations with modernity.

Eikelman and Piscatori (1996: 38–42) point at one of the results of the Islamic encounter with modernity: the objectification of religious knowledge. They point out that basic questions—'What is my religion?', 'How do my beliefs guide my conduct?'—come to the fore in the consciousness of a large number of believers. These 'objective' questions are specifically modern, and they increasingly shape the discourses and practices of Muslims across the world, rendering it a self-contained system that its believers can describe, characterise and distinguish from other belief systems. Eikelman and Piscatori also point out the process of democratisation of Islamic theology as a result of the Islamic encounter with modernity (ibid.).

In contrast with the early ages where Islamic knowledge was the monopoly of a limited number of jurists, Islamic knowledge and practices have in contemporary times been democratised among the common people. A number of structural elements of European modernity such as higher education, print capitalism, urbanisation and the expansion of technologies have contributed to the objectification and democratisation of religious knowledge. Such a process, Hefner (1998: 98) notes, is not a reaction against but a response to the modern world—the most successful religious refigurations thrive by drawing themselves down into mass society and away from exclusive elites, if and when the latter lose their hold on popular allegiance.

Robinson (2008) has extensively dwelt on these fundamental changes brought into the Islamic traditions as a result of its encounter with modernity. He points out that the reformist movements, though aimed at opposing the Western cultural and political hegemony, also made use of Western knowledge and technology to drive forward their purposes and came to be fashioned in part by their interaction with it. He further lists out five changes that the encounter with modernity brought about in Islamic subjecthood:

(a) the ending of a total authority of the past as Muslims sought new ways of making revelation and tradition relevant to the present;

> (b) the new emphasis on human will as Muslims realised that in a world without political power it is only through their will that they could create an Islamic society on earth; (c) the transformation of the self, achieved through willed activity, leading to self-reflectiveness, self-affirmation and growing individualism; (d) the rationalisation of Islam from scripturalism to its formation in to an ideology; (e) and finally a process of secularisation involving a disenchantment of the world, which arguably has been followed by a re-enchantment. (Robinson 2008: 261)

Each of these points elaborated by Robinson has its own specific manifestation in varied socio-historic contexts, thereby rendering an easy generalisation regarding the exact nature of change happening within Muslim society impossible. The rejection of the chain of *isnad* (holy transmit) of Islamic knowledge as the repository of religious authority is one such fundamental change brought about by the reformist movements within Islam. These changes materialised basically through two processes: one, by the jettisoning of the reformers of much of the medieval scholarship of Islamic world and, second, through the vigorous adoption of print. This process, as Eikelman and Piscatori (1996: 43) elaborate, contributed to the objectification and the radical democratisation of Islamic knowledge. Democratisation also leads to an increasing awareness about the necessity and possibilities of the instrumentality of human will. Professing and practising 'true Islam' is seen as the only option of bringing back the golden era of the Islamic past and the onus is laid squarely on the individual's shoulders. Hence, it becomes the religious and moral obligation of Muslims, irrespective of gender or other differences, to understand religion personally and practise it properly. This aspect, as elaborated by Robinson (2008), brought about possibilities of multiple and varied forms of religious expressions outside the boundaries of traditional Islamic schools. Yet another impact of modernity is the increasing tendency of self-reflexivity and self-consciousness, whereby the ordinary things of daily life were subjected to increasing scrutiny and examination.

The impact of rationalism as a contribution of Western modernity has had a tellingly different orientation and purpose in the discourse of Islamic reformism. Instead of the typical European rationality that questioned religious faith in favour of scientific reason, rationality within Islamic reformism developed a scriptural faith in the Quran and Hadith, thereby condemning all local manifestations of Islamic faith as irrational. Instead of using rationality to question the basic tenets of Islamic religiosity and piety, it was used to distinguish between the 'true' Islamic practices from the 'irrational' and 'corrupt' aberrations of Islam. This process followed the reification of Islam in which submitting to God became an act of will rather than the unquestioning following of the folkways of the faith (Eikelman and Piscatori 1996: 38).

It is evident from the arguments of the Mujahid activists that these processes identified by scholars as the hallmarks of Islamic reformism are reflected in their articulation of Islamic religiosity and their Islamic activism. For each of these volunteers, Islamic dawa is not a passive process but the result of a constant act of reflexivity; submitting to God is an act of will rather than a docile and unconscious process. They liberally use the language of rationalism as inherently ingrained in the true Islamic spirit rather than seeing them as antithetical. This rationalism, they argue, makes them good Muslims, capable of creatively interpreting Islam for the greater glory of Allah and directing dawa for the well-being and uplift of human beings.

The Islamic encounter with modernity also brought in the process of secularisation among Muslim societies across the world. Though there are several scholars who fervently argue that Islam is inherently anti-secular and the secularisation thesis of Max Weber simply does not work in Muslim societies (Gellner 1991; Huntington 1993; Lewis 2002; Weiner 1987), it is evident that Muslim societies across the world are undergoing the process of secularisation, albeit not the way it has been defined by classical sociologists including Weber. Critics of the secularisation theory point at its specific Christian origin and its inability to engage with religions such as Islam and Hinduism, where even the distinction between private and public spheres becomes difficult.

It is evident that the story of secularism in countries like India debunks the central tenets of the secularisation theory such as the decline of religion and its constriction in private life. The resurgence of religion in the United States, Latin America, Asia and Africa, particularly after the 1980s, made even the staunch supporters of the secularisation theory revisit their thesis, and resultantly, more nuanced engagements with religion are being made in this post-secular context (Habermas 2006).

At the same time, the experiences of multi-religious societies like India also offer important caveats for the theory of post-secularism as these societies were never secular in the Western sense of the word and renewed forms of engagement between the secular and the religious have been important markers of these societies in contemporary times. Several scholars have begun to argue that while paying attention to the larger theoretical debates about the compatibility of secularism with Islam, what is of utmost importance is to closely understand the complex negotiations between religious communities and the political projects of secularism. For example, Bangstad (2009) criticises Asad for treating Western and non-Western societies as reified, essentialist categories to argue for the incommensurability of secularism with the latter and exhorts the need to adopt a nuanced approach to postcolonial societies to see the substantial cultural and political transformations brought into them in terms of ideologies and democratic practices, which cannot be distinguished as Western or non-Western, especially in an increasingly interconnected global world. He argues for the 'anthropology of secular as a vernacular practice to explore and understand the concepts and practices of secularism and the secular that Muslims bring to the table—whether these concepts are based on notions of convergence or incommensurability between what is defined as "Islamic", the secular and secularism' (ibid.: 201). A series of studies has specifically adopted this method where the focus is not on the overarching conceptual questions related to the compatibility between Islam and secularism, but on the everyday practices of specific Muslim communities in particular socio-political contexts, which necessitates a careful treading with the principles and practices of secularisation, often reflected as the art of surviving in a multi-religious society. Soares and Otayek (2007: 17) have argued for the appreciation of Islam mondain, referring to the 'ways of being Muslims that exist in secular societies and spheres, without necessarily being secular'. Similarly, Hansen (2000), in his ethnographic work on the Muslims of Mumbai, has elaborated the mechanisms through which Muslims make use of secular democratic processes to ensure their citizenship rights.

Conclusion

The palliative care activism of the Mujahid volunteers, carried out with an explicit secular ethos and modalities while retaining its religious inspiration and ideals, for me, opens up ways of thinking the fraught relationship between Islam and secularisation. Notwithstanding the claims over the incompatibility between the two, owing to different historical contexts, it is imperative to look at the myriad Muslim communities that are under the constant process of engaging with the secularisation process. This study also highlights the significance of the specific historic trajectories of Islamic theological as well as organisational strands that are capable of producing highly divergent practices and interpretations of Islam in different socio-political contexts. The advent of reformism and the counter-initiatives, in various hues and shades, and the concomitant process of secularisation within Muslim communities in India and the constant engagement with a multi-religious society and secular state are important factors in the creation of such diversity.

It is evident that conventional questions like the commensurability of Islam with secularism or secularisation are now passé. Ever since the decisive intervention of Asad in treating religion as a discursive tradition, such questions have lost their relevance, and what are significant are the questions that explore specific manifestations in diverse locales that define categories like 'religious', 'secular' and 'Islamic' in specific ways. The palliative care volunteers of the Mujahid organisations continue to vouch by their religious affinity and inspiration, and are in the constant process of exploring more meaningful ways of living as true Muslims. Simultaneously, reflecting the decisive shifts in their religious articulation in the era of late modernity in a multi-religious society and secular state, they embrace secular modalities and ethos for their activism in the public sphere and continue to live as 'true Muslims'.

Notes

1. Zakat is derived from the word *zaka*, which means 'to purify', and it implies that by giving up, one purifies the portions that remain.
2. Dawa is mentioned in the Quran (14: 46) as God's 'call' to human society to find in Islam the true religion, and the term has developed over centuries into an explicit ideology of proselytism. Eickelman and Piscatori (1996) observe that while education on Islam remains a central feature of dawa, social welfarism is increasingly associated with this term.
3. While zakat is considered as an obligation for every Muslim, sadaqa is the more voluntary giving of alms.

References

Ahmad, Irfan. 2010. *Islamism and Democracy in India: The Transformation of Jamaat-e-Islami*. New Delhi: Permanent Black.

Asad, Talal. 1986. *The Idea of Anthropology of Islam*. Washington, DC: Center for Contemporary Arab Studies, Georgetown University.

Bangstad, Sindre. 2009. 'Contesting Secularism/s: Secularism and Islam in the Work of Talal Asad', *Anthropological Theory*, 9 (2): 188–208.

Eikelman, D. F., and J. Piscatori. 1996. *Muslim Politics*. New Jersey: Princeton University Press.

Gellner, Ernest. 1991. 'Islam and Marxism: Some Comparisons', *International Affairs*, 67 (1): 1–6.

Habermas, Jürgen. 2006. 'Religion in the Public Sphere', *European Journal of Philosophy*, 14 (1): 1–25.

Hansen, Thomas Blom. 2000. 'Predicaments of Secularism: Muslim Identities and Politics in Mumbai', *The Journal of the Royal Anthropological Institute*, 6 (2): 255–72.

Hefner, Robert W. 1998. 'Multiple Modernities: Christianity, Islam and Hinduism in a Globalising Age', *Annual Review of Anthropology*, 27: 83–104.

Huntington, Samuel P. 1993. 'The Clash of Civilizations', *Foreign Affairs*, 72 (3): 22–28.

Kumar, Suresh. 2012. 'Public Health Approaches to Palliative Care: The Neighbourhood Network in Kerala', in Libby Sallnow, Suresh Kumar and Allen Kellehear (eds), *International Perspectives in Palliative Care*, pp. 98–119. New York: Routledge.

Kumar, Suresh and N. Mathew. 2005. 'Neighbourhood Network in Palliative Care', *Indian Journal of Palliative Care*, 11 (1): 6–9.

Lewis, Bernard. 2002. *What Went Wrong? The Clash between Islam and Modernity in the Middle East*. New York: Oxford University Press.

Madan, T. N. 1997. *Modern Myths and Locked Minds*. New Delhi: Oxford University Press.

———. 2006. *Images of the World: Essays on Religion, Secularism and Culture.* New Delhi: Oxford University Press.

Nandy, Ashis. 1990: 'The Politics of Secularism and the Recovery of Religious Tolerance', in Veena Das (ed.), *Mirrors of Violence: Communities, Riots and Survivors in South Asia*, pp. 69–93. New Delhi: Oxford University Press.

Osella, Filippo and Caroline Osella. 2008. 'Islamism and Social Reform in Kerala, South India', *Modern Asian Studies*, 42 (2/3): 317–46.

Paleri, A. K., and Numpeli Mathew. 2005. 'The Evolution of Palliative Care in North Kerala', *Indian Journal of Palliative Care*, 1 (1): 15–18.

Rajagopal, M. R., and Suresh Kumar. 1999. 'A Model for Delivery of Palliative Care in India: The Calicut Experiment', *Journal of Palliative Care*, 15: 44–49.

Reetz, Deitrich. 2006. *Islam in the Public Sphere; Religious Groups in India, 1900–1947.* Oxford: Oxford University Press.

Robinson, Francis. 2008. 'Islamic Reform and Modernities in South Asia', *Modern Asian Studies*, 42 (2/3): 259–81.

Santhosh, R. 2013. 'Contextualizing Islamic Contestations: Reformism, Traditionalism and Modernity among Muslims of Kerala', *Indian Anthropologist*, 43 (2): 25–42.

Sanyal, Usha. 1996. *Devotional Islam and Politics in British India: Ahmad Riza Khan Barelwi and His Movement, 1870–1920.* New Delhi: Oxford University Press

Soares, Benjamin and René Otayek (eds). 2007. 'Introduction: Islam and Muslim Politics in Africa', in *Islam and Muslim Politics in Africa*, pp. 1–26. Basingstoke: Palgrave Macmillan.

Stjernsward, James. 2007. 'Palliative Care: The Public Health Strategy', *Journal of Public Health Policy*, 28 (1): 42–55.

Taylor, Charles. 1999. 'Modes of Secularism', in Rajeev Bhargava (ed.), *Secularism and Its Critics*, pp. 31–53. New Delhi: Oxford University Press.

Turner, Bryan S. 2001: 'Cosmopolitan Virtue: On Religion in a Global Age', *European Journal of Social Theory*, 4 (2): 131–52.

Vijay D., and K. Mukta. 2009. 'Framing and Diffusion of the Palliative Care Movement in Kerala, India', unpublished paper.

Weiner, Myron. 1987. 'Political Change: Asia, Africa and the Middle East', in Myron Weiner and Samuel Huntington (eds), *Understanding Political Development*, pp. 33–64. London: Little Brown and Company.

Notes on the Editors and Contributors

Anindita Chakrabarti is Associate Professor of Sociology, Department of Humanities and Social Sciences, Indian Institute of Technology, Kanpur.

Suchandra Ghosh is Assistant Professor of Sociology, Jhargram Raj College (Girls' Wing), Vidyasagar University.

T. Hashim is UGC post-doctoral Fellow in Sociology, Pondicherry University, Puducherry.

Shahul Ameen K. T. is Assistant Professor, School of Livelihoods and Development, Tata Institute of Social Sciences, Hyderabad Campus.

Aditya Kapoor is Assistant Professor of Sociology, Department of Sociology, Central University of Punjab, Bathinda.

R. Santhosh is Assistant Professor, Department of Humanities and Social Sciences, Indian Institute of Technology, Madras.

Aleena Sebastian is Programme Coordinator, Shaheen Women's Resource and Welfare Association (NGO), Hyderabad.

Sudha Sitharaman is Professor, Department of Sociology, Pondicherry University, Puducherry.

Index